Discourse and Democracy

SUNY series in Social and Political Thought
Kenneth Baynes, editor

Discourse and Democracy

Essays on Habermas's *Between Facts and Norms*

EDITED BY

René von Schomberg
and
Kenneth Baynes

STATE UNIVERSITY OF NEW YORK PRESS

Published by
State University of New York Press, Albany

© 2002 State University of New York

All rights reserved

Printed in the United States of America

For information, address State University of New York Press,
90 State Street, Suite 700, Albany, NY, 12207

Production by Diane Ganeles
Marketing by Patrick Durocher

Library of Congress Cataloging-in-Publication Data

Discourse and democracy : Essays on Habermas's Between Facts and Norms / edited by
René von Schomberg and Kenneth Baynes.
    p. cm. — (SUNY series in social and political thought)
    Includes bibliographical references and index.
    ISBN 0–7914–5497–5 (alk. paper) — ISBN 0–7914–5498–3 (pbk. : alk. paper)
    1. Habermas, Jürgen. Faktizität und Geltung. 2. Sociological jurisprudence. 3.
Democracy—Social aspects. 4. Rule of law—Social aspects. I. Schomberg, René
von. II. Baynes, Kenneth. III. Series.

L372.H333 D57 2002
340′.115—dc21
                                                                  2002021021

10 9 8 7 6 5 4 3 2 1

Contents

IV. Interview

Acknowledgments

The editors are grateful for permission to publish the following articles.

Peter Dews "Law, Solidarity and the Tasks of Philosophy," *Theoria* 88 (1996).

Jürgen Habermas, "A Conversation about Questions in Political Theory," in *A Berlin Republic: Writings on Germany* (Lincoln: University of Nebraska Press, 1997).

Ingeborg Maus, "Popular Sovereignty and Liberal Rights," *Cardozo Law Review* 17 (1998).

William Rehg and James Bohman, "Discourse and Democracy: The Formal and Informal Bases of Legitimacy in *Between Facts and Norms*," *Journal of Political Philosophy* 4 (1996).

William Scheuerman, "Between Radicalism and Realism: Critical Reflections on *Between Facts and Norms*," in *Habermas: Critical Essays*. Peter Dews, ed. (New York: Blackwell, 1999).

Introduction

Between Facts and Norms: Contributions to a Discourse Theory Law and Democracy is Jürgen Habermas's most important work since the publication of his *magnum opus*, *The Theory of Communicative Action*. In it he returns directly to questions in political and legal theory—in particular, the character of the liberal democratic state in capitalist society—that shaped his first and highly controversial book, *The Structural Transformation of the Public Sphere*. In this new study, however, he is able to pursue his earlier interest in the dynamic relations among law, politics, and society not only from the perspective of his general theory of communicative action but also with the wisdom and hindsight of thirty years of further analysis and reflection. The result is a wide-ranging and deeply informed account of the limits and possibilities of a democratic politics that attempts neither to avoid nagging questions about political legitimacy nor to become hopelessly utopian in the face of empirical realities. The chapters contained in this volume offer, from a variety of different perspectives and addressing a number of different issues, an initial assessment of Habermas's most recent proposal.

Even for those already familiar with the scholarly breadth of Habermas's theory of communicative action, the range of disciplines drawn upon in *Between Facts and Norms* can be overwhelming. He moves seemingly without effort among the philosophy of language, social theory, and political theory, as well as among debates in legal and constitutional thought—American and European—and among interpretations of the development of modern law and its relation to the idea of democracy and democratic legitimacy. Though we cannot attempt to summarize Habermas's project in any detail here—see the chapters in part I—, it may be helpful to point out that one of Habermas's basic aims is to remind us of the inseparable (conceptual) connections between the rule of law (*Rechtsstaat*) and the idea of democracy or, as he puts it, to show that "the rule of law cannot be had or maintained without radical democracy" (xlii). Hence, interpretations of the Constitution that see it as simply a limitation or constraint on the idea of (popular) sovereignty and interpretations of (popular) democracy that do not acknowledge the medium of law (*Recht*, including the guarantee of "subjective liberties") as the necessary means through which the "public autonomy" of the citizenry is secured both miss the interdependent relation between law and democracy required if either is to be legitimate. Habermas develops this general thesis at a number of levels, including a reconstruction of the relation between law and morality within his own model of communicative action, an interpretation of contemporary debates between liberals and civic republicans (or communitarians), a reconstruction of different legal paradigms, and even a provocative rereading of Immanuel Kant's own political theory. He also attempts to develop the implications of this general thesis for a model of "deliberative democracy," a reconstruction of the constitutional separation of powers and account of constitutional adjudication, and an analysis of the role of "civil society" in a satisfactory account of democratic legitimacy. Of course, his analyses can be criticized with respect to any of these themes—as in fact several of the contributors to this volume do—but it is also important to keep in mind the general aim of his work since it is finally in view of it, we believe, that the value of this work must prove itself. Our brief introduction attempts to locate Habermas's contribution with respect to one strand in these current political discussions, namely, models of deliberative democracy. We will also highlight briefly some of the themes found in the various contributions to this collection.

Within the context of discussions about deliberative democracy, a central and difficult concern for normative political theory at least since Jean-Jacques Rousseau reappears: the connection between democratic process (or popular sovereignty) and justice or "political rightness." Democracy means rule by the *demos* or "people" and this suggests that citizens must be the authors, in some "nonfictively attributable sense," Frank Michelman, of the laws that constitute their polity.[1] Yet it is far from clear precisely how political rightness and "rule by the people" are to be related since most deliberativists—and indeed most democrats—do not regard the outcome of any given democratic procedure as just or right simply because it issues from that process. Moreover, even if one regards democracy as an at best imperfect procedure, it is still not clear how democratic process itself is a constitutive (and thus ineliminable) element in a conception of political rightness—rather than, say, the best available means to an end specified in a process-independent way. Yet it is just this claim regarding the constitutive role of democratic process in a conception of political rightness that is the hallmark of Habermas's concept of deliberative democracy.

Moreover, this problem is particularly acute for deliberative theorists such as Habermas since populists of a more positivist bent tend simply to identify justice with the popular will, while more traditional *liberal* democrats (or "rights fundamentalists") tend to downplay the importance of demo-

cratic process.[2] The relation between liberal principles of right and democratic process thus appears to be largely contingent, and at least the attraction
of the benevolent (liberal) despot looms on the intellectual horizon. Neither
of these options is available to deliberativists like Habermas, however, since
they seem to insist upon both a deontological conception of political rightness (like liberals) and the indispensability of democratic process to that conception of political rightness. Deliberativists are, thus, faced with a unique
challenge not found in other democratic conceptions, which motivates the
following sorts of questions: How is this ideal of democratic polity even *conceptually* possible? How can political rightness, in some deep or constitutive
sense, be "process bound" and yet, in another sense, be associated with a
deontological notion of "right reason" that is process independent? Is political rightness process dependent or process independent?[3]

The conception of a procedural democracy and deliberative politics
developed in *Between Facts and Norms* is decidedly "deliberativist" and thus
gives rise to the sort of paradox just indicated. On the one hand, Habermas
displays a commitment to the deontological strain in deliberativist thought in
his claim that the ideal of a procedural democracy can be derived via reflection on the presuppositions of communicative reason and action. On the
other hand, Habermas apparently also insists upon the indispensability of
actual democratic process to ascertain and give content to the fundamentally
"unsaturated" (125) scheme of rights derived in that manner. Habermas
writes; "Individual private rights cannot even be adequately formulated, let
alone politically implemented, if those affected have not first engaged in
public discussions to clarify which features are relevant in treating typical
cases as alike or different, and then mobilized communicative power for the
consideration of their newly interpreted needs (450).

It seems, then, that Habermas's desire to embrace both elements in the
deliberativist position leads to what can be called the "regress problem":
Only the people in the collective exercise of their private and public autonomy can define what their legal rights are; yet, it would also seem that in
order for the people to give expression to their will, a legitimate political
order must already be presupposed.[4] As Habermas, puts it, "The idea of the
rule of law sets in motion a spiraling self-application of law" (39). Yet, as
many critics have asked, just how is this "circular" account of the relation
between democracy and constitutionalism (and, relatedly, public and private
autonomy) to be conceived? And how does a deliberative politics differ from
more traditional models?

These questions point to an important and difficult issue at the heart of
a secular (e.g., non-natural-rights-based) account of democracy. However,
the difficulty is not limited to deliberativists alone but is one that confronts
all modern, secular accounts of political legitimacy: How, for example, shall

"rights fundamentalists" determine their preferred set of rights or the appropriate weighing or balancing of rights and majority rule? Furthermore, since it is not a difficulty limited to deliberative models of democracy, it is not one that is limited to questions of conceptual possibility. Rather, it is to be found at the level of "middle-range" theorizing that attempts to spell out the institutional conditions for such a self-referential, self-limiting process of democratic law making.[5] The primary task is to specify the institutional design—together with the reasons for it—that are most likely to realize the abstract ideals mirrored in an (equally ideal) set of procedures.[6] An adequate assessment of Habermas's deliberative model, then, requires an understanding of his own description of democracy as "procedural." In what sense is his idea of a deliberative politics inescapably "process-bound"?

"Procedural" and "proceduralist" are among the most commonly used adjectives in Habermas's *Between Facts and Norms*. He broadly contrasts his preferred "proceduralist legal paradigm" to the liberal and welfarist paradigms (409). He speaks of a "procedural understanding of the constitution" (246); a "proceduralist" view of constitutional adjudication," a proceduralist understanding of law (409); a proceduralist theory of politics (273); and a procedural interpretation of popular sovereignty (Appendix I). He also describes his own conception of democracy as "proceduralist." Within the context of German discussions, it is clear that Habermas seeks to distance himself from a material value-ethics interpretation of the law and political process, interpretations inspired by the work of Max Scheler and Nicolai Hartmann (254). Habermas also uses the term *procedural* to distinguish his own conception of the democratic process from liberal and republican alternatives. This is, in part, to distance his own view from one that takes as fixed and given a "prepolitical" set of (natural) rights and from the view that the democratic process derives its legitimacy "from the prior agreement of a presupposed substantial-ethical community"—that is, from a prior agreement on a conception of the good. Thus, Habermas writes, "a consistent proceduralist understanding of the constitution bets on the intrinsically rational character of the procedural conditions grounding the supposition that the democratic process as a whole facilitates rational outcomes. In that case reason is embodied solely in the formal-pragmatic facilitating conditions for deliberative politics" (285).

However, within the wider context of legal and democratic theory, the term *procedural* is ambiguous and there are many different conceptions that have been described as proceduralist that differ importantly from Habermas's own. For example, in his influential essay, "Is Democracy Special?" Brian Barry describes his own conception as proceduralist which he understands to mean a rejection of "the notion that one should build into 'democracy' any constraints on the content of the outcomes produced, such as substantive equality, respect for human rights, concern for the general welfare, personal liberty, or the rule of law. The only exception (and these are significant) are those required by democracy itself as a procedure."[7] While the question of what is "required by democracy itself as a procedure" is itself a matter of much debate, Habermas's conception of democracy is not procedural in this sense. It clearly has more substantive normative content than Barry would grant.

Furthermore, even more normatively rich procedural conceptions, such as Peter Singer's conception of democracy based on a notion of "fairness as compromise" or John Ely's "process-oriented approach" to the Constitution and constitutional review, fall short of Habermas's conception.[8] For these conceptions, the democratic process consists of a set of rules and procedures that are supposed to weigh equal preferences whose formation is largely exogenous to the democratic process itself. Each person should be granted the opportunity to register her preference and no person's preference should count for more than another person's. The conceptions thus operate with an ideal of political equality understood in terms of the equal opportunity to influence political outcomes. A procedure is "fair" if it captures this notion of equal power. The difficulty with such conceptions, however, is that they remain relatively indifferent to the initial preferences that enter into the procedure.[9] A more in-depth and thus more adequate account would consider the formation and quality of preferences as well. To do this, the ideal of political equality must initially be conceived at a more abstract level and cannot be identified directly with the (procedural notion of the) equal opportunity to influence outcomes.[10]

Habermas's conception of democracy thus presupposes a more abstract ideal of political equality and this more abstract ideal in turn serves as a guide to indicate whether any proposed set of procedures is "fair." "The concept of democratic procedure itself relies on a principle of justice in the sense of equal respect for all" (266 and 103). The ideal of political equality is then not identified solely with a set of procedures that secures an equal opportunity (for any given preference) to influence outcome. In this sense, Habermas's procedural conception is perhaps closest to what Charles Beitz has called "complex proceduralism":

> Like other forms of proceduralism, [complex proceduralism] holds that democratic procedures should treat *persons* as equals; but it will not follow that the appropriate criterion for assessing procedures is the simple principle of equal power over outcomes. Instead, complex proceduralism holds that the terms of democratic participation are fair when they are reasonably acceptable from each citizen's point of view, or more precisely, when no citizen has good reason to refuse to accept them."[11]

In Habermas's conception, analogously, there are certain abstract ideals—in the last analysis an ideal of (public and private) autonomy or communicative freedom—that are identified prior to (and thus independent of) any proposed set of (ideal) procedures. It is these ideals that then confer a presumption of reasonableness or fairness on the proposed procedures.[12]

In sum, then, for Habermas, ideal procedures attempt to capture or express an ideal or model-conception of the citizen as free and equal or, what amounts to the same thing, an ideal of practical reason. This accounts for the "deontological" aspect of his thought. But in what way is democratic process constitutive of political rightness? Political rightness is process-dependent, we suggest, in two senses: First, the specification of a set of (ideal) procedures represents an attempt to "mirror" an interpretation of the requirements of right reasoning or, in other words, a model-conception of the citizen as free and equal. And, the claim must be, that this set of procedures captures these ideals better than a more determinate or substantive set of values is likely to do. Second, even the specification of these procedures remains nevertheless quite abstract and the "rights" they are said to express remain fundamentally "unsaturated." For Habermas, rights can acquire a concrete and determinate character only through the exercise of the citizens' collective autonomy. Only the citizens can legitimately determine what their rights shall be. Yet, to restate the "regress problem," how shall they do that unless they are already constituted as citizens?

Of course, when the issue is stated in such an abstract form it has the air of a deep and insurmountable paradox: The people cannot make laws unless they are already constituted as a people. But why is it necessary to end with the most paradoxical formulation? As John Rawls points out in a related context, we are not beginning at "ground zero." Rather, we have a history and tradition of Constitution-making, with its relative successes and failures, which can serve as a guide. Habermas's position appears to be the same: "'The system of rights does not exist in transcendental purity. But two hundred years of European constitutional law have provided us with a sufficient number of models. These can instruct a generalizing reconstruction of the intuitions that guide the intersubjective practice of self-legislation in the medium of positive law" (129). Furthermore, in attempting to give more specific content to that to which citizens could reasonably assent special attention should also be given to secure the conditions required for citizens to give (or contest) such agreement. Hence, the importance of the basic liberties (e.g., those contained in Rawls's First Principle). Thus, while the paradox of democracy and rights cannot be altogether eliminated, its initially immobilizing effect can be mitigated by attending to the problems and dynamics associated with various forms of institutional design.

Finally, there may not be a definitive or uncontestable answer to many questions concerning the indispensability of various social and economic guarantees, the regulation of speech, or the guarantee of various specific rights as preconditions for the democratic process. Yet it is not for that reason inconsistent or incoherent to regard these as matters that are basic matters of democratic debate while at the same time engaging in various critical efforts to convince the demos that the demos cannot, at this place and time, properly or genuinely exist without their recognition. Precisely such a strategy, it seems to me, is reflected in the best understanding of what Rawls calls "reflective equilibrium": It is an attempt to convince "us"—that is, we citizens who are asked to regard ourselves as simultaneously authors and subjects of the laws and "constitutional essentials" in question—that certain matters are of such deep importance that they should be constitutionally secured from what James Madison called the "mischiefs of factions." It is also, it would seem, not antithetical to democracy but rather democracy, most broadly conceived, at work.

The chapters gathered in the present volume all pursue, from various perspectives, issues raised by Habermas's deliberative or discursive conception of democracy. In "Deliberative Democracy and the Limits of Liberalism" Kenneth Baynes situates Habermas's model of deliberative democracy within the context of three ongoing discussions in contemporary political theory: the relation between constitutionalism (or basic rights) and democracy, the question of political neutrality, and the more recent discussion of identity politics. Baynes argues that the abstract character of Habermas's proceduralism is both its greatest strength and greatest weakness. On the one hand, it enables Habermas to outline a model of the political process that is not sectarian or deeply shaped by a particular conception of the good life. But, on the other hand, it is not clear that he has paid sufficient attention to the political values and cultural norms required for his model of "constitutional patriotism" to flourish. "Discourse and Democracy," by William Rehg and James Bohman, addresses concerns raised by the strong "epistemic" or cognitive model of democracy proposed by Habermas with its ideal of consensus or unanimity. They applaud its normative superiority to more aggregative models of the democratic process, but question whether Habermas has gone far enough in his attempts to incorporate into his theory what Rawls' describes as the "fact of reasonable pluralism." As an alternative to Habermas's strongly consensus-oriented model of public reason, they propose a weaker model of public reason that acknowledges the inevitably of pervasive conflict even at the level of moral principles and fundamental procedures. According to William E. Scheuerman, in "Between Radicalism and Resignation," *Between Facts and Norms* is, in contrast to *The Structural Transformation of the Public Sphere*, surprisingly ambiguous when it comes to an assessment of so-called actually existing democracies. On the one hand, Scheuerman detects a "socialist streak" in Habermas's suggestion that massive social inequalities would render the project of (radical) democracy impossible. Furthermore, in drawing upon Nancy Fraser's distinction between strong and weak publics to characterize the distinction between the formal (parliamentary) political system and the informal public sphere broadly conceived, Habermas clearly thinks that the normative reasons and deliberations must move from the informal public sphere of civil society *into* the administrative system. Yet, at other times, relying more on the recent work of Bernhard Peters, Habermas describes this formal/informal distinction in terms of a "center" and "periphery" that seems to privilege the parliament and administrative state over the more informal and "anarchic" institutions of civil society. This latter model, according to Scheuerman, threatens the more radical democratic project that informs other parts of Habermas's work.

In the second section of this volume, various historical and comparative studies are pursued. In a detailed discussion of Habermas's own "circular" analysis of the relation between democracy (popular sovereignty) and constitutionalism (basic rights), Ingeborg Maus in "Liberties and Popular Sovereignty," argues that Habermas offers a highly stylized caricature of the positions of both Rousseau and Kant. According to her, both theorists (though especially Kant) have a much more complex analysis of the relation between natural law and democratic legitimacy and one that in many respects was sensitive to the very same problems that confront Habermas. By contrast, in "Habermas, Hegel, and the Concept of Law," Andrew Buchwalter notes the conspicuous absence of Hegel from *Between Facts and Norms*. At least part of this absence, he contends, is to be attributed to Hegel's idealistic philosophy. However, as Buchwalter points out, there are nonetheless many affinities between Habermas's project in *Between Facts and Norms* and G.W.F. Hegel's *Philosophy of Right*. More importantly, though, Buchwalter also argues that when their positions diverge Hegel more often than not gains the upper hand. In particular, Buchwalter argues that Habermas's renewed appreciation for the socially integrative function of law still remains too "Kantian"—that is, abstract and procedural—in contrast to Hegel's subtle reflections (much indebted to Montesquieu) on the cultural dimensions of constitutionalism. In "Rawls and Habermas" Hauke Brunkhorst offers an initial comparison of these two contemporary political thinkers. He notes how a conception of public reason and deliberation figure prominently in each but suggests that Rawls's "political liberalism" with its "strategy of avoidance" and "overlapping consensus" is less able to explain how the two traditional ideals of autonomy—roughly, private liberties and political self-legislation—are to be successfully integrated into a contemporary political theory. Although not without its own internal difficulties, Habermas's theory looks more promising for this task.

The third section explores some of the wider implications of Habermas's communicative or discourse theory, especially as developed in *Between Facts and Norms*. In "Law, Solidarity, and the Tasks of Philosophy" Peter Dews offers a set of probing reflections on Habermas's current project. He begins with the shift (in *Between Facts and Norms*) to a more positive assessment of the role of law in modern society, noting that for Habermas the process of juridification is no longer an inevitable result of the colonization of the lifeworld (as it was in *The Theory of Communicative Action*). This leads him to reflect further on Habermas's account of social solidarity and his (perhaps too harmonistic) description of the relation between individualization (and guarantee of rights) and renewed sources of collective solidarity in the contemporary world. Finally, in a critical analysis of Habermas's own description of philosophy's dual role as "stand-in" and "interpreter," Dews suggests that Habermas may ascribe to philosophy a too limited or modest role in the task of articulating new forms of solidarity in contemporary life. In "Rational Politics?" Geert Munnichs compares Habermas's model of deliberative democracy to the economic model of democracy developed by Robert Dahl and others. He argues that Habermas is correct in pointing to the normative deficiencies of that earlier model but, in an interesting discussion of the changing role of political parties, Munnichs also argues that Habermas has not paid sufficient attention to the constructive role of political parties in the democratic process. He draws on the work of Claus Offe to suggest how political parties might continue to play a formative role in a less aggregative conception of the political process. In "The Disappearance of Discourse Ethics in *Between Facts and Norms*" Matthias Kettner considers some of the implications for Habermas's moral theory. In *Between Facts and Norms* Habermas now introduces the basic principle of discourse (D) as a normative principle prior to its further characterization as either a moral principle (as a principle of universalizability) or a principle of democracy. As Kettner points out, this is a significant shift from his earlier analysis and raises important questions about the kind of impartiality it enjoins. In connection with some other difficulties posed by the proliferation of types of discourses in *Between Facts and Norms*, Kettner further suggests that this work is threatened by the "disappearance of discourse ethics" altogether. Finally, in "The Erosion of our Value Spheres?" René von Schomberg contrasts Habermas's conceptual analysis of the differentiation of discourses to their actual dedifferentiation in the context of a society coping with scientific and moral uncertainties. He argues that society's reaction to risk and uncertainty, especially in science and ethics, exacerbates the erosion of value spheres and he considers whether the institutionalization of discourses—in part through the actions of administrative law—could address this growing social crisis.

The final section of this collection contains a lengthy interview with Habermas on *Between Facts and Norms,* "A Conversation about Questions of Political Theory." He discusses both the theoretical ambitions of his work and some of the practical consequences he hopes might be advanced by it. The interview not only clarifies Habermas's views on issues that are often misunderstood—concerning, for example, the idealizing assumption of an uncoerced community of communication—but also indicates the contribution he hopes his work will make to such current topics as globalization, European identity, and the future of the welfare state. As such, it constitutes a fitting conclusion to the present volume.

Notes

1. Frank Michelman, "How Can the People Ever Make Law?" in *Deliberative Democracy*, eds. James Bohman and William Rehg (Cambridge: Massachusetts Institute of Technology Press, 1997), p. 148.

2. A similar criticism of this sort of (roughly) "rights-based" liberal theory articulated by John Rawls, Ronald Dworkin or, for that matter, Nozick, can be found in Michael Walzer, "Philosophy or Democracy?" *Political Theory* 9 (1981): 379–399, as well as in the "strong democratic" theory of Benjamin Barber (see his "The Reconstruction of Rights," *American Prospect* (Spring 1991): 36–46.

3. In addition to the article by Michelman, "How Can the People Ever Make Law?" see David Estlund, "Beyond Fairness and Deliberation: The Epistemic Dimension of Democratic Authority," in *Deliberative Democracy*, eds. Bohman and Rehg.

4. For a similar "deconstructive" account of this paradox found in the act of constitution-making, see Jacques Derrida, "Declarations of Independence," *New Political Science* 15 (Summer 1986): 7–15. The paradox, of course, has a much longer history and is also expressed in the tension Sieyes noted in the distinction between the *pouvoir constitué* and *pouvoir constituant*; see Hannah Arendt, *On Revolution* (New York: Viking, 1963), pp. 160f. Jürgen Habermas's "circular" account of this process is discussed at length in the chapter by Ingeborg Maus in this volume.

5. See, for example, the recent edited volume by Robert Goodin, *The Theory of Institutional Design* (New York: Cambridge University Press, 1996), especially pp. 39f.

6. See as well, Joshua Cohen, "Deliberation and Democratic Legitimacy," in *Deliberative Democracy*, eds. Bohman and Rehg.

7. In *Philosophy, Politics, and Society*, ed. P. Laslett (Oxford: Blackwell, 1979), pp. 155–156.

8. See Peter Singer, *Democracy and Disobedience* (New York: Oxford University Press, 1974); and John Hart Ely, *Democracy and Distrust* (Cambridge: Harvard University Press, 1980).

9. See Charles Beitz, *Political Equality* (New Jersey: Princeton University Press, 1989), p. 82.

10. See, for example, Habermas's remark linking the notion of equal respect with the idea of reasons acceptable to all (BFN, 103).

11. Beitz, *Political Equality*, p. 23.

12. See *Between Facts and Norms: Contributions to a Discourse Theory of Law & Democracy*, 295; and Habermas, "Three Models of Democracy," *Constellations* 1 (1994): 6.

I

Initial Assessments of *Between Facts and Norms*

1

Deliberative Democracy and the Limits of Liberalism

Kenneth Baynes

Jürgen Habermas's *Between Facts and Norms: Contributions to a Discourse Theory of Law and Democracy* engages current discussions in Anglo-American political theory—especially concerning the nature and limits of liberal democracy—more extensively than any of his earlier works.[1] It should thus be possible to form an initial judgment about how his "discourse theory of law" and conception of "procedural democracy" might fare when confronted by some of the more pressing issues in liberal political theory. In these discussions three issues particularly stand out: First, there is a long-standing debate about the relation between democracy and other political ideals (e.g., political equality, the rule of law, and the guarantee of basic rights and liberties). Are these political values in deep conflict with the ideal of democracy, or can they be reconciled with one another in a more general interpretation of democracy?[2] Second, there has been a lengthy discussion about the ideal of liberal neutrality.[3] Is the claim that the liberal state should not act in ways intended to promote a particular conception of the good defensible when, on the one hand, the diversity of distinct cultures and life-forms are increasingly threatened by global markets and, on the other, the ethical foundations of liberal society are being called into question by nonliberal regimes? Third, as an extension of the critique of neutrality, the "dilemma of difference," as expressed by Martha Minow, poses a distinct challenge to liberal ideology: Must any attempt to address "difference" under the liberal ideals of equality, impartiality, and toleration necessarily perpetuate injustices and do violence to those categories and classes not traditionally recognized as within the norm? This issue has been raised particularly (though not exclusively) in recent feminist jurisprudence.[4] After briefly reviewing some of the main features of Habermas's procedural democracy, I will return to these three

15

issues to consider how they might be addressed from within the perspective of his discourse theory.

Within the context of American discussions, Habermas's use of the phrase "procedural democracy" could be misleading since it differs from the contrast between procedural and substantive democracy found, for example, in John Ely's account in *Democracy and Distrust* or in Brian Barry's influential essay, "Is Democracy Special?" Barry writes:

> I follow . . . those who insist that "democracy" is to be understood in procedural terms. That is to say, I reject the notion that one should build into "democracy" any constraints on the content of outcomes produced, such as substantive equality, respect for human rights, concern for the general welfare, personal liberty and the rule of law.[5]

Habermas's model is clearly not procedural in this sense since it draws upon the ideals of liberty and equality implicit in the idea of communicative reason (see 266 and 445). It presupposes as an element of practical reason an ideal of citizen's autonomy that should be reflected in an institutional design incorporating various practical discourses. Procedural democracy is thus closer to what Charles Beitz refers to as "complex proceduralism" which holds that "the terms of democratic participation are fair when they are reasonably acceptable from each citizen's point of view, or more precisely, when no citizen has good reason to refuse to accept them."[6] Habermas's proceduralism may also be compared to what has been called a "public reasons" approach. According to this approach, found in the work of John Rawls, Thomas Scanlon, Samuel Freeman, and others, democratic norms and procedures are said to be based on reasons that citizens can publicly affirm in view of a conception of themselves as free and equal persons.[7]

Habermas introduces his conception of procedural democracy by way of a contrast between two highly stylized alternatives: liberal and republican (or communitarian). These have become familiar reference points in recent discussions. Cass Sunstein, for example, has recently summarized the liberal model well: "Self-interest, not virtue, is understood to be the usual motivating force of political behavior. Politics is typically, if not always, an effort to aggregate private interests. It is surrounded by checks, in the form of rights, protecting private liberty and private property from public intrusion."[8] By contrast, republicanism characteristically places more emphasis on the value of citizens' public virtues and active political participation. Politics is viewed as a deliberative process in which citizens seek to reach agreement about the common good, and law is not seen solely as a means for protecting individual rights but as an expression of the common praxis of the political community.

Habermas's procedural democracy attempts to incorporate the best features of both models while avoiding the shortcomings of each. In particular, with the republican model, it rejects the vision of the political process as primarily a process of competition and aggregation of private preferences. However, more in keeping with the liberal model, it regards the republican vision of a citizenry united and actively motivated by a shared conception of the good life as inappropriate in modern, pluralist societies.[9] Since political discourses involve bargaining and negotiation as well as moral argumentation, the republican or communitarian notion of a shared ethical-political dialogue also seems to be too limited (285).

> According to discourse theory, the success of deliberative politics depends not on a collectively acting citizenry but on the institutionalization of the corresponding procedures and conditions of communication, as well as on the interplay of institutionalized deliberative processes with informally constituted public opinions. (298)

Thus, what is central is not a shared ethos, but institutionalized discourses for the formation of rational political opinion.

The idea of a suitably interpreted "deliberative politics" thus lies at the core of Habermas's procedural democracy. In a deliberative politics attention shifts away from the final act of voting and the problems of social choice that accompany it.[10] The model attempts to take seriously the fact that often enough preferences are not exogenous to the political system, but "are instead adaptive to a wide range of factors—including the context in which the preference is expressed, the existing legal rules, past consumption choices, and culture in general."[11] The aim of a deliberative politics is to provide a context for the possible transformation of preferences in response to the considered views of others and to the "laundering" or filtering of irrational and/or morally repugnant preferences in a manner that is not excessively paternalistic.[12] For example, by designing institutions of political will-formation so that they reflect the more complex preference structure of individuals rather than simply registering the actual preferences individuals have at any given time, the conditions for a more rational politics (i.e., a political process in which the outcomes are more informed, future-oriented, and other-regarding) can be improved.[13] One could even speak of an extension of democracy to preferences themselves since the question is whether the reasons offered in support of them are ones that could meet the requirements of public justification.[14] What is important for this notion of deliberation, however, is less that everyone participate—or even that voting be made public—than that there be a warranted presumption that public opinion be formed on the basis of adequate information and relevant reasons and that those whose interests are involved have an equal and effective opportunity to make their own interests (and the reasons for them) known.

Two further features serve to distinguish Habermas's model of procedural democracy and deliberative politics from other recent versions. First, this version of deliberative politics extends beyond the formally organized political system to the vast and complex communication network that Habermas calls "the public sphere:"

> [Deliberative politics] is bound to the demanding communicative presuppositions of political arenas that do not coincide with the institutionalized will-formation in parliamentary bodies but rather include the political public sphere as well as its cultural context and social basis. A deliberative practice of self-determination can develop only in the interplay between, on the one hand, the parliamentary will-formation institutionalized in legal procedures and programmed to reach decisions and, on the other, political opinion-building in informal channels of political communication. (274-275)

The model suggests a "two-track" process in which there is a division of labor between "weak publics"—the informally organized public sphere ranging from private associations to the mass media located in "civil society"—and "strong publics"—parliamentary bodies and other formally organized institutions of the political system.[15] In this division of labor, "weak publics" assume a central responsibility for identifying and interpreting social problems: "For a good part of the normative expectations connected with deliberative politics now falls on the peripheral structures of opinion-formation. The expectations are directed at the capacity to perceive, interpret, and present encompassing social problems in a way both attention-catching and innovative" (358). However, decision-making responsibility, as well as the further "filtering" of reasons via more formal parliamentary procedures, remains the task of a strong public (e.g., the formally organized political system).

Second, along with this division of labor between strong and weak publics and as a consequence of his increased acknowledgment of the "decentered" character of modern societies, Habermas argues that radical-democratic practice must assume a "self-limiting" form. Democratization is now focused not on society as a whole, but on the legal system broadly conceived (305). In particular, he maintains, it must respect the boundaries of the political-administrative and economic subsystems that have become relatively freed from the integrative force of communicative action and are in this sense "autonomous." Failure to do so, he believes, at least partially explains the failure of state socialism.[16] The goal of radical democracy thus becomes not the democratic organization of these subsystems, but rather a type of indirect steering of them through the medium of law. In this connection, he also describes the task of an opinion-forming public sphere as that of laying siege to the formally organized political system by encircling it with reasons without, however, attempting to overthrow or replace it.[17]

This raises a number of difficult questions about the scope and limits of democratization. Given the frequent metaphoric character of his discussion (see, e.g., the references to "colonization," "sieges," and "sluices"), it is not clear what specific proposals for mediating between weak and strong publics would follow from his model. Some have questioned, for example, whether he has not conceded too much to systems theory and Nancy Fraser, in an instructive discussion of Habermas's conception of the public sphere, raises the question whether there might not be other possible "divisions of labor" between strong and weak publics.[18] Habermas's response, I think, would be that an answer to these questions will not be found at the level of normative theory, but depends upon the empirical findings of complex comparative studies. However, a more general question that arises in connection with this model of democracy is whether Habermas's confidence in the rationalizing effect of procedures alone is well-founded. In view of his own description of "weak publics" as "wild," "anarchic," and "unrestricted" (308), the suspicion can at least be raised whether discursive procedures will suffice to bring about a rational public opinion. To be sure, he states that a deliberative politics depends on a "rationalized lifeworld" (including a "liberal political culture") "that meets it halfway."[19] But without more attention to the particular "liberal virtues" that make up that political culture and give rise to some notion of shared purposes, it is difficult not to empathize with Sheldon Wolin's observation concerning the recent politics of difference. Describing the situation of someone who wants to have his claim to cultural exclusiveness recognized while at the same time resisting anything more than minimal inclusion in the political community, Wolin exposes a disturbing paradox within it:

> I want to be bound only by a weak and attenuated bond of inclusion, yet my demands presuppose a strong State, one capable of protecting me in an increasingly racist and violent society and assisting me amidst increasingly uncertain economic prospects. A society with a multitude of organized, vigorous, and self-conscious differences produces not a strong State but an erratic one that is capable of reckless military adventures abroad and partisan, arbitrary actions at home. . . . yet is reduced to impotence when attempting to remedy structural injustices or to engage in long-range planning in matters such as education, environmental protection, racial relations, and economic strategies.[20]

Habermas no doubt shares some of these same concerns about the conditions necessary for maintaining a liberal political culture, and his own focus on the more abstract form of mutual recognition at the basis of a legal community may make the requirements for inclusion less demanding than Wolin suggests. The question nevertheless remains whether Habermas's almost exclusive attention to questions of institutional design and discursive procedures offers an adequate basis for dealing with this paradox or whether he must supplement his model with a more specific account of the "liberal virtues" or "ethical foundations" that must "meet these halfway."[21]

I would now like to consider how Habermas's theory fares with respect to the three issues noted in the introduction: the project of reconciliation, the question of liberal neutrality, and the dilemma of difference.

1. In *Between Facts and Norms*, Habermas introduces a novel attempt to reconcile the principle of democracy (or popular sovereignty) with a system of basic rights. His claim is that neither should be seen as subordinate to the other (as is generally the case in both republicanism and classical liberalism), but that they are equiprimordial or co-original (*gleichursprünglich*) (122) and "reciprocally explain each other (93). The system of rights is the "reverse side" (93) of the principle of democracy, and "the principle of democracy can only appear at the heart of a system of rights" (121).

More specifically, Habermas's claim is that the system of rights (along with the principle of democracy) can be developed from the interpenetration (*Verschränkung*) of the discourse principle and the legal form (121). As I understand it, this "derivation"—Habermas speaks of a logical genesis (*logische Genese*)— of a system of rights occurs in two stages: First, the notion of law cannot be limited to the semantic features of general and abstract norms. Rather, bourgeois formal law has always been identified with the guarantee of an equal right to subjective liberty.[22] This is reflected in Immanuel Kant's Universal Principle of Right (*Recht*) as well as in Rawls's First Principle both of which guarantee the greatest amount of liberty compatible with a like liberty for all. For Habermas this link between positive law and individual liberty means that insofar as individuals undertake to regulate their common life through the legal form they must do so in a way that grants to each member an equal right to liberty.

However—and this is the second step—although the legal form is conceptually linked to the idea of subjective rights, it alone cannot ground any specific right (128). A system of rights can be developed only if and when the legal form is made use of by the political sovereign in an exercise of the citizens' public autonomy. This public autonomy in the last analysis refers back to the discourse principle that implies the "right" to submit only to those norms that one could agree to in a discourse. Of course, in connection with the principle of discourse this "right" has only the "quasi-transcendental" status of a communicative act and does not carry with it any coercive authorization. It can acquire a coercive authorization only when, as the principle of democracy, it is realized in the legal medium together with a system of rights:

> The principle of discourse can assume through the medium of law the shape of a principle of democracy only insofar as the discourse principle and the legal medium interpenetrate and *develop* into a system of rights bringing private and public autonomy into a relation of mutual presupposition. Conversely, every exercise of political autonomy signifies both an interpretation and concrete shaping of these fundamentally 'unsaturated' rights by a historical law-giver. (128)

Habermas hopes in this way to have reconciled democracy and individual rights in a manner that does not subordinate either one to the other. "The system of rights can be reduced neither to a moral reading of human rights [as in Immanuel Kant and in the tradition of natural rights] nor to an ethical reading of popular sovereignty [as in Jean-Jacques Rousseau and in some communitarians] because the private autonomy of citizens must neither be set above nor made subordinate to their political autonomy" (104). Rather, the co-originality or "equiprimordiality" of the system of rights and the principle of democracy, which also reflects the mutual presupposition of citizens' public and private autonomy, is derived from this "interpenetration" of the legal form and the "quasi-transcendental" discourse principle that "must" occur if citizens are to regulate their living together by means of positive law.

Since Habermas claims that no one else has yet succeeded in this project of reconciliation (84), it may be useful to contrast his own position with two other recent attempts. In *Democracy and Its Critics* Robert Dahl recognizes the potential conflict between a "procedural" democracy and a "substantive" set of basic rights and attempts to resolve it by arguing that the right to self-government through the democratic process is basic and that other political rights can be derived from this fundamental right:[23]

> These specific rights—let me call them *primary political rights*—are integral to the democratic process. They aren't ontologically separate from—or prior to, or superior to—the democratic process. To the extent that the democratic process exists in a political system, all the primary political rights must also exist. To the extent that primary political rights are absent from a system, the democratic process does not exist.[24]

This strategy faces two serious objections. First, it is not clear whether other "nonpolitical" rights can be accounted for in a similar manner and, even if so, whether this would not amount to an instrumentalization of private autonomy for the sake of public autonomy. Second, although it is a "substantive" not a "procedural" account, Dahl's strategy suffers from a reliance on an "aggregative" conception of democracy that is in the end similar to Ely's procedural conception that was just referred to. This is suggested, for example, in his endorsement of a fairly utilitarian reading of the "principle of equal consideration of interests" in contrast to the autonomy-based conception implicit in Habermas's account.[25]

In a recent essay, Ronald Dworkin has also attempted to reconcile democracy and basic rights.[26] He begins with Ely's observation that many of the "disabling provisions" of the Constitution (roughly the Bill of Rights) may be seen as "functionally structural" to the democratic process and thus not in conflict with it. The right to freedom of expression is an example: "Since democratic elections demonstrate the will of the people only when the public is fully informed, preventing officials from censoring speech protects rather than subverts democracy. . . . So a constitutional right of free speech counts as functionally structural as well as disabling in our catalogue."[27] However, as Ely concedes, this strategy will not work for all the "disabling provisions"—for example, the establishment clause of the First Amendment or rights that regulate the criminal process—and so, Dworkin concludes, "Ely's rescue of democracy from the Constitution is only a partial success."[28]

Dworkin's own response to the "supposed conflict between democracy and a constitution" (330) begins by distinguishing between a "statistical reading of democracy" (i.e., the aggregative conception just referred to) and a "communal reading of democracy" (e.g., Jean-Jacques Rousseau's general will).[29] He then argues for a specific version of the latter that he calls "democracy as integration." This model is specified in connection with three principles: the principle of participation (requiring that each citizen have an equal and effective opportunity to make a difference in the political process), the principle of stake (requiring that each citizen be recognized or shown equal concern), and the principle of independence (specifying that each citizen be responsible for their own judgments). Dworkin then concludes that on this model many of the disabling provisions Ely rejected may be regarded as functionally structural and, hence, not antidemocratic: "On the communal conception, democracy and constitutional constraint are not antagonists but partners in principle."[30]

Dworkin's model is clearly preferable to aggregative conceptions. The three principles appeal directly to the ideals of autonomy and mutual recognition, and the analysis of democracy (as well as law) in connection with the integrity of a community's practices and attitudes points away from a metaphysical or substantialist conception of community. On the other hand, as he recognizes, his "principle of stake" threatens to become a "black hole into which all other political virtues collapse."[31] His response, however, which is to claim that the principle requires not that each citizen be shown equal concern but only that there exist a "good faith effort," threatens to undermine the public autonomy of citizens.

Habermas's proposal, by contrast, reconciles popular sovereignty and human rights in the sense that public and private autonomy are said to mutually presuppose one another. A virtue of the model is that it relates these ideals at an abstract level: Public and private autonomy are two dimensions of the fundamental "right" to communicative liberty as this is expressed in the legal form. If one begins with this notion of communicative liberty, it is possible to regard the constitution as a sort of "public charter" and the system of rights as a form of "precommitment" that citizens make in undertaking to regulate their common lives by public law.[32] As such the proposed reconciliation of democracy and rights neither undervalues public autonomy, nor overtaxes private autonomy. It is not based on a shared conception of the good, but on a more abstract form of recognition contained in the idea of free and equal consociates under law.

At the same time, the principal strength of this approach may also prove to be its greatest weakness. Given the abstract character of the reconciliation of public and private autonomy, it is difficult to determine how it might contribute to more specific constitutional debates, for example, regarding the interpretation of the establishment clause of the First Amendment, or the more specific scope and content of the right to privacy. Habermas would probably claim that the system of rights is "unsaturated" and needs to be filled in both with reference to a political community's particular tradition and history and in response to ongoing deliberations within the public sphere. This may be so, but it also seems reasonable to expect that the general proposal for a reconciliation of democracy and basic rights should provide some guidance to more specific debates about rights (e.g., would it support a constitutional right to abortion as a condition for securing the public autonomy of women?). I suspect, in fact, that the theory will be able to provide such guidance, but much more work still needs to be done in this "middle range" between general conceptions and the enumeration of specific rights and liberties.

2. Despite his emphasis on "weak publics" and pluralist civil society Habermas's model of procedural democracy and deliberative politics endorses a "nonrestrictive" or "tolerant" version of the principle of liberal neutrality (308ff.). This principle has been criticized by communitarians and others who argue that it is excessively individualistic or atomistic in its conception of the citizen and/or that it presupposes its own conception of the good and thus is inherently self-defeating (since it cannot allow for the promotion of values required for a liberal society).[33] In particular, it has been argued that the principle of liberal neutrality is not compatible with the state's pursuit of measures intended to promote or maintain a diverse civil society and robust

public sphere.[34] Is Habermas's endorsement of a principle of neutrality consistent with his affirmation of the value of a robust public sphere?

It is important that the meaning of liberal neutrality, at least on its best interpretation, not be misunderstood. First, the principle of neutrality is not itself a neutral or nonmoral principle. It does not imply a merely procedural neutrality with respect to whatever conceptions of the good life citizens may happen to have. Rather, it is an ideal introduced in conjunction with a principle of right (e.g., Kant's Universal Principle of Right or Rawls's Principle of Equal Liberty) and thus one that is biased against conceptions of the good that are incompatible with the basic rights and liberties specified by that principle.[35] Second, the principle of neutrality does not even require that the state treat equally any permissible conception of the good citizens may have or that the policies pursued by the state must have the same effect upon any and all (permissible) conceptions of the good life. This form of neutrality, which has been called "neutrality of effect" or "consequential neutrality," is both impractical and undesirable. Rather, what liberal neutrality entails is "neutrality of aim" or "neutrality of grounds" in the sense that arguments and considerations introduced in support of specific principles or policies should not appeal to particular conceptions of the good life but should regard all citizens and their (permissible) conceptions with equal concern and respect.[36]

Even on this interpretation the principle can be contested. Can policies be neutral in their justification in this way, or must not such claims to neutrality inevitably appeal to some (permissible) conceptions of the good over others? One version of neutrality, suggested by Bruce Ackerman's notion of "constrained conversation" and Rawls's "method of avoidance," is susceptible to this challenge since by unduly restricting the issues that can be placed on the political agenda or raised in public discussion there is the danger of reinforcing the status quo and inhibiting mutual understanding.[37] This strategy also suggests that there is a relatively fixed and clear distinction between those matters appropriate for public discussion and those that are not.

An alternative interpretation of liberal neutrality is able to avoid this objection. On this interpretation, the principle of neutrality is not understood as part of a general strategy of avoidance, but as part of what is required in showing equal concern and respect in a stronger sense: The state should not act in ways intended to promote a particular conception of the good life since that would constitute a failure to show each citizen equal concern and respect. Unlike the method of avoidance, this interpretation of neutrality does not require keeping controversial issues off the political agenda in order to avoid moral conflict. Rather, it is quite consistent with the view that the state act in ways intended to promote rational discussion in order to help resolve potentially divisive social and moral conflicts.[38] On this interpretation neutrality is compatible with the attempt to secure a form of mutual respect or "militant toleration" in which difference is not only tolerated, but in which individuals seek to understand one another in their differences and arrive at a solution to the matter at hand in view of their common recognition of one another as free and equal citizens.

It will perhaps be objected that this view leads beyond liberal neutrality to a liberal or "modest" perfectionism. In fact, a similar argument for a more robust and pluralist public sphere has recently been made by Michael Walzer.[39] As paradoxical as it may seem, in view of the tremendous "normalizing" effects of the market economy and bureaucratic state there is little reason to assume that either a robust and pluralist public sphere or the other general social conditions for a more deliberative politics can be secured without the (self-reflective) intervention and assistance of the state. However, while I have argued that the state may be justified in acting in ways to secure such forums, I do not see that this requires embracing a perfectionist account of liberalism rather than the alternative principle of neutrality that was just outlined. For, on this interpretation, the actions of the state are justified not because of their contribution to a particular way of life or conception of the good, but because robust and pluralist deliberative forums are necessary conditions for the effective exercise of basic rights of public and private autonomy. The state may at times be justified in acting in ways aimed at promoting or securing the conditions for a pluralist civil society not because it regards a pluralist society as a good for its citizens, but because it regards such conditions as requirements of practical reason in the sense that informed and reasonable deliberation could not be achieved without them.

3. Finally, issues raised in the critique of liberal neutrality reemerge in a heightened form in the "dilemma of difference." For the claim is now that the pursuit of "justice" through the bourgeois legal form (e.g., general law aimed at the guarantee of equal rights) necessarily devalues difference and does violence to individuals, groups, and practices that deviate from the established norm.[40] The dilemma of difference, which has been most extensively discussed in recent feminist jurisprudence, is inextricably entwined with the fundamental principle of legal equality. "Treat equals equally" requires a judgment about the respects in which two things are equal and what it means to treat them equally. But this gives rise to the following dilemma:

> By taking another person's difference into account in awarding goods or distributing burdens, you risk reiterating the significance of that difference and, potentially, its stigma and stereotyping consequences. But if you do not take another person's difference into account—in a world that has made that difference matter—you may also recreate and reestablish both the difference and its negative implications. If you draft or enforce laws you may worry that the

effects of the laws will not be neutral whether you take difference into account or you ignore it.[41]

Attempts to secure legal equality have generally pursued either an "assimilationist model" (which emphasizes the extent to which we are all alike) or an "accommodation model" (which seeks to create "special rights" on the basis of "real" differences). As some feminists point out, however, both models founder upon the same problem. In attempting to determine which differences deserve legal remedies and which should be ignored the background norms that establish terms of relevance and in light of which judgments of similarity and difference are made frequently go unchallenged.[42]

One response has been to resist the language of sameness and difference altogether and to pursue a critique of law from the point of view of domination instead.[43] However, once the problem is framed in this manner, that is, not as a problem of judgments of sameness and difference per se, but as a critique of the underlying norms and criteria guiding them, attention shifts to the process through which those norms have been defined. And here, I think, the strength of Habermas's approach emerges: The effort to secure equal rights and the protection of law for each citizen must go hand in hand with efforts to secure the exercise of the public autonomy of all citizens. Public and private autonomy mutually suppose one another and must be jointly realized to secure processes of legitimate lawmaking. With this model in view, one could then take up the suggestion of some feminists that the point is not for the law to be "blind" to difference, nor to fix particular differences through the introduction of "special rights," but "to make difference costless."[44]

With respect to these three challenges to liberal democracy, I conclude that the abstract and highly procedural character of Habermas's version of the project of radical democracy is its principal strength and weakness. Its strength is that, in connection with his theory of communicative reason and action, Habermas generates a unique and powerful argument for a model of democracy in which the public and private autonomy of citizens are given equal consideration. It generates an intersubjective account of basic rights and a procedural democracy more attractive than any of the liberal or republican accounts currently available. It also offers a strong argument for the design of institutions that will facilitate discussion based on mutual respect. On the other hand, the highly abstract character of the proposal suggests that more work still needs to be done if it is to contribute *directly* to more specific debates about basic rights, the "dilemmas of difference," or what counts as the appropriate correspondence (or "meeting halfway") of liberal virtue and institutional design which, as Habermas concedes, is required if his notion of a procedural democracy and deliberative politics is to be effectively realized in the contemporary world.

Notes

1. *Between Facts and Norms: Contributions to a Discourse Theory of Law and Democracy*, trans. William Rehg (Cambridge: Massachusetts Institute of Technology Press, 1996).

2. Two recent attempts at a reconciliation can be found in John Ely, *Democracy and Distrust* (Cambridge: Harvard University Press, 1980) and Robert Dahl, *Democracy and Its Critics* (New Haven: Yale University Press, 1989).

3. See, for example, the criticisms of communitarians (e.g., Charles Taylor) or "critical legal studies" (e.g., Mark Tushnet, *Red, White, and Blue* [Cambridge: Harvard University Press, 1988]).

4. See, for example, the articles collected in *Feminist Jurisprudence*, ed. Patricia Smith (New York: Oxford University Press, 1993); more generally, see Iris Young, *Justice and the Politics of Difference* (Princeton: Princeton University Press, 1990) and William Connolly, *Identity/Difference* (Ithaca: Cornell University Press, 1991).

5. See Ely, *Democracy and Distrust* and Brian Barry, "Is Democracy Special?" in *Philosophy, Politics, and Society*, ed. P. Laslett (Oxford: Blackwell, 1979), pp. 155–156.

6. Charles Beitz, *Political Equality* (Princeton: Princeton University Press, 1989), p. 23.

7. For examples of this "public reasons" approach, which is influenced by the work of John Rawls and Thomas Scanlon, see especially, Joshua Cohen, "Deliberation and Democratic Legitimacy," in *The Good Polity*, eds. Alan Hamlin and Philip Pettit (Blackwell, 1989), pp. 17–34 and several articles by Samuel Freeman, "Constitutional Democracy and the Legitimacy of Judicial Review," *Law and Philosophy* 9 (1990–1991): 327–370, "Original Meaning, Democratic Interpretation, and the Constitution," *Philosophy and Public Affairs* 21 (1992): 3-42, and "Reason and Agreement in Social Contract Views," *Philosophy and Public Affairs* 19 (1990): 122–157.

8. "Preferences and Politics," *Philosophy and Public Affairs* 20 (1991): 4.

9. Habermas cites Frank Michelman's "Law's Republic" as an example of this sort of republicanism; he might also have referred to some of the writings of Taylor. Habermas's own position seems closest, however, to the "Madisonian" republicanism of Sunstein; see "Beyond the Republican Revival," *Yale Law Journal* 97 (1988): 1539–1590.

10. See also B. Manin, "On Legitimacy and Political Deliberation," *Political Theory* 15 (1987): 338–368 and David Miller, "Deliberative Democracy and Social Choice," *Political Studies* 40 (1992), Special Issue, p. 54–67.

11. Sunstein, "Preferences and Politics," p. 5; see also Jon Elster, *Sour Grapes* (New York: Cambridge University Press, 1983).

12. See Robert Goodin, "Laundering Preferences," in *Foundations of Rational Choice Theory*, ed. Jon Elster, (New York: Cambridge University Press, 1985), pp. 75–101.

13. Specific proposals for realizing the ideals of a deliberative politics could range from something like James Fishkin's idea of a "deliberative opinion poll" to alternative procedures of voting and modes of representation; see Fishkin, *Democracy and Deliberation* (New Haven: Yale University Press, 1990), Ian McLean, "Forms of Representation and Systems of Voting," in *Political Theory Today*, ed. David Held, (Stanford, 1991), pp. 172–196; and Young, "Polity and Group Difference," *Ethics* 99 (1989): 250–274 (which discusses the question of special or group representation).

14. Although I think Donald Moon overestimates the dangers of "unconstrained conversation," especially for individual privacy rights, he points to the difficult question concerning the kinds of institutional design that are appropriate to help ensure that the deliberations conducted in an "unconstrained conversation" influence the process of decision making. Should there, for example, be a system of public voting? See "Constrained Discourse and Public Life," *Political Theory* 19 (1991): 202–229.

15. Habermas takes these terms from Nancy Fraser who used them to describe Habermas's two-track conception of the public; see "Rethinking the Public Sphere: A Contribution to the Critique of Actually Existing Democracy," in *Habermas and the Public Sphere*, ed. Craig Calhoun (Cambridge: Massachusetts Instiute of Technology Press, 1992).

16. See "What Does Socialism Mean Today?" *New Left Review* 183 (1990): 3–21.

17. see *Die Nachholende Revolution* (Frankfurt, Germany: Suhrkamp, 1990), p. 199 and *BFN*, 486–487.

18. Specific proposals for a shared "division of labor" can be found in recent discussions concerning "neocorporatist" and "associative" democracies; see especially, Joshua Cohen and Joel Rogers, "Secondary Associations and Democratic Governance," *Politics and Society* 20 (1992): 393–422, and the discussions that follow.

19. *BFN*, 302; compare also Habermas's corresponding remark that a postconventional morality "is dependent upon a form of life that meets it halfway. . . . There must be a modicum of fit between morality and socio-political institutions" [*Moral Consciousness and Communicative Action* (Cambridge: Massachusetts Instiute of Technology Press, pp. 207–208)] and the interesting article on this topic by Claus Offe, "Binding, Shackles, Brakes: On Self-Limitation Strategies," in *Cultural-Political Interventions in the Unfinished Project of Enlightenment*, eds. A. Honneth et al. (Cambridge: Massachusetts Instiute of Technology Press, 1992).

20. Sheldon Wolin, "Democracy, Difference and Re-cognition," *Political Theory* 21 (1993): 480.

21. I have in mind Ronald Dworkin's remarks on the "ethical foundations" of liberalism in "The Foundations of Liberal Equality," in *The Tanner Lectures* (University of Utah Press, 1990), v. 11 and Stephen Macedo's discussion in *Liberal Virtues* (Oxford: Clarendon, 1990); see also the related criticism of Habermas's "constitutional patriotism" from an Hegelian perspective in Andrew Buchwalter, "Hegel's Concept of Virtue," *Political Theory* 20 (1992): 576.

22. Some support for this claim can already be found in the fact that the German *Recht*, like the French *droit*, means "subjective right" as well as "objective law."

23. *Democracy and Its Critics*, pp. 169–170.

24. Ibid., p. 170.

25. For the principle of equal consideration of interests, see ibid., p. 85; for a similar criticism (to which I am indebted) see Cohen's review of *Democracy and Its Critics*, in *Journal of Politics* 53 (1991): 221–225.

26. "Equality, Democracy and Constitution: We the People in Court," *Alberta Law Review* 28 (1990): 324–346.

27. Ibid., p. 328.

28. Ibid.

29. Ibid., p. 330.

30. Ibid., p. 346.

31. Ibid., p. 339.

32. For this use of the notion of "precommitment" and the Constitution as a "public charter," see Freeman, "Original Meaning, Democratic Interpretation, and the Constitution."

33. See, for example, Taylor, "Cross-Purposes: The Liberal-Communitarian Debate," in *Liberalism and the Moral Life*, ed. Nancy Rosenblum (Cambridge: Harvard University Press, 1989); Joseph Raz, "Facing Diversity," *Philosophy and Public Affairs* 19 (1990): 3–46; and Michael Walzer, "The Communitarian Critique of Liberalism," *Political Theory* 18 (1990): 6–23. In the following section I draw at points on my "Liberal Neutrality, Pluralism, and Deliberative Politics," *Praxis International* 12 (1992): 50–69.

34. Walzer, "Communitarian Critique of Liberalism."

35. See "The Idea of an Overlapping Consensus," *Oxford Journal of Legal Studies* 7 (1987): 9.

36. Rawls, "The Priority of the Right and the Ideas of the Good," *Philosophy and Public Affairs* 17 (1988): 260-268; Peter de Marneffe, "Liberalism, Liberty, and Neutrality," *Philosophy and Public Affairs* 19 (1990): 253-274; and Kymlicka, "Liberal Individualism and Liberal Neutrality," *Ethics* 99 (1989), 883-884.

37. Bruce Ackerman, "Why Dialogue?" *Journal of Philosophy* 86 (1989): 5–32.

38. "Moral Conflict and Political Consensus," in *Liberalism and the Good*, eds. G. Mara, R. Douglas, and H. Richardson (New York: Routledge, 1991), pp. 125–147.

39. "The Communitarian Critique of Liberalism," p. 19.

40. See Young, *Justice and the Politics of Difference*; and Martha Minow, *Making all the Difference* (Ithaca: Cornell University Press, 1990).

41. Minow, "Justice Engendered," in *Feminist Jurisprudence*, ed. Patricia Smith, (New York: Oxford University Press, 1992), p. 232.

42. See Christine Littleton, "Reconstructing Sexual Equality," in *Feminist Jurisprudence*, ed. P. Smith (New York: Oxford University Press, 1992); Deborah Rhode, *Justice and Gender* (Cambridge: Harvard University Press, 1989); and Habermas's discussion in BFN, 409ff.

43. See Catharine MacKinnon, "Difference and Dominance," in *Feminism Unmodified* (Cambridge: Harvard University Press, 1987).

44. This position, which she calls the "acceptance model," is proposed by Littleton in "Reconstructing Sexual Equality." I do not mean to suggest (nor does Littleton) that this is an easy task for, as Taylor points out in a related discussion, there can arise conflicts between the "politics of equal dignity" and "the politics of difference"—conflicts, for example, between equal opportunity and cultural membership—that cannot easily be resolved (see *Multiculturalism and 'The Politics of Recognition'* [Princeton: Princeton University Press, 1992, p. 37]).

2

Discourse and Democracy: The Formal and Informal Bases of Legitimacy in *Between Facts and Norms*

William Rehg and James Bohman

Jürgen Habermas's *Between Facts and Norms* is a complex and multi-faceted work. In it, Habermas provides not only a philosophy of law but also a theory of deliberative politics for complex societies. According to many proponents of deliberative democracy, political decision making is legitimate insofar as it follows upon a process of public discussion and debate in which citizens and their representatives, going beyond their mere self-interest and limited points of view, reflect on the public interest or common good.[1] Habermas, however, is skeptical of Rousseauian and "civic republican" variants of such a theory of democracy. These interpretations of deliberative democracy suggest that political decisions express the substantive values and traditions of a homogeneous political community or a "general will."[2] Such motifs are not readily plausible in contemporary pluralist democracies, and in some cases the attempt to realize them have been nothing short of disastrous and have discredited radical democratic ideals.[3] Habermas's challenge, then, is to show how the core idea of radical democracy—that legitimate laws are authored by the citizens subject to them—can still be credible in complex and pluralist societies.

The counterintuitive concept of "subjectless communication" is central to Habermas's attempt to preserve an account of ideal democratic deliberation without recourse to a unitary popular will. Our aim in this chapter is both to explicate and to develop further this concept of deliberation as a way of preserving the core ideas of radical democracy. First, we situate the problem by elaborating the theory of discourse that provides Habermas with a more complex account of deliberation than found in civic republicanism. One can then understand the concept of "subjectless communication" as introducing further dimensions of social complexity within the process of democratic deliberation and decision making. We then argue that Habermas's strongly epistemic interpretation of this model engenders difficulties in dealing with contemporary value pluralism. These difficulties motivate a weaker epistemic conception of deliberative democracy that allows more room for ongoing disagreement and compromise. Revising the democratic epistemic ideals themselves makes them more plausible than Habermas's own strategy of accommodating strong ideals of consensus to the "unavoidable complexity" of modern society. In conclusion, we formulate a weaker version of the democratic principle and suggest its benefits for the empirical analysis of current institutions. We argue that such a weaker version of the democratic ideal of agreement remains consistently cognitivist and at the same time provides a better tool for criticizing the failures of actual democratic arrangements to promote public deliberation.

I

As an account of democracy in deliberative terms, Habermas's *Between Facts and Norms* is an attempt to hold onto a strongly normative account of legitimacy in the face of the complexity inherent in functionally differentiated, pluralist societies.[4] Deliberative models of democratic legitimacy are strongly normative, in the sense that they are supposed to go beyond utilitarian explanations of the rationality of collective decision making and their instrumental view of politics. Social choice theories, for example, typically conceive rational public choice as the aggregation of individual preferences; the paradoxes afflicting this approach, especially when it is applied to large-scale elections, are well-known.[5] On a deliberative view, it is crucial that citizens (and their representatives) test their interests and reasons in a public forum prior to deciding. The deliberative process forces citizens to justify their views about the best outcome by appealing to common interests or by arguing in terms of reasons that "all could accept" in public debate. Merely expressing a given preference as one's own will not, simply by itself, sway others to one's view.[6] As a result, the ensuing collective decision should in some sense reflect an interpretation of the common good that could be justified by public reasons, that is, ones that are generally convincing to everyone participating in the process of deliberation. Outcomes can be considered democratic either if citizens themselves are involved in the deliberation or if representatives make decisions that all citizens *would* agree to, given the time, knowledge, and the disposition to be "reasonable."[7]

The deliberative conception in this respect presupposes an account of how public deliberation makes an outcome more rational. The reasons given must meet the conditions of publicity, that is, they must be convincing to everyone.[8] One should not be surprised if such an account is "epistemic" in some sense: deliberation improves outcomes insofar as it helps decision makers construct an interpretation of the common good for all those affected by the matter at hand. Decisions can then be considered "correct" or not, at least in a broadly cognitive sense, depending on how well they reflect this common good. According to an "epistemic" conception of democracy, a legitimate political system should operate according to procedures that foster deliberation and increase the chances of arriving at correct (or valid, or true) decisions.[9] One need not think of the correct decision as a truth "out there," given prior to engaging in the procedures that discover it. In fact, deliberative theorists usually defend the view that it is procedural ideals, rather than outcomes, which constitute the decisive parameters for correctness.[10] Nor should one think of the common good in overly substantive terms, as though political deliberation primarily involved an authentic appropriation of already shared values or political ideals. While this may be part of the picture (as a necessary background of political culture), it is in general far too simplistic to capture the complexity of deliberation in contemporary institutions, such as the legislative processes in parliamentary bodies.

In this context, Habermas's "discourse theory of democracy" can be seen as an epistemic account that is both procedural and complex, for it explains the rationality of deliberation in terms of a complex of reason-giving procedures. This account starts with the idea that beliefs and actions have a rational character insofar as they can be supported publicly by good reasons. More technically, the formation of rational opinions and decisions must rest on validity claims to truth, rightness, and so forth, which can or at least could be justified before all competent persons with convincing reasons.[11] The exchange of reasons thus refers one to a *discourse* in which participants strive to reach agreement solely on the basis of the better argument. The rationally motivating character of such discourse rests on idealized procedural conditions that define "good reasons" and "better arguments" as those that survive an argumentative process that is free of coercion and open to all competent speakers.[12]

Habermas's account is internally complex, as we shall see, because different types of claims must be redeemed in different types of discourse. Before going into these, however, note how this concept of rational discourse actually defines valid outcomes in strongly cognitivist and consensual terms. Habermas's concept of discourse seems to imply, in principle, the possibility of full consensus toward something like the correct answer once ideal conditions are met. This cognitivist dimension is strongest in his concept of moral discourse, which pertains to norms of justice, that is, the regulation of interpersonal relations according to a mutual respect for persons. Such norms are justified if, and only if, everyone subject to them could assent on the basis of their own impartial judgment arrived at in an ideally unrestricted discourse in which the participants genuinely strive to reach a rational agreement. Rendered dialogic, the concept of insight that is operative here cannot be limited to the individual's head: being convinced is equally a matter of convincing others.[13] Nonetheless, each individual's conviction is a necessary condition for normative validity or rightness. This is, of course, a regulative ideal that is necessarily never realized in any actual discourse. This ideal status raises problems for the status of actual assent or dissent in real political discourse and debate, as we shall subsequently argue.

According to Habermas, political legitimacy can be reduced neither to moral discourse nor to substantive reflection on shared values. The validity of political decisions, and the legitimacy claim these entail, is more complex than classical natural law models allowed. It rests not only on moral reasons, but also on what Habermas calls "technical-pragmatic" and "ethical-political" reasons and even on bargaining and compromise.[14] The exact mix will no doubt depend on the complexities of the particular issue at stake.

To clarify this *complexity internal to rational discourse*, consider the following example, as a kind of idealized thought experiment, in which various discourses are intertwined. Imagine a society that is considering the adoption of a comprehensive health care plan. First, let us follow the public deliberation of one particular subgroup. Assume that everyone in the group eventually comes to agree, after conducting a *moral discourse*, that some revision of the health care system is morally required—that the present system does not meet the minimal needs of many citizens, and that this represents an injustice, a violation of the basic respect owed to all persons. (More precisely, we might assume that they agree that everyone's need for health care imposes on those who are better off an imperfect duty of benevolence.) They also agree, let us assume, that a centrally administered, "single-payer" system accords with the self-understanding and values of their particular society, say, the broadly shared value of public welfare provision (in contrast to a reliance on private organizations). This aspect of their agreement, which converges on shared, or overlapping, cultural values and identities, is the topic for what Habermas calls an *ethical-political discourse*. It is perhaps the closest he comes to assuming a substantive concept of the general will or a homogeneity of values. This has a harmless character, though, since it is simply a de facto overlapping consensus of values. Finally, assume that the group's own experts have reached agreement in a *technical-pragmatic discourse* regarding the best policies and strategies for realizing a government-administered health care program. The single-payer system is, all agree, the most efficient way to achieve the moral end of universal and sufficient coverage. To simplify matters at this stage, we assume that, in relation to the health care issue, the subgroup does not split over differences at the level of individuals' particular interests, needs, and preferences. Thus, in each type of discourse the members of the subgroup are able to reach full consensus on a solution that everyone finds rationally convincing. The strongly cognitive character of this agreement consists in the fact that "identical reasons are able to convince" everyone "*in the same way*" that a given solution is correct (339). Insofar as an issue can be discursively resolved, in other words, it should, at least in principle, command unanimous assent and be open to constant revision until it does.

Now let us broaden our thought experiment and introduce a further complication. Let us assume that there are different subgroups whose particular interests and values lead them to recommend somewhat different moral, ethical, and technical solutions (within the requirements set by justice and broader-shared identities and values). Even if we assume that everyone in this imaginary society has goodwill, is seeking the common good, and is committed to being reasonable, there may be differences among them that preclude such a strong consensus as that pictured within our homogenous subgroup. To this extent, different subgroups must *bargain* with one another in the search for a fair compromise. This compromise will be fair insofar as every group has an equal chance to influence the outcome (exactly how this equality is specified is a difficult question). Note that these discursive agreements with stronger epistemic status, insofar as they hold up across the subgroups as well as within them, set certain constraints on compromise, that is, the compromise must not violate requirements of justice or undermine the ethical values shared by all the groups, and it should be technically practical. As long as this is the case, the final outcome should be morally just, ethically authentic, technically expedient, and fair to all.

One might note yet another complication in passing: the outcome should be legally consistent with previous legislative acts, judicial precedents, and administrative practices, a requirement that must be worked out in *legal discourses*. The important general point is this: even these further complications do not seem to alter the counterfactual ideal of unanimity (unless perhaps legal discourses would be the exception). Compromises, insofar as they are based on conditions that all could accept as fair, should also command the approval of all those involved, even if their reasons for approval differ. Though the most minimal form of agreement, compromises remain democratic insofar as they conform to the general principle governing all of the interconnected discourses of public deliberation. Even if parties to a compromise do not agree for the *same reason*, they *all* nonetheless agree to the same policies. It is perhaps not entirely surprising, then, that Habermas's "democratic principle" defines a legitimate outcome in terms of unanimity: only those laws can claim to be legitimate that could meet with the assent of all citizens in a discursive law-making process that has been legally organized (110).

The reference to unanimity shows that this discourse-theoretical analysis, though internally complex, still refers to an abstract and singular set of idealizations. These idealizations cannot be empirically realized. Yet, precisely because they define rationality, they must somehow have an empirical effect on the real course of public deliberation if such deliberation is to be rational and thus fulfill the expectation of legitimacy. For example, an outcome that was based on the exclusion of an affected group would be prima facie suspect according to Habermas's democratic principle. But the strongly consensual and idealized character of this concept of discursive rationality raises a question: how can one hold onto such a strong ideal of reason under complex, pluralist circumstances that generally seem to preclude consensus? Habermas's concept of subjectless communication, along with his "two-track" model of democratic decision making, is meant to accomplish just this seemingly impossible task. According to this model, laws and political decisions in complex and pluralistic societies can be rational and thus legitimate in a deliberative democratic sense—thus, rationally authored by the citizens to whom they are addressed—if institutionalized decision-making procedures follow "two tracks." They must be both (1) open to inputs from an informal, vibrant public sphere and (2) appropriately structured to support the rationality of the relevant types of discourse and to ensure effective implementation. That is, political decision making in institutions must be open to an unrestricted public sphere, and yet structured in such a way as to be timely and effective (as well as coherent). In the next section we explain this model in greater detail and explain why Habermas thinks it is an answer to problems of social complexity and to the difficulties of public participation.

II

Habermas's differentiated account of discourse not only situates rationality in a set of historical and cultural practices; it also provides for a certain internal complexity in reason itself. But he must also meet the demands of *social* complexity if the idealized account is to be serviceable for real processes of deliberation and decision making. The discussion that follows bears primarily on deliberations that issue in *legislative decision making*, for this is where the claims of deliberative democracy must primarily prove themselves. Yet decisions about laws, whether taken by a legislature or through a popular referenda, almost never enjoy the universal consensus or direct participation projected by Habermas's ideals. Here the problem of participation in complex societies is the more basic one. In modern societies, citizens cannot literally come together to deliberate as a whole in any forum or particular body (170). The process of discourse itself is inevitably dispersed across a variety of fora: these include face-to-face interactions at home and work; larger meetings in the various informal voluntary associations and different levels of organization throughout civil society (clubs, professional associations, unions, issue-centered movements, etc.); the dissemination of information and arguments through the public media; and the complex network of government institutions, agencies, and decision-making bodies (see 359ff.). Even before dealing with the problem of dissent, a plausible concept of rational deliberation must somehow do justice to the complex and dispersed reality of real public discourse under contemporary social conditions.

In dealing with such complexity, a deliberative democratic view must hold three terms together in a certain tension. That is, it must link deliberation and decision making with the citizenry. The sheer size and complexity of society could tempt one to relegate deliberation so much to representatives that it would be difficult to call the account "democratic." An opposite error would be to underestimate complexity and locate deliberation primarily in the public sphere. Here one does not take sufficient account of the institutional requirements necessary for such deliberation to issue in effective decisions.[15] Yet a third error would be to overestimate the possibilities of bureaucratic control, thereby undermining popular sovereignty and the public control of decisions. The facts of complexity seem to present deliberative democracy with a Weberian dilemma: *either* decision-making institutions gain effectiveness at the cost of democratic deliberation, *or* they retain democracy at the cost of effective decision making. In either case, citizenship, deliberation, and decision making fail to be linked, so that the public sphere becomes powerless or the power of political institutions become reified.

Habermas solves this three-variable problem with a "two-track model," according to which Parliament and Congress provide an institutional focus for a broader, decentered "subjectless" communication dispersed across the public sphere and involving all citizens. On this view, institutional decision making depends on a broad and complex process of deliberation. That is, deliberation is not just the task of the better-informed representatives nor is it just the task of active citizens who merely delegate power of will to representatives as their agents.[16] As we shall see, the "subjectless" or "anonymous" character of such deliberation arises from the nature of social complexity. For the moment note that Habermas hopes to present a model of modern politics that is at once democratic, deliberative, and effective.

To see how Habermas's model solves this problem while meeting the challenge of social complexity, it helps to distinguish three types of pluralism: a plurality of procedural roles, a plurality of discursive perspectives, and a plurality of substantive opinions and arguments. At least in some measure,

Habermas's model explicitly recognizes each of these three forms of complexity and is formulated to provide a solution to the institutional dilemmas of each type, which threaten either the publicity of democratic procedures or the sovereignty of the citizenry.

The *plurality of procedural roles* involves something like a division of labor across levels of deliberation and decision. "*All* members must be able to take part in discourse, even if not necessarily in the same way" (182). Exactly how one spells out the different roles in a given deliberative process will depend not only on the issue and how a particular political system is structured, but also on theoretical perspective. Probably the most obvious and important differentiation is that between "weak" and "strong publics" (to use Nancy Fraser's terminology). This lines up with the two main components of Habermas's model, the informal public sphere and formal decision-making bodies. That is, a weak public is one whose "deliberative practice consists exclusively in opinion formation and does not also encompass decision-making," whereas strong publics, such as parliaments, can reach binding decisions and are institutionally organized to do so.[17] This distinction is not hard-and-fast inasmuch as citizens also occasionally decide matters through referenda; in addition, the general election of officials is a kind of decision making, and it is often related to deliberation about issues.[18]

Drawing on the recent work of Bernhard Peters, Habermas introduces a more fine-grained analysis of this relation between publics with a distinction between "center" and "periphery." He distinguishes institutional roles according to how close an actor or institution is to the "center" of the political apparatus (355ff.), and hence to the apex of decision-making power accumulated in the institution. At the center are those agencies with executive power along with the other branches of government; at the periphery lie opinion-forming publics containing a wide variety of nongovernmental organizations and groups. In a similar framework one might further distinguish positions according to their *power to decide* and their *influence on deliberation*.[19] Whereas political power, the ability to make binding decisions and execute government action, is found chiefly at the center, influence extends throughout society. In this context, influence refers to the ability to sway voters, persuade members of Congress, and so forth. Respected public figures, lobbyists, government watchdogs, and organizations like the League of Women Voters are examples of positions with more than usual influence. Their higher-profile position actually serves public deliberation inasmuch as it provides information shortcuts for voters who lack the time to research issues and candidates. In a sense, they make possible a broader participation in the deliberative process by making it easier for less informed voters to acquire information.[20] This reduction of costs is not without a certain danger of restricting public communication. Threats to this democratic sharing of information can come from the periphery when "private governments," such as corporations, seek to exploit problems related to information costs for their own purposes; or they may come from the center when bureaucracies permit only such information to be made public that produces "nondecisions," in Bachrach and Baratz's sense.[21]

The plurality of discursive perspectives reflects the internal differentiation of real discourse as it is associated with different social positions. That is, one can expect persons and groups in different social positions to highlight not only competing particular interests but also somewhat different values, different aspects of a given issue, and even different types of validity. If rational practical deliberation means that all the relevant aspects and perspectives on an issue are taken into account before reaching a decision, then we have to do here with a somewhat different division of labor from that already mentioned, that is, one that comes closer to the cooperative pooling of information than the fair distribution of procedural roles.[22] This is more than simply a difference of particular interests. On health care reform, for example, one would expect insurance companies (and their lobbyists in Washington) to emphasize the financial problems associated with reform, while doctors should cast their public contributions in terms of issues of medical treatment and professional autonomy. In other words, differences in interests can, taken together, motivate a broader search for relevant information and for better arguments on an issue.

This form of pluralism is not without its pitfalls. Interests can be concealed within each particular perspective in a way that distorts the deliberative process. Public interest groups then emerge to contest these "expert" accounts, challenging these sorts of associations in terms of the way in which the truth of their information is shaded in light of their current interests. Trust in such information comes less from such procedural roles and division of labor than from the capacity of such claimed expertise to withstand public scrutiny once the information is publicly accessible and pooled. Even so, not every deliberator will be able to judge the merits of these disputes in every respect, any more than they can determine the correctness of their own medical diagnoses. In these cases, institutional arrangements are democratic to the extent that they place the burden of proof on the "experts" to construct convincing public arguments in light of their well-warranted knowledge claims and not their special authority.

Insofar as this pluralism engenders conflicting arguments, it leads into the third form of pluralism. For the moment, though, we are interested in possibilities for a kind of cooperation that would be similar to the pooling of information. If this idea is plausible, then it suggests an intriguing interpretation of subjectless communication in informal public spheres. The public distribution of information and perspectives could be viewed as harboring a kind of communicative (or discursive) rationality, but not the idealized sense that requires complete understanding on the part of each citizen. The complexity of public spheres suggests a plethora of loosely connected and fragmented discourses in which various groups of individuals achieve partial insights into issues through discussion. But these groups may not fully grasp one another's views. As a result, they would not have a complete and definitive insight into the common good. The idea of subjectless communication thus suggests that public reason is an emergent property of a diffuse network of discourses. More specifically, if one assumes that for any given problem or issue, there are a number of considerations (corresponding to the different validity spheres, as well as to different interest positions, values, etc.), then there "exists" a public "potential of reasons" that individuals will draw upon in different ways and to differing degrees, some stressing efficiency considerations, other moral ones, and so on. To the extent that communication channels are open across these different publics, one might imagine that these reasons are "made fluid" and "interact" through the individuals and groups that represent them to one another. This suggests a deliberative twist on the idea of "aggregation." That is, one might think of an informed "public opinion" as a kind of "aggregation" of reasons that develops as people gradually become aware of an issue.[23] An opinion poll coming at the end of such communication would then have a certain rational quality to it: to the degree that the public sphere is open and vibrant, this aggregate should be more likely to reflect the weightier, sounder reasons—without one having to assume that every, or even any single individual has an insight based on a grasp of all the relevant considerations as required by the discursive ideal itself.[24] For this reason, Habermas calls such public opinion "anonymous," since it is not located in any individual or groups of individuals. It is "decentered" into the network of communication itself, suggesting a different and weaker conception of publicity than the highly idealized one of discursive agreement.

Political life under the condition of perspectival pluralism may not normally be so cooperative as this image of information pooling suggests. On the contrary, one more often associates different social positions with a further type of pluralism, the *plurality of substantive opinions and arguments*. Precisely this "fact of pluralism" is what makes majority rule necessary to conclude real deliberation. As we will see, this raises more problems than Habermas seems to realize. But, by itself, it need not undermine Habermas's strongly consensual account of discourse. Majoritarian decision making is compatible with ideal consensus if the better arguments—the arguments that *would* eventually lead to full consensus under ideal conditions—are more likely to be those that sway the majority. This sounds compatible with the concept of subjectless communication just developed. Condorcet's Jury Theorem might provide a probabilistic analogy here, cast in epistemic terms.[25]

However, a majority will not even be a probable indicator of rational consensus if the conditions of undistorted discourse are seriously violated. The pluralism of competing arguments, values, and interests is actually an important safeguard, then, for it makes it less likely that a majority will reflect a false consensus. To the extent that there are competing counterpublics, or *subaltern counterpublics*, to use Fraser's term, it is less likely that false arguments and attempts to exclude some groups will go unchallenged. Aside from this critical function, multiple publics have an important role even in egalitarian and multicultural societies, in that they help citizens form their own identities and find proper expression for their needs.[26]

We can now state more precisely how the discursive idealizations already elaborated in this chapter can be brought into a relation with real public deliberation. To start with a broad characterization, it is precisely the presence of "discursive structures" that gives the rather chaotic mix of roles, positions, and arguments an epistemic character, so that one can be justified in supposing that the resulting political decisions are reasonable. This "structuralist approach," as Habermas calls it, locates public reason not in a general will—which would have to be indicated by empirical majorities or discerned by representative bodies—but in the *discursive structures* that link public with legislature.[27] This has somewhat different implications for the two main components in Habermas's model, the informal public sphere and formal decision making. In both cases, however, the basic idea is to foster processes of communication and to design institutional procedures that at least make it more likely that political decisions will be based on reasons that would counterfactually correspond to those emerging from a discourse both open to all and free of coercion.[28]

Let us start with the public sphere. To function properly for democracy, a vibrant public sphere must, according to Habermas, "not only detect and identify problems but also convincingly and *influentially* thematize them, furnish them with possible solutions, and dramatize them in such a way that they are taken up and dealt with by the parliamentary complex" (359). This description presents four, more or less realizable, functional requirements for a democratic public sphere. (1) The public sphere must be receptive to broadly relevant problems as they are perceived by citizens in their everyday life (364–366). (2) In order to be receptive, the public sphere must be rooted in a robust civil society and in an open, pluralist culture. As used in this context, "civil society" refers to the various informal voluntary associations that provide individuals with sympathetic audiences before which they can articulate their experiences, needs, and identities.[29] These first two conditions ensure that everyone is potentially included in public discourses, that is, has some initial avenues for voicing his or her concerns and suggestions. (3) The various informal publics generated by these different associations must be at least partly open to one another, so that an exchange of arguments and viewpoints can occur in the public sphere: "boundaries inside the universal public sphere as defined by its reference to the political system remain permeable in principle."[30] These conditions show that civil society by itself is insufficient for deliberative democracy without a unifying public sphere. A rich associational life does not promote deliberation without an overarching public sphere that unites these "partial societies" and avoids the "mischief of factions."[31] Only in this way can arguments be challenged by counterarguments and transform citizens' views. (4) Finally, the public sphere must be relatively free of serious distortions and blockages in communication. At the very least, this means that in critical moments it must be possible for the public sphere to mobilize itself and place issues on the agenda. It also means that the mass media, which plays a central role in the dissemination of arguments and information, cannot simply be controlled, restricted, or distorted by powerful social interests.[32]

Hence, by way of the various informal organizational avenues for voicing concerns and contributing arguments and proposals, a vibrant public sphere ensures that public deliberation does not exclude any citizens and their viewpoints. If the public sphere takes the lead in rendering deliberation inclusive, then formal legislative bodies focus this deliberation for purposes of decision making. This focusing has two aspects. First, in a well-functioning system, all the relevant information, arguments, and viewpoints should come together in the legislative body (with the help of research staffs, government statistical bureaus, lobbyists, etc.). Second, members of Congress and Parliament should be able to give the relevant arguments a more focused and detailed consideration than can citizens who are enmeshed in other pursuits.[33] In effect, the inclusive participation of *citizens* in the public sphere is thereby translated into the inclusion of *arguments* in Parliament and in other deliberative bodies.[34] This can be further elaborated as four conditions that are roughly parallel to the conditions on a well-functioning, vibrant public sphere: (1) Legislative bodies must be open or "porous" to more widespread public discourses. Social critics can then perform the task of introducing new themes and interpretations into the discourse of the legislative public. (2) This openness places certain technical conditions on the composition of legislative bodies, so as to ensure adequate representation of views and interests. These conditions will ensure that public opinion appropriately guides decision making. (3) There must be a real exchange of arguments with deliberative uptake among legislators, so that the weaker arguments are screened out and the better ones survive and sway the majority (see, e.g., 307 and 340). (4) Finally, it is important to design procedural mechanisms that compensate for the distorting effects of self-interest and power, so that the chances are increased that the stronger arguments will in fact prevail at the moment of decision.[35]

III

We now have Habermas's basic model of deliberative democracy in broad outline: democratic procedures should allow a broadly based, subjectless public communication to be institutionally channeled toward specific decisions backed by socially effective power; insofar as discursive structures govern this whole process, the process itself is rational and its outcomes, reasonable to all citizens.

However, there are two ways of interpreting this reasonability. One account in emphasizes procedures of deliberation itself. But the discourse theory already discussed in this chapter, which issues in a democratic principle oriented toward unanimity, highlights *the outcome* as one upon which all citizens would ideally converge. Even if this outcome is constructed rather than discovered, it amounts to something like a "right answer," or at least implies a *singular* concept of public reason.[36] From this standpoint, discursive processes make sense precisely in the pursuit of consensus on right answers. Even if we reject the idea that a political question has a *single* right answer, Habermas's account at least requires that deliberation should delimit that *set* of solutions that can satisfy moral, ethical, and pragmatic conditions of acceptability. With such general constraints in place, it is then possible to resolve any further differences by compromise or concession. (In the health care debate, a requirement of universal coverage acts as just such a constraint on public compromises.) Communicative structures and procedural designs thus have a rationalizing effect on politics because they help voters and their representatives at least to begin to converge on cognitively persuasive outcomes. Even if Habermas's model makes considerable concessions to the complexity and plurality of actual, situated deliberation, *at the ideal level* it concedes nothing. The rational character of decentered, "subjectless" public deliberation still depends on the same discursive idealizations that stand in tension with the facts of pluralism and complexity, such as the need for compromise even on moral issues. To put it another way, real plurality is "transsubstantiated" into idealized unanimity, and thereby rationalized.[37] This sort of transformation of disagreements seems to require three rather strong assumptions about argumentation, each of which is open to serious challenge when applied to political deliberation.[38]

First, for unanimity to be possible in the political arena, Habermas must assume that there are no intractable conflicts between different types of discourse. The problems posed by such conflicts among the values of different practical perspectives have been the focus of considerable philosophical attention recently. Moral theorists, for example, have examined the possibility of intractable conflicts between impartial morality, desires for happiness, and the demands of interpersonal bonds (e.g., between friends). In legal and political theory, one thinks of the possible conflicts between individual rights and collective benefits, or those between liberty and equality.[39] In the political context, Habermas's discourse theory handles such conflicts either by optimistically differentiating among types of issues that are "self-selecting" or by constructing a hierarchy of discourses (with moral discourse at the top, followed by ethical discourse, etc.).[40] Where these mechanisms fail—as Habermas has recently admitted they may—one must simply rely on institutional procedures to decide the question.[41] But such procedures are not based on a meta- or superdiscourse with the authority to arbitrate disputes between types of discourse. Such a superdiscourse would require practical reason to have a unity that is no longer possible today; as Habermas puts it, we "cannot speak of practical reason in the singular."[42] Although this pluralist view of practical reason is widespread in contemporary moral and political theory,[43] it would seem to pose a particular problem for Habermas. For it undermines his view of political consensus, which presupposes potential unanimity in the choice among types of discourses and criteria among those deliberating in the public sphere. Disputes at this level are literally arguments without a home—there is no place where they can be discursively adjudicated. Should they prove to be more than occasion exceptions, then the consensual basis of legitimacy would be in jeopardy.

The second assumption is related to the first. Habermas's idea that democratic results are susceptible to unanimous approval, at least in principle, implies that citizens can always clearly separate the rational-discursive aspects of issues from those aspects that require compromise. In his reply to critics in the 1994 "Postscript" to *Between Facts and Norms*, Habermas shifts from distinguishing separate types of discourse to "analytical aspects" of problems: "Political questions are normally so complex that they require simultaneous treatment of pragmatic, ethical and moral *aspects*."[44] Precisely because moral and ethical-political issues still can be separated by competent participants in discourse, at least analytically, conflicts can be avoided. Citizens do not have to compromise their moral integrity or their self-understanding as members of a given country (135–138, 182). Furthermore, if the technical-pragmatic aspects are dealt with by experts, then they too need not compromise their professional integrity. At worst, more particularistic values and aspects of identity, or one's particular interests, may have to yield before moral and ethical-political considerations. At least in principle, the capacity of each citizen to separate aspects of problems keeps them from having to compromise their deepest values and thus to avoid deep conflicts with one another.

This second assumption may undermine the ability of discourse theory to deal with contemporary pluralism. Moreover, it may even underestimate the potentials for disagreement implied by Habermas's discourse theory itself.

For Habermas grants that the moral point of view is internally related to need-interpretations and thus to "ethical" values. More precisely, moral norms regulate matters in the equal interest of all, and on almost any plausible reading it is difficult to separate the determination of what is equally in each individual's interest from how individuals perceive and evaluate those interests. But if, as he also maintains, one cannot always expect unanimity on substantive values and questions of identity—especially when the values are not shared by the whole group—then there is an opening within *moral* discourse for disagreements resistant to argumentative resolution. This implies that on some justice issues, citizens could find themselves in irreconcilable but *reasonable* disagreement.[45] Now according to Habermas, participants can overcome such conflicts to the extent that they can separate out the particularistic sources of conflict and strike a fair compromise, or to the extent that they can frame the issue at a more abstract level that allows for resolution from the standpoint of impartiality or neutrality (while leaving the ethical conflicts themselves unresolved). Indeed, the very legitimacy of law requires citizens to assume that such resolutions are at least possible in principle.[46] But in cases where subcultural ethical values and particular identities affect the very interpretation of justice and impartiality, then consensus would seemingly require different groups first to resolve those ethical differences behind their competing views of justice—a task one need not assume is possible in principle. Even aside from this problem, however, one may ask whether it is possible or reasonable to expect citizens to treat their moral identities as Habermas's account of abstraction requires.

Third, Habermas makes strong assumptions about ideal convergence toward the correct answer, even in cases of incomplete deliberation. Convergence of public opinion seems required even under nonideal, actual epistemic conditions. If deliberation within legislatures and among voters is to improve the chances that majority outcomes are correct, then one seemingly must make a rather strong assumption about the relation between incomplete deliberation in a group and the majority's likelihood of being swayed toward the correct view of a matter. After a period of debate, voters—even in parliaments—may still have only an imperfect grasp of the relevant information and arguments. Incomplete deliberation, even if open and inclusive, does not necessarily increase the chances that the better arguments will prevail. There is no guarantee under the less than ideal conditions of incomplete deliberation and information that there will be any view at all toward which the majority of citizens will converge, of if there is, that this view is the correct one. Moreover, such convergence still does not follow even under the further counterfactual assumption that public discourse is ideology-free, that is, free of undetected restrictions in communication. Incompleteness by itself may well make the deliberation underdetermining, even if good arguments are

available. One might say, then, that Habermas's linkage between real decen-
teredness and ideal convergence requires the Socratic assumption that the
likelihood of a majority's converging upon the better argument is proportion-
al to the amount, or length, of deliberation.[47]

IV

If the foregoing assumptions should prove difficult to defend at many
points and at different levels, especially in view of the depth of contemporary
multicultural pluralism, then one has good reason to provide a weaker interpretation of epistemic deliberation than Habermas's. This weaker reading
does not deny that public reason is singular in some respects and on certain
issues—in fact it presupposes this in order that citizens still can deliberate in
a civic public sphere. But merely deliberating together in a common public
sphere does not presuppose ideal convergence, even in principle. The weaker
reading thus makes more room for pluralism, including moral pluralism, than
does the stronger interpretation of unanimity.

The key to a weaker reading is this: to consider a political decision legitimate, citizen-deliberators need not make the strong assumption that their
deliberative process makes it more likely that the outcome is one on which
everyone would ultimately and ideally *converge*. Rather, it is enough for them
to assume that, given the conditions of deliberation, outcomes and decisions
allow an *ongoing cooperation with others* of different minds that is at least *not
unreasonable*. Citizens are justified in making this corrigible supposition, for
all practical purposes, if the deliberative process satisfies at least three closely related conditions. First, the discursive structures of informal and formal
deliberation make it less likely that irrational and untenable arguments will
decide outcomes. Second, decision-making procedures are structured to allow
possibilities for revisions—of arguments, decisions, and even procedures—
that either take up features of defeated positions or better their chances for
being heard. Third, deliberative decision-making procedures are broadly
inclusive, so that minorities may reasonably expect that they will be able to
affect future outcomes in ways that they have not been able to so far. This is
not, to be sure, a full account of rational cooperation—for that one would have
to bring in the costs of noncooperation and presence of basic-rights guarantees. But, as we shall argue, it does broaden the normative account of legitimacy to recognize forms of compromise that are not simply based on strategic calculations.

In any case, the first condition implies that the various institutions and
publics outlined in this chapter have, in the first instance, a *negative* and hence
critical function. That is, they are meant to elevate debate to a civil and pub-

lic level by ensuring that simple and crude appeals to prejudice can be publicly challenged and undermined, that subtle and not-so-subtle coercion will be exposed and contested, and that unjustifiable exclusionary mechanisms will be eliminated and corrected. On many issues, vigorous pursuit of these measures may suffice to produce a positive consensus. But this need not be the case, and reasonable disagreements may still persist. That, however, is just the point: that all *un*reasonable disagreements, as well as unreasonable *agreements*, be eliminated.

With the elimination of unreasonable appeals to fear, prejudice, and ignorance, many citizens may transform their preference and beliefs and adopt substantively different positions. But this depends on many empirical factors and need not necessarily always be the case. On the contrary, it may be that people retain their original views, only now supported by even better and hence more reasonable arguments that only sharpen existing conflicts. Discursive structures, in other words, primarily raise the level of debate, even when they do not produce agreement. Insofar as a vibrant public sphere contains a variety of arenas and publics that submit unreflective views to criticism, insofar as institutional checks screen arguments against careful and public scrutiny of the facts and a representative inclusion of different constituencies, insofar as the mass media is not myopic, it should be more difficult for proposals and candidates to carry the day on the basis of empty rhetoric. To borrow Robert Goodin's phrase, making reasons public may "launder" them, "filtering the inputs" of public deliberation about conflicts through public testing.[48]

The second condition, revisability, appears in a number of forms, one of which is already implicit in the first condition. Precisely because the public testing of reasons and outcomes in effect "launders" majority views, it makes it possible for minorities to influence the set of reasons that justify outcomes. Thus, the fact that rational deliberation is guided by publicity can engender a revision of *substantive arguments*, which, even if it does not terminate in consensus, can bring positions closer together so that a kind of moral compromise becomes possible. We will illustrate this momentarily. Often, however, one associates revisability simply with the change of earlier outcomes through the repetition of the procedure (or through the use of an alternative procedural route). Democratic procedures typically allow for this in many different ways, such as periodic elections, the repeal of laws, legal review, and constitutional amendments.[49] Finally, revisability can also touch the procedures themselves: democratic procedures may be revised in order to re-establish the equal power of minorities to influence deliberative outcomes in the face of contingent social and demographic facts that may undermine cooperation. If such facts make minorities permanent, democratic institutions will not be "well-ordered" in John Rawls's sense; they will not ensure the political equality necessary for mutual cooperation. In each of these forms, revisability has the effect of "compel[ling] the majority to take the minority into account, at least to a certain extent."[50] For example, the extension of the equal protection clause in the New Deal to include economic rights helped redress social imbalances that undermined equal participation in political procedures.[51]

The possibility of having one's (defeated) position taken into account, as well as other forms of revisability, points to the third condition, inclusivity. With substantive revisions, for example, minority positions have a role in shaping majority outcomes. The future possibility of reversing majorities means that minorities are not permanently excluded from decision making, and that procedural revisions are introduced precisely to safeguard this possibility by increasing voting equality. In general, more inclusive deliberative and decision-making procedures make it more likely that citizens will overcome both their myopia and ethnocentrism. For example, knowing that their decisions may have to be revised to maintain publicity and equality, citizens will think of their democratic practices in an inclusive and future-oriented way. They will also regard themselves as potentially occupying the minority position; even if they are in the majority for now, this alone does not lend their arguments epistemic force as necessarily the better ones.

This weaker epistemic conception opens up a space for forms of compromise that go beyond the balance of interests envisioned by Habermas. Here we will simply illustrate how a kind of "moral compromise" becomes possible insofar as deliberation allows citizens to see that an opposing view is not simply based, at least in any obvious way, on self-deception or prejudice. This makes it easier to search for a common framework that is accepted by each group for *different* reasons but allows opposing groups to maintain social cooperation.[52] Moral compromises seek to change the framework for ongoing deliberation in such a way that each can continue to cooperate from their own diverse perspectives. Here the idea of a "framework" includes both the pool of available reasons and the procedures of deliberation itself—two elements that are often only analytically distinguishable. Hence successful moral compromise must expand the pool of available reasons in order to get beyond the incompatibility of current interpretations, and it must be procedurally fair.

This is in fact the way in which constitutional assemblies have proceeded historically. They did not produce a single, coherent set of principles, but a complex patchwork of compromises and even conflicting values. For example, Federalists and anti-Federalists together constructed the framework of constitutional checks and balances in such a way as to reflect both their principles. Third-party mediation of conflicts may also illuminate the sorts of devices that promote moral compromises. For example, the Camp David accords can be seen as a successful moral compromise in which President Carter did not proceed by way of abstract principles. He slowly constructed an alternative framework in communication facilitated by a changing negotiation text. Once this device overcomes the initial incompatibilities, it may then be possible to deliberate in common about a new moral framework, with new rules of cooperation and new forms of justification. What is interesting about this procedure of compromise formation is that it does not require an assumed background consensus; each party can modify the text according to their own values and principles, and the result does not necessarily reduce the plurality of points of view in the same way as impartiality implies. The text is precisely the ongoing framework of deliberation, which in each round must be modified enough to assure continued cooperation by both sides.[53]

In sum, one would expect such mechanisms for cooperation and compromise to become particularly important when political decisions concern difficult issues of justice, which for Habermas does not allow for compromise. Suppose, for example, that I vote in the minority on an issue that I consider a question of justice. If the lack of open discussion leads me to believe the majority has largely been swayed by passion, prejudice, or ignorance, or perhaps manipulated by powerful interests that control access to the mass media, then on both the strong and weak interpretation of rational deliberation I have good reason to question the legitimacy of the outcome, and my compliance with the decision should be grudging at best. But if on the contrary there was an open and honest treatment of the issue prior to the vote, then I am less justified in my suspicions about the legitimacy of the outcome. Even if I still disagree with the majority, I can at least see that their position can be argued in public. Moreover, procedures used to construct compromises can allow minorities to accept decisions based on future oriented considerations, such as revision or the building of new coalitions. If I take the unanimity requirement in Habermas's democratic principle at face value, however, then I would seemingly always be justified in questioning the very *legitimacy* of all majoritarian outcomes, no matter how well-debated and revisable. By contrast, if I accept a weaker reading of legitimacy, I can dispute the ultimate correctness of the outcome (which seems open to reasonable dispute in this case) and still acknowledge that the outcome has legitimacy insofar as it is not obviously unreasonable. I can also reasonably expect that such outcomes may be revised in the future and thus that my continued cooperation and participation may even effectively bring such changes about if my reasons are publicly convincing.

V

The discursive process of working out a moral compromise suggests a solution to the problems of complexity and pluralism that remain in

Habermas's notion of deliberative democracy. In *The Theory of Communicative Action*, Habermas spoke of the need for "reversing step by step the strong idealizations by which the concept of communicative action has been built up."[54] Such a process of "de-idealization" of the theory of communicative rationality is necessary to bring its analyses closer to the complexity of actual social situations. This reversal must be done, however, "without sacrificing all theoretical perspectives for analyzing the coordination of interactions." *Between Facts and Norms* represents Habermas's own extended attempt to do just that through understanding the intermediate status of the law. His insistence on unanimity in his formulation of the democratic principle reflects the determination to maintain his theoretical perspective. However, this insistence is not only theoretically unnecessary; it is also empirically implausible for a democratic theory appropriate to contemporary social conditions. We have argued that Habermas has not gone far enough with his program of "reversing the idealizations of the theory," beginning with his identification of unanimous agreement under ideal conditions with the rationality of outcomes of political discourse. But, as the problems of moral compromise show, pluralism and complexity require abandoning precisely the assumptions underlying this ideal.

We propose three weaker assumptions about complex political discourse in their place. Pluralism and complexity do not require that we abandon the theory or its approach to deliberative democracy, but that we weaken the strong assumptions that support unanimity as the guiding principle for democratic deliberation.

First, conflicts between types of discourses and hence disputes about what sorts of claims are involved in an issue are ineliminable in pluralistic societies. Rather than being the subject of a "precommitment" to liberal principles and removed from public debate, they fall within the bounds of reasonable disagreement.[55] Such conflicts do indeed produce enduring problems and domains of social life whose boundaries are constantly contested. In these "hard cases" and "essentially contested issues," it is not always possible to separate epistemic, or discursive, aspects of the problem from those settled by bargaining or compromise.[56] Examples of these sorts of issues include enduring disputes about the boundaries of the private and public sphere, or religious and secular domains. Cultural identities are connected precisely to how people make such distinctions among social domains and types of reasons, and thus disputes will emerge about how citizens draw these boundaries differently in pluralist societies.

Second, it follows from this first assumption of pluralism that democratic deliberation does not require, as Habermas sometimes believes, agreements about how to make distinctions among different aspects of problems. Citizens can deliberate about these issues from many different perspectives, since they are capable of entering into a variety of different types of discourses on the same topic. Citizens are able to deliberate well and to solve disputes only if they are able to distinguish appeals to reasons from appeals to prejudices in the pluralist civic public sphere. This capability will enable them to see that their differences, no matter how deep, are connected with positions that can at least be argued in public, even if the arguments are not conclusive for all citizens. Only if citizens understand each other in this way can they correctly identify when reasonable disagreement is at stake in their political discourse. Publicly establishing that competing views can each be argued in public, rather than convergence on consensus, then becomes the modest goal of dialogic deliberation among pluralist citizens. Such an argument may prepare the way for both parties to recognize the need to consider a new view that both ultimately may recognize as correct. More often, however, reasonable disagreements can be settled by moral compromise.

Third, even incomplete deliberation represents an epistemic gain on the weaker view, so long as it is open and inclusive to all reasons. These gains should be put negatively, however. Under pluralist conditions, incomplete public deliberation acts as a filter upon the acceptability of the reasons that are the source of potential conflict. After open public deliberation and dialogue, citizens will be less likely to accept reasons that appeal to ideologies, passions, or interests. Being able to see issues from a variety of perspectives and points of view will help such publicly irrational reasons lose their motivating force. At the very least, bad arguments are less likely to be acceptable to a democratic majority after vigorous deliberation and dialogue, and in this way citizens will be motivated to revise those beliefs, practices, and norms that depend upon such reasons even if they are not the subject of the original issue in dispute. Losers in incomplete deliberation may bring about wide changes of this sort. For important cases of public unreason and ideological restrictions of communication, the weaker version of the democratic principle still performs the critical functional of identifying unreasonable disagreement, without sacrificing the normative analysis of cooperation and coordination.

Between the full consensus that correctness would entail and the elimination of obvious sources of unreason, there is room for a form of moral compromise that does not sacrifice rational integrity. This might partly explain why citizens more readily accept unfavorable institutional outcomes when these have been preceded by discourse or opportunities to voice their disagreements.[57] On our revised view, Habermas's ideal of deliberative democracy helps us to understand why majority rule must always be linked with the free and open public sphere, in which we can cooperate but not necessarily agree with each other. Only if he revises his principle of democracy and removes the strong condition of unanimity can Habermas solve the problems of complexity that he sets for himself. Only then do the resources of public, "subjectless" communication provide a plausible empirical defense of the relevance of the ideals of radical democracy for complex and pluralistic societies. The weaker arguments that we have offered are thus not only more defensible and consistent. They also better fulfill Habermas's own goals of reversing the idealizations of his theory, reconstructing the potential for rationality built into current democratic institutions, and defending the heritage of radical democracy under contemporary conditions.

Notes

* The authors would like to express their appreciation to R. Randall Rainey, Larry May, William O'Neill, Timothy Clancy, Mark Burke, and Thomas McCarthy for commenting on earlier versions of this essay.

1. See, for example, Joshua Cohen, "Deliberation and Democratic Legitimacy," in *The Good Polity*, eds. A. Hamlin and P. Pettit (New York: Oxford University Press, 1989), pp. 17–34; James S. Fishkin, *Democracy and Deliberation: New Directions for Democratic Reform* (New Haven, 1991); John S. Dryzek, *Discursive Democracy: Politics, Policy, and Political Science* (Cambridge: Cambridge University Press, 1990); for the relation to representation, see Cass R. Sunstein, "Interest Groups in American Public Law," *Stanford Law Review* 38 (1985): 29-87; for a close study of deliberation in Congress, see Joseph M. Bessette, *The Mild Voice of Reason: Deliberative Democracy and American National Government* (Chicago: University of Chicago Press, 1994). For an account of deliberative democracy in complex and pluralist societies, see James Bohman, *Public Deliberation* (Cambridge: Massachusetts Institute of Technology Press, 1996).

2. Rousseau's account of the "general will" in his *Contrat Social* is sometimes interpreted this way; for Habermas's critique, see *BFN*, 100–104. For Habermas's earlier critique of Rousseau, see Habermas, "Legitimation Problems of the Modern State," in *Communication and the Evolution of Society* (Boston: Beacon, 1979), p. 186. For an historical overview of republicanism and its influence, see Frank Michelman, "The Supreme Court 1985 Term—Forward: Traces of Self-Government," *Harvard Law Review* 100 (1986): 4–77; also his "Political Truth and the Rule of Law," *Tel Aviv University Studies in Law* 8 (1988): 281–291. Habermas includes Benjamin R. Barber, Michelman, Michael Sandel, and Charles Taylor among "civic republicans"; most communitarians could also be included.

3. Among many recent examples is the former Yugoslavia, where newly formed nations have defined the common good in ethnic terms and enacted constitutions on the basis of ethnicity. To be sure, many civic republicans do not require such an oppressive degree of homogeneity; for example, Michelman, "Law's Republic," *Yale Law Journal* 97 (1988): 1493-1537, strives to formulate a pluralist, inclusive version of civic republicanism; cf. also Taylor, "The Politics of Recognition," in

Multiculturalism, ed. Amy Gutmann (Princeton: Princeton University Press, 1994), pp. 25–73.

4. Habermas critically appropriates Niklas Luhmann's conception of social complexity. For a clear statement of the special problems of functional differentiation and complexity for democracy, see Danillo Zolo, *Democracy and Complexity* (University Park: Pennsylvania State University Press, 1992), especially chapter 3; for a criticism of Habermas's claims about the "unavoidable complexity" of modern societies, see Bohman, *Public Deliberation*, chapter 4. For a criticism of the macrosociology behind more skeptical views of democracy, see Bohman, *New Philosophy of Social Science: Problems of Indeterminacy* (Cambridge: Massachusetts Institute of Technology Press, 1991), chapter 4.

5. The problems primarily have to do with the interpretation of voting results. For a brief introduction with further literature, see Ian McLean, "Forms of Representation and Systems of Voting," in *Political Theory Today*, ed. David Held (Stanford: Stanford University Press, 1991), pp. 172–196; for a more detailed, accessible introduction, see William H. Riker, *Liberalism Against Populism: A Confrontation Between the Theory of Democracy and the Theory of Social Choice* (Prospect Heights, Ill.: Waveland, 1982). On the debate between social choice conceptions and deliberative models, see not only Riker but also Joshua Cohen, "An Epistemic Conception of Democracy," *Ethics* 97 (1986): 26–38; Russell Hardin, "Public Choice versus Democracy," and the reply by Thomas Christiano, "Social Choice and Democracy," both in *The Idea of Democracy*, eds. David Copp, Jean Hampton, and John E. Roemer (Cambridge: Cambridge University Press, 1993), pp. 157–172 and 173–195; also Jack Knight and James Johnson, "Aggregation and Deliberation: On the Possibility of Democratic Legitimacy," *Political Theory* 22 (1994): 277–296.

6. See Cohen, "Deliberation and Democratic Legitimacy," pp. 24–25.

7. For the theory of representation in the U.S. Constitution, see Bessette, *Mild Voice*, chapter 2. For an account of the role of representation in complex societies, see Robert Dahl, *Democracy and Its Critics* (New Haven: Yale University Press, 1989), 311–341.

8. For a more detailed account of the mechanisms that enable public reasons to be convincing, see Bohman, *Public Deliberation*, chapter 1.

9. Besides Cohen's "Epistemic Conception," see David Estlund, "Making Truth Safe for Democracy," in *Idea of Democracy*, eds. Copp, Hampton, and Roemer, pp. 71–100. Estlund argues that an epistemic account need not be authoritarian or elitist. For an account of Habermas's writings on democracy prior to *Between Facts and Norms* in terms of an epistemic conception of democracy, see Bohman, "Participating in Enlightenment: Habermas' Cognitivist Interpretation of Democracy," in *Knowledge and Politics*, eds. M. Dascal and O. Gruengard (Boulder, Colo.: Westview Press, 1988), 264–289. For Habermas's generally positive assessment of Cohen's views, see *BFN*, 304ff.

10. See Cohen's "Deliberation and Democracy"; also "Epistemic Conception," p. 32, in which the standard of correctness is defined in terms of "an ideal procedure of deliberation." A process view of political knowledge is also defended by Barber, *Strong Democracy: Participatory Politics for a New Age* (Berkeley: University of California Press, 1984), pp. 167–198.

11. See Habermas, *The Theory of Communicative Action*, 2 vols., trans. Thomas McCarthy (Boston: Beacon, 1984; 1987), 1:1–42, and 273–337.

12. For a sketch of these procedural idealizations, see Robert Alexy, "A Theory of Practical Discourse," in *The Communicative Ethics Controversy*, eds. Seyla Benhabib and Fred Dallmayr (Cambridge: Massachusetts Institute of Technology Press, 1990), pp. 151–190.

13. For a more in-depth treatment of this point, see William Rehg, *Insight and Solidarity: A Study in the Discourse Ethics of Jürgen Habermas* (Berkeley: University of California Press, 1993), part 1.

14. For the following description of discourse and bargaining, see *BFN*, 151-168.

15. Habermas sees a tendency toward this error in Hannah Arendt's republicanism; *BFN*, 146–152; see also his "Hannah Arendt: On the Concept of Power," in Habermas, *Philosophical-Political Profiles*, trans. F. Lawrence (Cambridge: 1985), pp. 173–189. For an account of the tension between deliberation and democracy in the Constitution, see Bessette, *Mild Voice*, chapters 1–2.

16. See *BFN*, 170–186 for a two-track interpretation of the U.S. system, see Bruce Ackerman, "Neo-federalism?" in *Constitutionalism and Democracy*, eds. J. Elster and R. Slagstad (Cambridge: Cambridge University Press, 1988), pp. 153–193. See also Ackerman, *We the People*, vol. I (Cambridge: Harvard University Press, 1991). For the use of the principal-agent distinction from contract law as a way of understanding representation as a form, of delegation, see Bernhard Peters, *Integration moderner Gesellschaften* (Frankfurt, Germany: Suhrkamp, 1993), pp. 284ff.

17. See Nancy Fraser, "Rethinking the Public Sphere: A Contribution to the Critique of Actually Existing Democracy," in *Habermas and the Public Sphere*, ed. Craig Calhoun (Cambridge: Massachusetts Institute of Technology Press, 1992), pp. 109–142; here p. 134. Habermas appropriates Fraser's analysis in FG, 373.

18. Samuel L. Popkin, *The Reasoning Voter: Communication and Persuasion in Presidential Campaigns* (Chicago: University of Chicago Press, 1991), provides a detailed account of the "low-information" rationality characterizing voters' reasoning in presidential elections.

19. Habermas seems to suggest this very distinction in *BFN*, 363–364.

20. Popkin, *Reasoning Voter*, pp. 47–49. For various analyses of democracy from the standpoint of information dissemination, see *Information and Democratic Processes*, eds. John Ferejohn and James Kuklinski (Urbana: University of Illinois Press, 1990).

21. For an account of how nondecisions can be explained in terms of restrictions in public communication, see Bohman, "Communication, Ideology, and Democratic Theory," *American Political Science Review* 84, no. 1 (1990): 93–104.

22. On the concept of information pooling, see *Information Pooling and Group Decision Making*, eds. B. Grofman and G. Owen (Westport, Conn.: JAI Press, 1983).

23. If this use of "aggregation" sounds novel, it is not without precedent; see David Estlund, "Democracy without Preference," *Philosophical Review* 99 (1990): 397–423, who argues that aggregative mechanisms need not be antithetical to deliberation on the common interest; this is also one of the main points of Johnson and Knight's argument in their "Aggregation and Deliberation." Recent work on information pooling and Condorcet's jury theorem are in a similar vein (see notes 23 and 26).

24. This extends some cautious remarks in *BFN*, 362–363; see also p. 341: "to the degree that practical reason is implanted in the very forms of communication and institutionalized procedures, it need not be embodied exclusively or even predominantly in the heads of collective or individual actors." The possibility of a rational public opinion is disputed in the literature: Bessette, *Mild Voice*, pp. 212–218, is rather skeptical, whereas Barber, *Strong Democracy*, is quite optimistic; see especially chapter 10. Fishkin's idea of a "deliberative opinion poll" represents an intermediate position; see his *Democracy and Deliberation*, pp. 1–13 and 81–104. A normative theory of public deliberation is not necessarily committed to the anti-skeptical view.

25. According to Condorcet's mathematical analysis of voting, if the average individual voter in a group has a better than 50 percent chance of voting "correctly" on a question, then the probability that a majority will be correct rapidly approaches certainty as the size of the group increases. For a brief presentation of Condorcet's probabilistic analysis of voting, see Duncan Black, *The Theory of Committees and Elections* (Cambridge: Cambridge University Press, 1958), pp. 159–180. On the possibility of applying this to a deliberative conception of democracy, see Bernard Grofman and Scott Feld, "Rousseau's General Will: A Condorcetian Perspective," *American Political Science Review* 82 (1988): 567–576; and David Estlund, Jeremy Waldron, Bernard Grofman, and Scott Feld, "Democratic Theory and the Public Interest: Condorcet and Rousseau Revisited," *American Political Science Review* 83 (1989): 1317–1340; on the compatibility of a Condorcetian analysis with opinion leaders, see Estlund, "Opinion Leaders, Independence, and Condorcet's Jury Theorem," *Theory and Decision* 36 (1994): 131-162.

26. Fraser, "Rethinking the Public Sphere," pp. 122–128. Here, too, "counterpublics" are not sufficient for democracy for the same reason that civil society is insufficient; the plurality of publics is democratic only if they are within an open civic public sphere, a point that is overlooked by Joshua Cohen and Joel Rogers, "Secondary Associations and Democratic Governance," *Politics and Society* 20 (1992): 393-472. We thus distinguish not only "strong" and "weak" publics, but also specialized and "civic" public spheres. Deliberative democracy depends on the existence of a larger, unifying civic public of all citizens.

27. "[T]his model takes a *structuralist approach* to the manner in which institutionalized opinion- and will-formation is linked with informal opinion-building in culturally mobilized public spheres. This linkage is made possible neither by the homogeneity of the people and the identity of the popular will, nor by the identity of a reason that is supposedly able simply to *discover* an underlying homogeneous general interest. . . . If the communicatively fluid sovereignty of citizens instantiates itself in the power of public discourses that spring from autonomous public spheres but take shape in the decisions of *democratically proceeding* and *politically responsible* legislative bodies, then the pluralism of beliefs and interests is not suppressed but unleashed and recognized in revisable majority decisions as well as in compromises. For then the unity of a completely proceduralized reason retreats into the discursive structure of public communication," *BFN*, 186; also 184–186).

28. "The exercise of political rule is oriented to and legitimated by the laws citizens give themselves in a discursively structured opinion- and will-formation. . . . The rational acceptability of outcomes reached in conformity with [democratic] procedure follows from the institutionalization of interlinked forms of communication that . . . ensure that all relevant questions, topics, and contributions are brought up and processed in discourses and negotiations on the basis of the best available information and arguments." (*BFN*, 170)

29. "Civil society is composed of those more or less spontaneously emergent associations, organizations, and movements that, attuned to how societal problems resonate in the private life-spheres, distil and transmit such reactions in amplified form to the public sphere. The core of civil society is comprised of a network of associations that institutionalizes problem-solving discourses on questions of general interest inside the framework of organized public spheres." (*BFN*, 366; see also 367–373) See also Fraser, "Rethinking the Public Sphere," pp. 121–128. On this concept of civil society, see especially Jean Cohen and Andrew Arato, *Civil Society and Political Theory* (Cambridge: Massachusetts Institute of Technology Press, 1992). In this quotation, Habermas is distinguishing public spheres according to their scope.

30. *BFN*, 373. Also, "In complex societies the public sphere . . . represents a highly complex network that branches out into a multitude of overlapping international, national, regional, local, and subcultural arenas. . . . Moreover, the public sphere is differentiated into levels according to the density of communication, organizational complexity, and breadth. . . . Despite these manifold differentiations, however, all the partial publics constituted by ordinary language remain porous to one another." (*BFN*, 373-374).

31. For a criticism of civil society theorists along these lines, see Bohman, *Public Deliberation*, chapter 2.

32. "The mass media ought to understand themselves as the mandatary of an enlightened public whose willingness to learn and capacity for criticism they at once presuppose, demand, and reinforce; like the judiciary, they ought to preserve their independence from political and social actors; they ought to look after the public's concerns and proposals in an impartial manner and . . . bring a demand for legitima-

tion and more intense criticism to the political process" (*BFN*, 378). On the mass media, see also *BFN*, 368 and 376–380; on mobilization of the public sphere, social movements, and agenda-setting, see 380-384.

33. See Bessette, *Mild Voice*, chapter 8; as Bessette points out, however, even the individual member of Congress is overtaxed by the complexity and quantity of the information and arguments affecting legislation; see p. 156. In this sense, congressional deliberation and decision making does not entirely escape the conditions of decentered subjectless communication; see *BFN*, 184. Note that Habermas formulates this focusing function in terms of the difference between discovery and justification: the meaning of institutionalized democratic procedures in strong publics "consists less in discovering and identifying problems than in dealing with them—it has less to do with becoming sensitive to new ways of looking at problems than with justifying the selection of a problem and the choice among competing proposals for solving it" (*BFN*, 307).

34. Habermas makes this point more or less explicitly with regard to ethical and moral discourses: "Discourses conducted by representatives can meet this condition of equal participation on the part of all members [i.e., citizens] only if they remain porous, sensitive and receptive to the suggestions, topics and contributions, information and arguments that flow in from a discursively structured public sphere" (*BFN*, 182); and "representation can only mean that with the election of parliamentary delegates, one provides for the broadest possible spectrum of interpretive perspectives to be anticipated from the inclusion of the self-understandings and world-views of marginal groups" (*BFN*, 183).

35. Habermas refers to this last condition as "countersteering"; see *BFN*, 327–328. The "steering" is done by "systemic" and hence noncommunicative power; "countersteering" derives from communicatively generated power. This power is supposed to be able to override the limitations that systemic power imposes on discourse and hence ultimately upon deliberative outcomes.

36. See Bohman, "Public Reason and Cultural Pluralism: Political Liberalism and the Problem of Moral Conflict," *Political Theory* 23 (1995); the designation of public reason as "singular" derives from John Rawls, *Political Liberalism* (New York: Columbia University Press, 1993), p. 220, where Rawls argues that "there is but one public reason."

37. This move provokes a general criticism of consensus theories in Bernard Manin, "On Legitimacy and Political Deliberation," trans. Elly Stein and Jane Mansbridge, *Political Theory* 15 (1987): 338-368; here 342.

38. For criticisms of the assumptions that follow, see Thomas McCarthy, "Practical Discourse: On the Relation of Morality to Politics," in his *Ideals and Illusions: On Reconstruction and Deconstruction in Contemporary Critical Theory* (Cambridge: Massachusetts Institute of Technology Press, 1991), pp. 181-199; David Ingram, "The Limits and Possibilities of Communicative Ethics for Democratic Theory," *Political Theory* 21 (1993): 294-321; McCarthy, "Legitimacy and Diversity:

Dialectical Reflections on Analytic Distinctions," *Habermas on Law and Democracy*, eds. Michel Rosenfeld and Andrew Arato (Berkeley: University of California Press, 1998); and Bohman, "Public Reason and Cultural Pluralism."

39. See, for example, Ronald Dworkin, *Taking Rights Seriously* (Cambridge: Harvard University Press, 1978); in moral theory, see Stuart Hampshire, *Morality and Conflict* (Cambridge: Harvard University Press, 1983), as well as the extensive literature on the "ethics of care."

40. See *BFN*, 155, 159f., 164f., and 167; also Habermas's "Reply to Participants in a Symposium," in *Habermas on Law and Democracy*, pp. 428-430.

41. Habermas, "Reply to Participants," pp. 429–430.

42. See ibid., pp. 428–433; also his article, "On the Employments of Practical Reason," in *Justification and Application*, trans. C. Cronin (Cambridge: Massachusetts Institute of Technology Press, 1993), especially pp. 16ff. In the latter work, Habermas argues that "there is no meta-discourse on which we could have recourse to in order to justify the choice between different forms of argumentation" (p. 16); rather than resolve this in terms of a kind of logical self-selection, however, he went on to give a realist account of problems, which "thrust themselves upon us; they have a situation defining power. . . ." (p. 17).

43. In his "Reply to Participants," Habermas is responding in particular to Gunther Teubner's position. But there are many current philosophical discussions of conflicts between "irreconcilable values." Besides Hampshire, *Morality and Conflict*, see, for example, Bernard Williams, *Moral Luck* (New York: Cambridge University Press, 1981); Michael Walzer, *Spheres of Justice* (New York: Basic, 1983); Thomas Nagel, "The Fragmentation of Value," in *Mortal Questions* (Cambridge: Cambridge University Press, 1979), 128-141; Thomas Nagel, *The View from Nowhere* (New York: Oxford University Press, 1986); Nagel, *Equality and Partiality* (New York: Oxford University Press, 1991); and Joseph Raz, *The Morality of Freedom* (Oxford: Oxford University Press, 1986), especially chapter 13. We need not defend the strong thesis of value incommensurability to make our point here; value pluralism requires only that there are incompatible values and that cultural pluralism heightens such conflicts. For the distinction between "incommensurable" and "incompatible" values, see Steven Lukes, "Understanding Moral Conflict," in *Liberalism and the Moral Life*, ed. N. Rosenblum (Cambridge: Harvard University Press, 1989), pp. 133ff. While incommensurability rules out compromise (which requires the possibility of creating some common currency), incompatibility does not.

44. Habermas, "Postscript," in *BFN*, p. 452.

45. See McCarthy, "Practical Discourse," pp. 182–192; McCarthy proposes an even stronger criticism of Habermas along these line in "Legitimacy and Diversity"; for a more optimistic view, see Rehg, *Insight and Solidarity*, chapter 4; in Habermas see *Theory of Communicative Action*, vol. I, p. 20; and "Wahrheitstheorien," in *Vorstudien und Ergänzungen zur Theorie des kommunikativen Handelns* (Frankfurt, Germany: Suhrkamp Verlag, 1986), pp. 127–183, here pp. 166–174.

46. See Habermas, "Reply to Participants," pp. 390–404; abstraction is exemplified when a society solves conflicts between different religious practices by recognizing an impersonal right of all groups to religious freedom; in "Reply to Participants" we read that the impartial standard for abstractions of this sort is the "equal right of different groups to coexist."

47. A strong assumption of this sort is also required if one wants to solve problems of instability by resort to deliberation (and not simply in terms of institutional design); see Knight and Johnson, "Aggregation and Deliberation," pp. 278–285.

48. Robert Goodin, "Laundering Preferences," in *Foundations of Social Choice Theory*, eds. J. Elster and A. Hylland (Cambridge: Cambridge University Press, 1986), pp. 75–102. This "cleansing," or filtering, effect of making preferences public should not be overestimated. It is limited only to those bad reasons and arguments that participants can detect; many prejudices and false ideological beliefs, however, may be too widely shared to be filtered simply by being made public. Moreover, such filtering may only reinforce preferences that are widely shared and those false beliefs that are publicly acceptable. These and other insidious community-wide restrictions in communication require social critics and social movements to make them part of public discourse.

49. Habermas also acknowledges this point in a general way in "Reply to Participants," p. 395.

50. Manin, "On Legitimacy and Political Deliberation," pp. 360–361.

51. This is argued by Ackerman, *We the People*, 1:38ff.

52. See Bohman, "Public Reason and Cultural Pluralism."

53. For an excellent account of the use of this device in the Camp David negotiations, see Howard Raiffa, *The Art and Science of Negotiations* (Cambridge: Harvard University Press, 1982), pp. 205–217.

54. Habermas, *Theory of Communicative Action*, 1:330.

55. For this view of constitutional rights and principles as "precommitments," see Samuel Freeman, "Reason and Agreement in Social Contract Views," *Philosophy of Public Affairs* 19 (1990): 122–157; and Jon Elster, *Ulysses and the Sirens* (Cambridge: Cambridge University Press, 1979), pp. 94ff. Our weaker epistemic view rejects such arguments as inconsistent with the sort of deliberation demanded by moral pluralism.

56. On what it would mean for an issue to be "essentially contested," see W. B. Gallie, "Essentially Contested Concepts," *Proceedings of the Aristotelian Society* 56 (1955–1956): 167–198. For a more recent treatment, see William Connolly, *The Terms of Political Discourse* (Lexington: Heath, 1974). As against both Gallie and Connolly, we do not draw skeptical conclusions about politics; moral compromises have epistemic weight. On boundary disputes, including abortion, see Kent Greenawalt, *Religious Convictions and Political Choice* (Oxford: Oxford University Press, 1988);

besides seeing a role for religion in inevitable disputes about "the borderline status" of events, persons, or things (e.g., those about birth and death, fetuses, or animal rights), Greenawalt grants religious conviction a public role so long as the religious reasons can be made "publicly accessible."

57. For a survey of empirical research on this topic, see E. Allen Lind and Tom R. Tyler, *The Social Psychology of Procedural Justice* (New York: Plenum, 1988). Another area of empirical research that supports this view is the phenomena of "cheap talk," in which preplay communication among strategic actors increases the likelihood of mutually beneficial outcomes; even without effective sanctions, it helps coordinate expectations among the players. See James Johnson, "Is Talk Really Cheap?" *American Political Science Review* 87, no. 1 (1993): 74–85.

3

Between Radicalism and Resignation:
Democratic Theory in Habermas's
Between Facts and Norms

William E. Scheuerman

A conformist political theory is no theory.
—Franz Neumann[1]

In 1962, a relatively unknown scholar published a contribution to democratic theory destined to generate something of a sensation in the still rather staid intellectual universe of postwar Germany. Appearing a mere thirteen years after the reestablishment of liberal democracy in Germany, the thirty-three-year-old Jürgen Habermas's landmark *Structural Transformation of the Public Sphere* focused on precisely those features of contemporary democracy that the young author's more conservative scholarly peers tended to downplay.[2] Influenced significantly by the neo-Marxism of the Frankfurt school, Habermas argued that contemporary democracy exhibited a number of troublesome tendencies: a catastrophic fusion of state and society, unforeseen by classical liberal theory, had resulted in the disintegration of the very core of liberal democratic politics, a public sphere based on the ideal of free and uncoerced discussion. In Habermas's scathing account, mounting evidence suggested that liberal democracy was evolving toward a new and unprecedented form of authoritarianism, a mass-based plebiscitarianism in which privileged organized interests linked hands (by means of what Habermas polemically described as "neofeudal" institutions fusing public and private power) in order to perpetuate social and political domination. Relying on the most advanced empirical American social science, Habermas argued that an ossified and inflexible political system, in which decisions increasingly were "legitimated" by means of subtle forms of mass persuasion, functioned alongside a profit-hungry mass media that trivialized public life in order to thwart democratic aspirations. The autonomous "bourgeois public sphere" of the late

61

eighteenth and early nineteenth centuries had been jettisoned for the "manipulated public sphere" of organized capitalism.

Habermas's study struck a raw nerve in the young German polity. Particularly in the context of a political system in which traditional cleavages seemed increasingly muted—recall Willy Brandt's 1961 comment that "in a sound and developing democracy it is the norm rather than the exception that the parties put forward similar, even identical demands in a number of fields"[3]—Habermas's analysis of the decline of a critical public sphere seemed prescient. Within a few years, the influence of Habermas's work was already manifest in political tracts, sometimes far more radical in character than his own study, written by those who openly identified with Germany's burgeoning New Left.[4]

Thirty years after the publication of his first major work, Habermas's *Between Facts and Norms: Contributions to a Discourse Theory of Law and Democracy* revisits many of the core concerns of his original contribution to democratic theory.[5] Once again, Habermas hopes to offer a conception of *deliberative democracy* capable of providing a guidepost for a revised critical theory. Indeed, the analytical framework of his recent contribution to democratic theory is infinitely more subtle than its predecessor, chiefly because Habermas himself has conceded that *The Structural Transformation of the Public Sphere* was seriously flawed.[6] Thus, his recent works articulates a sophisticated neo-Kantian brand of contract theory in dramatic contrast to the Hegelian-Marxism at the core of his original foray into democratic theory. Even more striking, the normative and institutional specifics of the discursive conception of the "public sphere" introduced, but inadequately developed in Habermas's 1962 work, are elaborated in great detail here. *Between Facts and Norms* also breaks dramatically with what Habermas has recently described as a form of crude "holism" implicit in traditional democratic socialism, according to which a more or less homogeneous "macrosubject" ("the people") is outfitted with the task of establishing a perfectly transparent, democratically planned economy in order to achieve full autonomy; Habermas now believes that this ideal, which clearly motivated his 1962 inquiry, fails to provide sufficient independence for the "system imperatives" of modern markets and bureaucracies. For Habermas, radical democracy has to come to grips with the exigencies of social complexity. The failure to do so can prove disastrous, as demonstrated by Soviet-style state socialism.[7] Finally, missing from *Between Facts and Norms* is a problematic feature pivotal to the dramatic texture of his 1962 study: an exaggerated contrast between a stylized freewheeling "bourgeois public sphere," described in a surprisingly sympathetic light, and the bleak reality of contemporary capitalist democracy, described in tones reminiscent of the apocalyptic cultural criticism of the early Frankfurt school. To his credit, Habermas now avoids the oftentimes tortured historical claims that rightly garnered so much criticism for *The Structural Transformation of the Public Sphere*.[8]. The democratic theory of *Between Facts and Norms* rests on an impressive attempt at rigorous political and social theorizing, not idiosyncratic myths about a liberal bourgeois "golden age."

But my concern here is not with explaining the conceptual advances of Habermas's *Between Facts and Norms* vis-à-vis *The Structural Transformation of the Public Sphere*. Scholars sympathetic to Habermas's project have already done so.[9] Instead, I would like to pursue an alternative line of inquiry. My guess is that Habermas's recent book is unlikely to ignite anything on the scale of the response ignited by his 1962 study. One might simply chalk this up to its immense intellectual complexity; *Between Facts and Norms* is accessible to only a minuscule group of scholarly experts. But it may also point to a profound weakness in Habermas's contemporary democratic theory, namely, its failure to give adequate expression to legitimate unease and anxiety about the fate of representative democracy at the end of the twentieth century. Despite rapidly growing evidence of widespread dissatisfaction with the operations of contemporary capitalist democracy, Habermas's work at times offers a surprisingly moderate and even conciliatory picture of "real-existing" democracy. In my view, Habermas's justified acknowledgment of the *intellectual* virtues of liberal and democratic thought à la John Stuart Mill or John Rawls, and his justified attempt to correct the theoretical failings of his early forays into democratic theory, seems to have generated a troubling side effect: an inadequately critical assessment of "real-existing" capitalist democracy.

Let me be more specific. In his eagerness to integrate a mind boggling array of alternative legal and political theories, *Between Facts and Norms* ultimately offers a deeply ambiguous account of modern democracy. Habermas's democratic theory now lends itself to two competing—but probably incompatible—interpretations, in part because Habermas undertakes to develop his model of deliberative democracy by relying on a series of politically and intellectually inconsistent views. First, *Between Facts and Norms* at times seems to point to the outlines of an *ambitious* radical democratic polity, based on far-reaching social equality, and outfitted with far-reaching capacities for overseeing bureaucratic and market mechanisms. Yet Habermas never adequately develops this line of inquiry. Despite his repeated attempts to overcome a false juxtaposition of normativity to facticity, this model remains at the level of an abstract "ought." Second, Habermas simultaneously suggests a *defensive* model of deliberative democracy in which democratic institutions exercise at best an attenuated check on market and administrative processes, and where deliberative publics most of the time tend to remain, as Habermas himself describes it, at rest (*im Ruhezustand*) (379). In my view, this second model risks abandoning the critical impulses that have motivated Habermas's intellectual work throughout his impressive career.

I begin with a brief introduction to the general features of Habermas's model of deliberative democracy before turning to an analysis of its inconsistent "critical" and "uncritical" renditions. Finally, I point to the possible sources of this tension in the conceptual structure of *Between Facts and Norms*. In particular, I hope to suggest that Habermas never offers an adequate analysis of the interface between democratic and administrative authority.

I

For Habermas, the normative core of modern democracy is best captured by the principle that "[o]nly those laws can claim legitimate validity if they meet with the agreement of all legal consociates in a discursive law-making procedure that in turn has been legally constituted."[10] Despite the immense complexity of Habermas's attempt to explicate this (deceptively simple) statement in *Between Facts and Norms*, the broad outlines of his institutional vision of deliberative democracy are relatively straightforward. Habermas develops what he describes as a "two-track" model of representative democracy, in which an "organized public" (consisting of legislative bodies and other formal political institutions) functions alongside an "unorganized public," a broader civil society in which citizens rely on a panoply of devices (including political associations and the mass media) to take part in freewheeling political debate and exchange. Formal political institutions do play a key role by "focusing" the process of public opinion formation and then codifying the results of that process by giving them a binding legal form, but Habermas's model places special weight on the importance of civil society: it is the freewheeling character of discourse outside the formal political arena that now takes on the absolutely pivotal role of identifying, thematizing, and interpreting political concerns.[11] Indeed, Habermas tends to wax enthusiastic about what he describes as the refreshingly "chaotic" and even "anarchic" nature of deliberation in civil society.

Habermas repeatedly describes civil society as "anonymous" and even "subjectless" in order to break with a long tradition in political theory that misleadingly conceptualizes "the people," in an overly concretistic way, as a unitary, collective sovereign. By more fully acknowledging the profoundly pluralistic and decentered quality of public life in modern democracy, Habermas hopes thereby to respond to theorists of difference who have worried about the potentially antipluralistic implications of the tendency, probably most evident in *The Structural Transformation of the Public Sphere*, to privilege a single, homogeneous public sphere engaged in the quest for rational agreement or unanimity.[12] Now, Habermas openly concedes that it only makes sense to talk of a diversity of public spheres, and in *Between Facts and Norms* he seems eager to show that complex processes of bargaining and compromise—dramatically distinct from the Rousseauian model of politics that haunted some of his previous works[13]—have a legitimate and even noble place to play in modern democracy.

But the anonymous character of civil society by no means renders it impotent. Explicitly building on Hannah Arendt's famous delineation of power from violence, Habermas describes civil society as the prime generator of what he calls "communicative power," according to which deliberation and action in concert are essential for understanding the *origins* of political power, though by no means the *exercise* or *use* of power. For Arendt, *"[p]ower* corresponds to the human ability not just to act but act in concert. Power is never the property of an individual; it belongs to a group and remains in existence only so long as the group keeps together."[14] In Habermas's view, Arendt thereby identifies the roots of power in uncoerced communication; she grasps the centrality of "the power of communication aimed at mutual understanding" (148). Communicative power constitutes a "scarce good" that state administrators rely on, but are unable to produce on their own (146–151). In this model, political power possesses a dualistic structure. Communicative power can only be effectively employed in complex modern societies by means of administrative bodies and forms of decision making that rest on strategic and instrumental-rational forms of action: "The legitimating ideals of administration are accuracy and efficiency. Administrators are to discover and undertake those actions that will be instrumental to the achievement of specific ends."[15] Thus, the nature of administrative power conflicts with the logic of communicative power, which is ultimately based—for Habermas as for Arendt—on relations of mutual recognition and respect.[16] Modern democracy thus seem paradox-ridden to the extent that it requires forms of (administrative) power structurally incommensurable with the very (communicative) power that alone make democratic deliberation possible in the first place; for Habermas, this is one of the more obvious manifestations of the tension between facticity and validity that he thematizes in the extremely demanding theoretical reflections found in the work's initial chapters.

For Habermas, in some distinction to Arendt, the medium of law plays a central role in transforming communicative power into administrative power. Crucial to *Between Facts and Norms* is the simple idea that law lies at the very intersection between communicative and administrative power. One of the most important implications of this insight is that the fate of representative democracy and the rule of law are intimately linked. Insofar as law potentially functions as a successful connecting-link or bridge between communicative and administrative power, the seeming paradoxes of modern democracy *are* surmountable. Communicative and administrative power should be able to cooperate fruitfully in the service of the plurality of deliberative "networks" that make up civil society. For Habermas, not only does Arendt fails to acknowledge adequately the autonomous dynamics of administrative power (and thus the paucity of legal analysis in her writings), but her republican streak leads her to envision "power" as a more or less spontaneous expression of a substantive common will.[17] In an extremely complicated discussion that I cannot do justice to here, Habermas tries to counter this view by arguing that communicative power combines otherwise distinct (in his terminology; "moral," "ethical," and "pragmatic") forms of deliberation: politics concerns questions of *moral fairness* guided by a rigorous neo-Kantian criteria of universalizability, questions of *cultural value and identity* concerned with arriving at an "authentic self-understanding" and that legitimately allow for a loosening of the tough standards of moral discourse, as well as *pragmatic* attempts to reach practical compromises that give equal weight to all relevant interests (155). Thus, political deliberations involve the quest for reaching an uncoerced, reasonable common understanding on normative matters *as well as* somewhat less pristine processes of mutual bargaining and compromise. In any case, crucial to this process is that we have "a warranted presupposition that public opinion be formed on the basis of adequate information and relevant reasons, and that those whose interests are involved have an equal and effective opportunity to make their own interests (and the reasons for them) known.[18] Habermas thus deserves to be grouped among those defending what has come to be described as a "public reasons" approach in political theory.

II

So much for the bare outlines of Habermas's democratic theory. What then is problematic about it?

At first, *Between Facts and Norms* seems to offer an ambitious interpretation of the idea of a two-track model of deliberative democracy. First, Habermas emphasizes that *all* manifestations of political power ultimately must derive from communicative power; even if indirectly, administrative power needs to legitimize itself by reference to discursive processes based in civil society (169). In particular, this is guaranteed by the principle of the legality of the administration. The medium of law merely *transfers* or *translates* communicative power into administrative power. The primacy of deliberatively derived law assures that communicative power effectively "determines the direction" (187) of the political system; in another formulation, Habermas claims that communicative power maintains or asserts (*behaupten*) itself against administrative and market mechanisms (299). Habermas by no means intends thereby to question the relative autonomy of complex markets and bureaucracies from the integrative force of communicative action. Nonetheless, some formulations in *Between Facts and Norms* suggest that their autonomy can legitimately be contained by means of a relatively *far-reaching* set of deliberatively derived democratic checks and controls on their operations. This is arguably a model not only, as Habermas himself tends to describe it, in which a "balance" has been achieved between communicative power, on the one side, and money and administrative power, on the other, but in which communicative power gains a preeminent position in relation to administrative and market processes (151), without thereby unduly impinging on the underlying dynamics of market and administrative subsystems.

Habermas builds on the work of socialist-feminist theorist Nancy Fraser, who has openly criticized Habermas's concessions to systems-theory *à la* Luhmann and has often sought to rework Habermas's theory in a more explicitly anticapitalist gloss than Habermas himself.[19] Habermas's most obvious debt to Fraser is his use of her distinction between "weak" and "strong" publics. For Fraser, weak publics simply refer to those unburdened by the immediate task of formal decision making, whereas strong publics (most importantly: elected legislatures) are those "whose discourse encompasses both opinion formation and decision making."[20] Both in chapters 4 and 7 of *Between Facts and Norms*, Habermas reproduces this formulation: for him as for Fraser, parliament at times is conceived as an *extension* of the deliberative networks constitutive of civil society, as an "organized middle point or focus of a society-wide network of communication" (182). Parliament is merely a technical device necessary in large, complex societies to "focus" the process of political debate and exchange, but this technical feature need not extinguish parliament's own deliberative attributes.[21] The task of making sure that parliamentary bodies are, in Habermas's expression, "porous" to civil society, is thus eminently realistic in light of the fact that there is nothing *structurally* distinct between weak and strong publics. In both, communicative power is predominant.

Fraser's original essay never adequately addresses the possibility that strong publics might be forced to realize communicative power in a manner distinct from the "anarchic" associational life found in civil society. But one can imagine that she might accept Habermas's gloss on her views in certain passages of *Between Facts and Norms*: in parliament, time constraints necessitate that actors are less concerned with the "discovery and identification than the treatment (*Bearbeitung*)" of problems, "less with developing a sensibility for new problem positions than with justifying the choice of problems and deciding between competing solutions" (307). Parliament serves as a site for impressive debate and exchange, even if the imperatives of the formal decision-making process reduce the "wild" and "anarchic" features in civil society. Habermas also suggests that "deciding between competing solutions" is likely to heighten the importance of *compromise* within the "strong" parliamentary public. But he can be interpreted as arguing that this need not vitiate his (and Fraser's) ambitious view of parliament as a deliberative policy-making body. Here, a compromise is "fair" when in accordance with three conditions: (1) it provides advantages to *each* party, (2) it tolerates no "free riders," and (3) it makes certain that no one is exploited in such a way as to force them to give up more than they gain by compromise (166). As Stephen K. White has noted, this theory of compromise means that "it is the privileged agent who is confronted with the choice of . . . demonstrating to what degree his inequality can be discursively justified," of showing that it is in accordance with standards of procedural equality, participation, nondeception, and nonmanipulation.[22] In this model, the process of reaching and then defending any particular compromise seems unlikely to entail the suppression of deliberation. On the contrary, it seems destined to encourage debate insofar as citizens are required by it to consider whether compromise procedures actually compensate for "asymmetrical power structures"(177), as Habermas demands that they must.

For our purposes, this last condition is most telling. Crucial to Fraser's discussion of weak and strong publics is the insight that "where societal inequality persists, deliberative processes in public spheres will tend to operate to the advantage of dominant groups and to the disadvantage of subordinates."[23] Thus, the achievement of a truly freewheeling civil society, as well as a parliament responsive to its dictates, demands that we radically challenge asymmetries of social power; Habermas's discussion of "fair" compromise can be interpreted as an illustration of this more general—and implicitly quite ambitious—point. Here again, Habermas reproduces Fraser's explicitly socialist argument: "*All* members of the political community have to be able to take part in discourse, though not necessarily in the same way" (182). In order for this requirement to gain substance, an egalitarian social environment needs to have been achieved: "Only on a social basis that has transcended class barriers and thrown off thousands of years of social stratification and exploitation" can we achieve a fully thriving civil society (308). At another juncture Habermas describes the merits of a civil society "adequately decoupled" from class structures, and then he adds that "social power should only manifest itself [in civil society] to the extent that it enables and does not *hinder* the exercise of citizenship" (175).

Deliberative democracy, it seems, *does* in fact need to break with what Karl Marx once described as the "prehistory" of class society. Although

Habermas seems allergic to the conceptual paraphernalia of traditional left-wing political theory, he does imply at many junctures that the socialist tradition's aspiration to destroy illegitimate socioeconomic inequality is anything but exhausted. On the contrary, this undertaking arguably takes on *renewed* significance in his work given the tremendous emphasis placed on civil society in it. To the extent that civil society is especially vulnerable to the pathologies of class domination, then it would seem incumbent on a democratic theory that places special emphasis on the importance of unhindered debate within civil society to salvage something of the socialist critique of the crippling inequalities of capitalist society, even if we now surely need to acknowledge the undeniable virtues of complex markets and bureaucracies in modern society.[24]

Habermas is right in following Fraser in focussing on the social barriers to deliberative democracy: the idea of a freewheeling deliberative democracy remains ideological as long as avoidable social inequalities undermine the deliberative capacities of the vast majority of humanity.[25] My concern is merely that *Between Facts and Norms* has nothing adequately *systematic* in character to say about "social asymmetries of power," let alone how we might go about counteracting them. Habermas points to the need for an account of how (1) capitalist domination undermines democratic deliberation and (2) some egalitarian alternative to existing capitalism alone can allow deliberative democracy to flourish. Alas, no such account is offered in his study. Indeed, matters may be complicated by the strikingly Weberian overtones of Habermas's definition of social power: "I use the expression 'social power' as a measure of an actor's chances to achieve his interests in social relations against the opposition of others" (192). Does this definition provide the best starting point for making sense of what Marxists have traditionally described as "structural" inequalities in economic power? I do not mean to trivialize the difficulty at hand here: in the wake of the demise of Marxist class theory, we still lack an adequate theory of social stratification.[26] Yet without some analysis of this sort, many of Habermas's more interesting proposals risk representing precisely what he seem so intent on avoiding in *Between Facts and Norms*: *normative aspirations* having at best a tangential relationship to the operations of real-existing capitalist democracy (373).

Many political scientists would, of course, legitimately note that Habermas's model of parliament as a focal point for meaningful debate represents at best an *ideal* of how parliament should operate.[27] Most parliaments today continue to rubber-stamp decisions that have been made elsewhere, by the upper divisions of the state bureaucracy working alongside the representatives of powerful organized social groups, in a manner not altogether unlike that described by the young Habermas in *The Structural Transformation of the Public Sphere* in 1962. Similarly, we would be hard-pressed to identify compromises in contemporary democracy that live up to the demanding standards of Habermas's model of just compromises. Amid the vast economic inequalities of contemporary capitalism, compromise often inevitably means that some group give up more than they gain: one only need recall the crippling "compromises" forced upon welfare state "clients" by neoliberal governments in recent years.

At worst, Habermas's comments about "social power" represent little more than a rhetorical leftover from the Hegelian-Marxism of *The Structural Transformation of the Public Sphere*. At best, they represent a starting point for a revised critical theory of contemporary capitalism—a critical theory that Habermas's *Between Facts and Norms* very much needs.

III

But Habermas's theory of deliberative democracy also lends itself to an alternative reading. Especially in the final chapters of *Between Facts and Norms*, Habermas is intent on showing that his theory has "empirical referents and represents more than a series of normative postulates" (451). However understandable, this move generates a real problem for Habermas: it leads him to an interpretation of the two-track model that stands in a profound tension to his initial reconstruction of Fraser's socialist-feminist democratic theory. Moreover, this revised model makes too many concessions to the often-times woeful conditions of "real existing" capitalist democracy—woeful realities, I should add, with which an ever-increasing number of our fellow citizens are rightfully becoming frustrated.[28]

The interpretation of Habermas's model along these potentially radical and socially critically lines suffers from an obvious flaw. Habermas's comments on the interface between communicative and administrative power are more ambivalent than I just suggested.[29] As I noted, at some junctures he argues that communicative power can rely on the medium of law to *determine* administrative power. Yet at many other junctures, Habermas offers a more modest view of the scope of communicative power: communicative power "more or less"(!) programs, and merely "influences" and "countersteers" administrative power. In any event, communicative power "itself cannot 'rule' (*herrschen*), but only steers the use of administrative power in certain directions" (300, 444). In this second line of argumentation, the significance of deliberative democratic processes within Habermas's overall model seems substantially reduced. Here, communicative power functions to "lay siege" in a defensive manner to the exercise of administrative power. But it is utopian to hope that communicative power can gain the upper hand in relation to bureaucratic (and market) mechanisms. In this final section, I hope to show that this ambiguity stems from a fundamental conceptual tension within Habermas's argument. For now, let me just suggest that Habermas's institutional gloss on his two-track model of democracy in the concluding chapters of *Between Facts and Norms* takes a substantially less ambitious form than what was just described.

In chapter 8, Habermas once again elaborates on his two-track model. But now Fraser's radical democratic socialism fades into the background. In its place, Habermas relies extensively on the work of Bernhard Peters, a German sociologist who has devoted much of his impressive intellectual ability over the course of the past decade to developing a critique of precisely those types of radical democratic arguments so important to writers like Fraser. Habermas here relies on a study that Peters himself openly describes as a contribution to a revised version of "realist" democratic theory, albeit of a "strongly modified normative" variety.[30] Like Habermas, Peters worries about the normative deficits of systems theory; in contradistinction to writers like Fraser, Peters thinks that critical theory remains excessively mired in unrealistic, radical liberal and radical democratic fantasies. In the spirit of Joseph Schumpeter, Peters argues that traditional normative interpretations of liberal democracy are essentially mythical in character: the idea of competent deliberative parliaments, deriving their authority from freewheeling political exchange among autonomous publics, and capable of determining administrative action by means of clearly formulated general rules, "has never even been approximately realized."[31] Despite its tremendous influence on democratic theory, "[i]t was not even defended as a normative political model—perhaps excepting certain short-lived constitutional doctrines influenced by Rousseau during the French Revolution (Sieyes, *The Constitution of 1791*)."[32] For Peters, the main source of the limits of every "idealized model of a democratic cycle of power" (like that already described in this chapter) is "the extremely limited capacities for communication and problem resolution," intrinsic to the communicative channels described by it, in relation to the actual decision-making needs of modern representative democracy.[33] Thus, both traditional democratic theory—and radical contemporary proposals hoping to salvage its more ambitious normative aspirations—must be discarded. In its place, we need a model of democracy, a "very abstract, topological description of the political process," more in tune with the complex dynamics and exigencies of modern democracy.[34]

Peters is no conservative in the mode of Schumpeter. To his credit, Peters openly admits that his description of the operations of real-existing democracy may include "contingent" elements.[35] But the polemical orientation of his book means that he has little to say about such elements. Bent on purging the specter of radical democracy from critical theory, Peters at times seems far more interested in pointing to the "rational" character of the democratic status quo than with elaborating its ills; the burden of proof lies with radical democrats critical of contemporary capitalist democracy. Although this view arguably provides a valuable immunization against irresponsible utopianism, it tends to lead him to downplay worrisome trends in contemporary capitalist democracy—just to name the most obvious: continued declines in participation rates, polls suggesting growing dissatisfaction with traditional legislative devices, and the resurgence of far-right-wing movements pandering to xenophobia and racism.

Alas, Habermas opts to reproduce the core of Peters's realist-inspired model of democratic decision making by simply superimposing it onto Fraser's model (355). Inevitably, this produces a real set of tensions in Habermas's argument. The "two tracks" described by Habermas thus ultimately refer not only to Fraser's distinction between weak and strong publics, but to Peters's idiosyncratic delineation of the political "center" from the "periphery." In Peters's model, the "center" consists, most importantly, of parliament, the administration, and the judiciary. The "periphery" refers to a host of associations and organizations (1) concerned with "the definition, aggregation, and articulation of interests and demands in relation to the decision making processes of the center" or (2) functioning to bring about the "realization of public functions" within selected spheres of social activity.[36] Autonomous publics and communicative networks make up *part* of the periphery, but Peters seems more interested in those actors identified by traditional political science, such as political parties, interest groups, and private associations. In order for decisions to take a binding form, they need to pass through the channels (*Schleusen*) of the center. But in contrast to traditional liberal democratic models, these channels are located at many different (administrative, legislative, and judicial) points within the "polycentric" decision-making center found within every modern representative democracy.

Even at this minimal descriptive level, Habermas's use of Peters leads the former to modify his initial account of the two-track model. Whereas his original gloss on Fraser made civil society the primary site for the "perception and thematization" of problems, here Habermas uses the same words to describe parliament's functions (373, 430). Moreover, now it is the administration that is seen as possessing the most impressive capacity for handling and resolving problems (*Problemverarbeitungskomplexität*); earlier in his study, that quality was attributed to parliament (307 and 355). At first glance, this may seem like a trivial shift. But in fact, it anticipates a dramatic revision that only becomes fully manifest in the proceeding stages of Habermas's argument: parliament becomes the administration's junior partner in the legislative process, and deliberative civil society is removed an additional step from the actual decision-making process, thereby substantially attenuating its influence over the exercise of political authority. In light of Peters's unabashed attempt to break with traditional "myths" of parliamentary sovereignty, this move is unsurprising. Given Habermas's purportedly critical aspirations, it is far more surprising.

Peters openly argues that the political center inevitably gains independent status in relation to the periphery. Habermas accepts this view without showing sufficient concern for its potentially worrisome implications for democratic politics. In the course of what Habermas describes as "normal" politics, the deliberative periphery inevitably plays a minor role in determining the policy making process. The autonomization (*Verselbständigung*) of the center vis-à vis the periphery is inevitable considering the complexity of modern social life (356–359 and 380–887). Most of the time, "courts reach decisions, bureaucracies prepare statutes and budgets, party organizations organize electoral campaigns, and clients influence 'their' administrators" (357), and civil society is unavoidably left at the wayside. Indeed, not only civil society, but even those elements of the "center" most closely tied to civil society, lose the central place attributed to them in traditional democratic theory: "the power and initiative to get problems on the agenda and then decide on them lies with the government and administration to a greater extent than the parliamentary complex" during moments of political normalcy (380). According to Habermas, only during "exceptional" situations do communicative processes within civil society and parliament again seem to take on a renewed significance for decision making; only during moments of heightened conflict, in periods of crisis, does the legislature finally have "the last word" and then "*actually determine* the direction" of political decisionmaking (357).

What concrete evidence does Habermas provide to demonstrate the empirical relevance of this model? (Recall that Habermas wants to show that his vision of deliberative democracy has "long gained a footing" [317]. This does not only mean that the self-understanding of modern liberal democracy is best captured by the idea of a two-track deliberative democracy; it also implies that empirical tendencies within contemporary democracy should correspond to his model.) The proliferation of autonomous social movements in civil society over the course of the last decades (especially the peace, women's, and ecological movements) proves that (1) the periphery of civil society often can succeed in thematizing issues ignored by the decision-making center; and (2) the political center remains "porous" to civil society, especially when a "growing awareness of a relevant societal problem generates a *crisis consciousness* on the periphery" (382).

Habermas's argument here represents an astonishing sleight of hand. Peters never claims that his account is radical-democratic; Habermas seems to think that it is. Nor does Habermas see any problem with synthesizing Fraser's democratic socialism and Peters's cautious brand of democratic realism; I wonder how Fraser and Peters would feel about this. Unsurprisingly, Habermas's model is Janus-faced. At times, he speaks the language of radical democracy, while at other junctures, his defense of what amounts to an administratively dominated "normal" politics is arguably less ambitious, in crucial respects, than the liberal democratic models of classical authors like John Stuart Mill or Alexis de Tocqueville.[37] The paradoxes here are striking: Habermas began his career as one of the most perceptive critics of "realist" democratic theory.[38] Is he now willing to engage in a rehabilitation of realist theory, as long as it is packaged in the impressive learning of critical social theory?

Even if we ignore this analytic tension in *Between Facts and Norms*, another problem become apparent as well. In short: this second version of Habermas's two-track model exhibits a number of immanent flaws. No *systematic* empirical argument is offered in support of the claim that it actually corresponds to the workings of contemporary liberal democracy; passing reference to a panoply of left-liberal social movements hardly constitutes adequate evidence for an empirical claim as ambitious as this one. After all, one might legitimately interpret the proliferation of social movements in recent years (as well as the increasingly widespread dependence on civil disobedience, which for Habermas represents the clearest instrument by which social movements have mobilized public opinion) in a somewhat less positive light as well. Whatever their undeniable merits, these movements may *also* provide evidence for *worrisome* tendencies within contemporary representative democracy: precisely because the "center" has gained exorbitant power in relation to the "periphery," extraparliamentary social movements, engaging in illegal action, have emerged to fill the gap left by a formal political system increasingly dominated by ossified parties and organized vested interests. Similarly, civil disobedience often represents what Habermas himself calls "the final instrument" (462) by which political groups hopes to *ward off* state action that they consider altogether unbearable; this would seem to be a rather *defensive* form of political action to emphasize in order to demonstrate the continued vitality of civil society in contemporary democracy. In a truly thriving deliberative democracy, one would hope that citizens need not engage too often in peaceful lawbreaking in order to gain attention.[39]

Habermas's argument here begs a host of unanswered questions. How can we make sure that civil society will reactivate itself during moments of crisis?[40] Habermas refers to the importance of liberal political culture as a precondition for this (382). But as Ken Baynes has noted, Habermas has very little to say about the specifics of such a culture.[41] Indeed, there may be something downright *un*realistic about the logic of Habermas's borrowing from "realist" theory: can a public sphere at rest (*Öffentlickeit im Ruhezustand*) effectively tolerate the exercise of de facto political power by isolated political elites without risking its own disintegration (380)? Tocqueville's warnings about "democratic despotism" should come immediately to mind here: why wouldn't political elites take advantage of a situation characterized by a "public in dormancy" in order to exacerbate privatistic tendencies? Habermas claims that a political system temporarily dominated by the "center" by no means necessarily means that illegitimate social power has gained undue influence within the political complex (356). But his explanation here tends to be disappointing, particularly in light of the prescient concerns expressed elsewhere in his work about the dangers of social asymmetries of power for civil society: we can rest assured that social power will not be able to gain illegitimate influence as long as the periphery is able and effective to identify outbreaks of illegitimate social power and then counteract them" (358 and 442). But what if social inequality simultaneously distorts the operations of civil society itself?[42]

Sometimes *Between Facts and Norms* does present a refreshingly honest assessment of worrisome trends within contemporary democracy. Habermas offers a clear-headed discussion of a capitalist mass media that trivializes public debate and cultivates cultural and political illiteracy; he notes that political parties too rarely serve as a meaningful device for guaranteeing the supremacy of communicative power; he concedes that cynical brands of systems theory have some real empirical correlates in contemporary democracy. In short, he still defends some of the critical elements of his empirical account of contemporary democracy in *The Structural Transformation of the Public Sphere*. But Habermas now seems so intent on proving that his own model "represents more than a set of normative postulates" that he ignores the possibility that his use of Peters's *empirical description* risks forcing him to make unnecessary concessions to the sad state of real-existing capitalist democracy.

IV

For Habermas, law—and, more specifically, legislative bodies like an elected parliament—mediates between communicative and administrative power: law-making bodies depend on communicative power in order to issue norms, which then are rendered binding by the coercive apparatus of the modern state. The ambiguities that I have just described in my exegesis ultimately revolve around the nexus between communicative and administrative power. At some junctions, Habermas seems to point to parliament as the main site for lawmaking; at others, he accepts the "realist" view that parliamentary sovereignty is little more than a moldy liberal myth. Sometimes parliament is envisioned as an extensive of a deliberative civil society; at other times, parliament's deliberative capacities are demoted in order to accentuate its pragmatic qualities and to distinguish it from the "anarchic" processes of deliberation and exchange found within civil society. Habermas tends to emphasize the virtues of a deliberative civil society; at the same time, he is willing to admit that civil society inevitably has little real impact on state action during the course of "normal" democratic politics. Habermas hopes to show that communicative power can be "transcribed" into administrative power. But he does not seem altogether sure *exactly* how weak publics, strong publics, and administrative bodies should interact in order to bring about this translation.

The immediate source of this tension is not hard to find. Habermas conceives of his project as an attempt to overcome the one-sidedness of both normative theories allegedly blind to the exigencies of empirical reality (e.g., Rawls and Ronald Dworkin) and social-scientific theories lacking the most minimal normative sensitivity (e.g., the German systems theorists Luhmann and Willke). In the process, he devotes an enormous amount of energy to an immanent reconstruction of competing views in order to demonstrate how (1) they repeatedly succumb to one of these two flaws and (2) ultimately their underlying insights can best be integrated into his own thematization of the relationship between *facticity* and *validity*. As a consequence, most of Habermas's own ideas here are formulated by means of an *exegesis and reconstruction of competing theories*. There is no question that Habermas is a masterful practitioner of this craft. But in light of the *fundamental* dissimilarities between theories discussed by Habermas, there is a real danger that either (1) something essential is lost in the translation of these ideas into Habermas's own; or (2) the integrity of competing theories is preserved, but at the cost of attempting a synthesis of that which probably cannot be synthesized. Indeed, isn't that precisely what we find in Habermas's model of a two-track deliberative democracy, where radical democratic socialism and democratic "Realism" are oddly transformed into intellectual allies?

In the space remaining here, I cannot develop this methodological criticism with adequate care. But it is striking that Habermas's analysis of communicative power is derived from normative theorists (most importantly. Arendt), whereas his discussion of administrative power is drawn from a tradition of social scientific inquiry oblivious to normative questions (e.g., Luhmann). Habermas himself repeatedly emphasizes the incongruities between these two traditions; as he repeatedly shows in *Between Facts and Norms*, both are blind to the merits of the other. In light of this, it should not surprise us that his own attempt to integrate these traditions at times may reproduce something of the original incongruity between them. More specifically: Habermas's description of communicative and administrative power at many junctures tends to posit the existence of a *fundamental* dissimilarity between them. Communicative power rests on action in concert, deliberation oriented toward mutual understanding; it depends on what Hegel famously described as "mutual recognition." In stark contrast, administrative action relies on strategic-rationality, takes an unavoidably hierarchical form, and it is concerned first and foremost with efficiency (16–51, and 187). Given Habermas's insistence on a fundamental difference between these two forms of power, is not the task of translating communicative into administrative power inevitably destined to remain highly enigmatic? Does not this undertaking risk approximating the alchemist's attempt to "transform" simple metals into silver—that is, an inevitably doomed attempt to transform one set of elements into an altogether different set? No wonder Habermas at times stumbles in his description of the interface between communicative and administrative power: he may have defined the task in such a manner as to render it virtually impossible to solve.[43]

Of course, the liberal tradition long provided an easy answer to the question of how communicatively derived legislative power could be successfully transformed into administrative action so as to guarantee that the latter does not infringe on the former: if we insist that legislation take the form of cogent, general norms, then we can make sure that administrative power can be effectively regulated in accordance with the preferences of democratically elected legislative bodies. Although I believe that Habermas is too quick to dismiss the contemporary merits of this traditional argument, he certainly *is* right in suggesting that it at least seems anachronistic in light of the proliferation of vague and open-ended legal clauses and concepts in twentieth-century law.[44] For Habermas, the ongoing deformalization of law suggests that we need to reconceive the traditional idea of the separation of powers in such a way so as to de-emphasize the orthodox emphasis on generality within legal statutes; this view purportedly rests on an overly "concretistic" reading of the separation of powers (187–193 and 437–445).

So Habermas argues in the final pages of *Between Facts and Norms* for a restatement of the idea of a separation between distinct *institutions* (the legislature, judiciary, and administration branch) in terms of a distinction between alternative *forms of communication* and different *ways of making use of reasons and arguments*. Regardless of their *concrete location* within the state apparatus, forms of action deserve to be described as "legislative," "administrative," and "judicial" to the extent that they make use of forms of argumentation that Habermas sees as capturing the core of what traditional liberal theorists envisioned by means of each of the individual "instances" of the separation of powers. In turn, such forms of action then rightfully deserve to be institutionalized in such a way so as to correspond to the logic of the form of communication at hand:

Laws regulate the transformation of communicative power into administrative power in that they come about according to a democratic procedure, ground a legal protection guaranteed by impartially judging courts, and withhold from the implementing administration the sorts of reasons that support legislative resolutions and court decisions. These normative reasons belong to a universe within which legislature and judiciary share the work of justifying and applying norms. An administration limited to pragmatic discourse must not disturb anything in this universe by its contributions; at the same time, it draws therefrom the normative premises that have to underlie its own empirically informed, purposive-rational decision making. (192).[45]

Legislative power is best captured by the idea of communication involving the justification of norms (*Normanwendungsdiskursen*), which—as we have seen—makes use of diverse (moral, ethical, and pragmatic) forms of deliberation (192 and 437–438). The gist of Habermas's rather complicated argument here is that we need to consider the possibility of extending communicative forms of this type *whenever* problems at hand require a legislative resolution—for example, when administrators are confronted with a choice of mutually incompatible collective goals in such a way as to explode the boundaries of traditional conceptions of administrative action. In order finally to do justice to a political system in which legislation occurs at many different interstices of the governmental apparatus, central parliaments need to consider the possibility of openly delegating and decentralizing legislative authorities and then organizing them in such a way as to subject them to deliberative democratic procedures (437–438).

Habermas's suggestion here is surely a provocative one. Indeed, if it could be successfully undertaken, it might very well serve as an antidote to some of my criticisms: if deliberative democratic ideals could be institutionalized within the very *core* of the state bureaucracy, then Habermas's description of an administratively dominated "normal" politics might begin to seem somewhat less worrisome than what I have just suggested. Then the "normal" rule of the "state administration" need not necessarily entail a realist-inspired corrosion of deliberative democracy.[46]

But his argument here also points to a familiar weakness in *Between Facts and Norms*. Given the immense complexity of Habermas's text, it is easy to miss the tremendous significance of his discussion of a reformed separation of powers for the structure of his overall argument: it is supposed to represent nothing less than an *institutional* solution to the problem of transforming communicative power into administrative power. But, once again, Habermas has far too little to say about the specifics of his agenda here. Even if we are willing to concede the virtue of integrating deliberative democratic elements into the administration, does that necessarily solve the problem of how communicative power is to be effectively *translated* into administrative power? Habermas's proposal is not meant to deny that we still need to acknowledge the autonomous logic of the administrative system; instead, it only claims that what we today describe as the state administration or bureaucracy undertakes legislative tasks that should be organized in accordance with the principles of deliberative democracy. So perhaps this argument simply shifts the *locus* of the interface between communicative and administrative power from the nexus between parliament and the administrative apparatus to *within* the administration itself. If so, we still need an analysis of how deliberative processes then can effectively "steer" and "bind" decisions within the administration itself. In fairness, Habermas *alludes* to a growing number of experiments (e.g., participation by clients in administrative bodies, ombudsmen, and administrative hearings) with the "democratization" of administrative and judicial instances (440). But his examples have now long been established in many administrative practices of the advanced democracies of the west. Does anyone really believe that more ombudsmen or administrative hearings can really protect us from what Habermas himself describes as the "crisis-tendencies" of modern representative democracy?[47] What about more ambitious experiments in political and social democracy? Habermas does not a priori exclude them; he tells us that a careful brand of "institutional fantasy" is appropriate for the examination of such proposals (441). Unfortunately, it is just such "institutional fantasy" that is absent from Habermas's own argument here—notwithstanding its tremendous importance for his own ambitious attempt in *Between Facts and Norms* to reconceive the project of modern representative democracy.

Notes

I would like to thank Iris Young for her helpful comments on an earlier draft of this chapter.

1. Franz L. Neumann, *The Rule of Law Under Siege: Selected Essays of Franz L. Neumann and Otto Kirchheimer*, ed. William E. Scheuerman (Berkeley: University of California Press, 1996), p. 197.

2. Jürgen Habermas, *The Structural Transformation of the Public Sphere*, trans. Thomas Burger (Cambridge: Massachusetts Institute of Technology Press, 1989).

3. Cited in: Otto Kirchheimer, *Politics, Law, & Social Change: Selected Essays of Otto Kirchheimer*, eds. Frederic S. Burin and Kurt L. Shell (New York: Columbia University Press, 1969), p. 331.

4. See, for example, Johannes Agnoli and Peter Brückner, *Die Transformation der Demokratie* (Frankfurt, Germany: EVA, 1968).

5. Habermas, *Between Facts and Norms: Contributions to a Discourse Theory of Law and Democracy*.

6. Habermas, "Further Reflections on the Public Sphere," in *Habermas and the Public Sphere*, ed. Calhoun; pp. 421–461.

7. See also Habermas, "What Does Socialism Mean Today? The Rectifying Revolution and the Need for New Thinking on the Left," *New Left Review*, no. 183 (September–October, 1990).

8. Wolfgang Jäger, *Öffentlickeit und Parlamentarismus* (Stuttgart, Germany: Kohlhammer, 1973) is good on this score: Jäger shows that Habermas's model of the bourgeois public sphere is a myth not unlike that constructed by Carl Schmitt in order to discredit contemporary democracy. Unfortunately, Jäger's work is little known in the English-speaking intellectual world; this may explain the relatively modest character of criticism of the historical structure of Habermas's study, see Craig Calhoun, ed., *Habermas and the Public Sphere* (Cambridge: Massachusetts Institute of Technology Press, 1992). For an interesting discussion of the similarities and dissimilarities of Habermas's and Schmitt's historical accounts of modern democracy see Hartmuth Becker, *Die Parlamentarismuskritik bei Carl Schmitt und Jürgen Habermas* (Berlin: Duncker & Humblot, 1994).

9. For a helpful brief overview of Habermas's study, see Peter Dews, "Agreeing What's Right," *London Review of Books*, May 13, 1993. More ambitiously, see Kenneth Baynes, "Democracy and the *Rechtsstaat*: Habermas's *Faktizität und Geltung*," in *The Cambridge Companion to Habermas* ed. Stephen K. White (Cambridge: Cambridge University Press, 1995); James Bohman, "Complexity, Pluralism, and the Constitutional State: On Habermas's *Faktizität und Geltung*," *Law and Society Review* 28, no. 4 (1994); and Michel Rosenfeld, "Law as Discourse: Bridging the Gap Between Democracy and Rights," *Harvard Law Review* 108, no. 5 (March 1995). These thoughtful discussions address many elements of Habermas's complicated argument that I necessarily leave unexamined here. See also the special issue of *Philosophy and Social Criticism* no. 4 (1994) devoted to Habermas's legal theory. For a discussion of Habermas that does an excellent job of placing Habermas within (1) debates in twentieth century German legal thought and (2) jurisprudential debates between positivists and natural lawyers, see David Dyzenhaus, "The Legitimacy of Legality," *Archiv für Rechts- und Sozialphilosophie* (forthcoming, 1996).

10. *BFN* 110. See also Baynes, who offers a fine introductory discussion of its broader complexities, including the question of its relationship to Habermas's conception of communicative rationality. For Habermas, communicative rationality refers to the basic idea that

> Communication is not reducible to getting someone to believe something. For Habermas, it consists (paradigmatically) in reaching an understanding

with someone about something, where "reaching an understanding" draws upon (unavoidable) suppositions constitutive for a weak and fragile (but nonetheless socially effective) form of mutual recognition: To reach an understanding with someone about something implies that one is also prepared to provide warrants for the claims raised . . . should they be contested and that one recognizes the other as someone who is free to take a Yes/No position with respect to those claims. Baynes, "Democracy and the *Rechtsstaat*," pp. 203 and 208.

Here, I have chosen to bracket many of the fundamental questions concerning the normative roots of democratic politics in Habermas's concept of communicative rationality, not because I consider them unimportant, but because I think that an adequate vision of modern democracy ultimately should offer a convincing institutional model as well as an impressive account of its normative core. In addition, it seems to me that Habermas scholarship too often downgrades "mere" institutional questions: too often, something of the academic philosopher's traditional snobbishness toward her empirical-minded cousins in political science can be detected here.

11. Habermas has been influenced here by the important study by Jean Cohen and Andrew Arato, *Civil Society and Political Theory* (Cambridge: Massachusetts Institute of Technology Press, 1992).

12. Nancy Fraser, "Rethinking the Public Sphere: A Contribution to a Critique of Actually Existing Democracy," in Calhoun, *Habermas and the Public Sphere*, pp. 109-142. In a more general vein; see Iris Young, *Justice and the Politics of Difference* (Princeton: Princeton University Press, 1990). For a discussion of *Between Facts and Norms* that claims that Habermas's recent work remains inadequate on this count see Bohman, "Complexity, Pluralism, and the Constitutional State; pp. 920–928.

13. Seyla Benhabib, *Critique, Norm, and Utopia: A Study of the Foundations of Critical Theory* (New York: Columbia University Press, 1986), pp. 309-316. I will discuss Habermas's model of a "fair compromise" in greater detail in the next section.

14. Hannah Arendt, *On Violence* (New York: Harcourt, 1970), p. 44. Habermas here downplays elements of Arendt's conception of the public sphere that conflict with his emphasis on uncoerced dialogue. Benhabib, "Models of Public Space: Hannah Arendt, the Liberal Tradition, and Jürgen Habermas," in *Habermas and the Public Sphere*. More generally on Arendt and Habermas, see the study by Maurizio Passerin d'Entreves, *The Political Philosophy of Hannah Arendt* (New York: Routledge, 1994).

15. Jerry Mashaw, *Due Process in the Administrative State* (New Haven: Yale University Press, 1985), cited in *BFN* 187.

16. Thus, Habermas argues that radical democracy today must take a "self-limiting" form: neither administrative bodies nor markets can be *immanently* organized in accordance with the principles of communicative power.

17 See also Habermas, "Hannah Arendts Begriff der Macht," in his *Philosophisch-politische Profile* (Frankfurt, Germany: Suhrkamp, 1981).

18. Baynes, "Democracy and the *Rechtsstaat,*" p. 216.

19. Fraser, *Unruly Practices: Power, Discourse and Gender in Contemporary Social Theory* (Minneapolis: University of Minnesota Press, 1989), pp. 113–190. On the ills of systems theory for Habermas, see also Thomas McCarthy, "Complexity and Democracy: The Seducements of Systems Theory," in his *Ideals and Illusions: On Reconstruction and Deconstruction in Contemporary Critical Theory* (Cambridge: Massachusetts Institute of Technology Press, 1991).

20. Fraser, "Rethinking the Public Sphere," p. 134

21. This comes out most clearly in Habermas's detailed discussion of parliament in chapter 4. There, he explicitly locates different (moral, ethical, and pragmatic) forms of political argumentation *within* formal parliamentary bodies, and then suggests that each form of deliberation has particular implications for the institutionalization of deliberative legislative bodies. Pragmatic activities (concerned primarily with reaching compromises) justifies a system of fair, equal, and secret elections, "[f]or the participation in a fairly organized system of compromise demands the equal representation of all affected" (181). Ethical debates concerning the "authentic self-understanding" and "collective identity" of a particular people requires that "*[a]ll* members of the community . . . take part in discourse." Thus, deliberations of this type, "which are only representative in character because of technical reasons," cannot be organized according to a traditional model of an elected representative as a "stand-in" for those represented. Parliamentary debate can only constitute "the organized middle point or focus of a society-wide network of communication" (181). A similar vision of the legislature as a deliberative *extension* of civil society derives from the nature of moral discourses: "Here representation can only mean that the choice of representatives should function to guarantee the broadest conceivable spectrum" of interpretative perspectives, particularly those of marginal groups. The strict universalizability requirements of moral discourse for Habermas demand that the voices of even those groups that may not even make up a particular community (e.g., refugees or resident aliens) need to be heard within the halls of parliament (225).

22. Stephen K. White, *The Recent Work of Jürgen Habermas: Reason, Justice, & Modernity* (Cambridge: Cambridge University Press, 1988), pp. 76-77.

23. Fraser, "Rethinking the Public Sphere," pp. 122–123.

24. For an important recent attempt of this type, see Alec Nove, *The Economics of Feasible Socialism* (London: Routledge, 1991). It would be interesting to know Habermas's view of this genre; he utterly ignores it in his written work.

25. For a thoughtful critical analysis of Habermas's theory in light of recent developments in the international capitalist political economy, see Neil Brenner and John P. McCormick, "Habermas's *Facticity and Validity* and the Historical-Geographical Limits of Contemporary Democratic Theory" (Manuscript, 1996).

26. Cohen, *Class and Civil Society: The Limits of Marxian Critical Theory* (Amherst: University of Massachusetts Press, 1982).

27. The literature here is vast. For a recent summary, see E.N. Suleiman, ed., *Parliaments and Parliamentarians in Democratic Politics* (New York: Holmes and Meier, 1986). For an argument suggesting that even the relatively impressive American Congress exhibits evidence of parliamentary decay, see Theodore Lowi, *The End of Liberalism* (New York: Norton, 1979).

28 What I have in mind here is a massive empirical literature that suggests two different points: first, democratic processes continue to be undermined by social and economic inequalities that too often mean that the voices of the socially vulnerable are inadequately represented in the halls of government. A good deal of the political science literature on this topic suggests that this familiar problem has been exacerbated over the course of the last twenty years, as economic inequality has increased and neoliberal governments have dismantled welfare state-type decision-making devices that often provided real—though inadequate—representation to socially subordinate groups. Second, growing evidence suggests that contemporary liberal democracy may be experiencing a crisis of legitimacy of sorts: even in the most stable liberal democracies, voting rates are on the decline, and many polls suggest growing unease and dissatisfaction with the workings of parliamentary government. In short, a growing number of citizens are seeking to "disengage" themselves from the workings of representative democracy to an extent arguably unprecedented since World War II. How serious this crisis will turn out to be in the developed capitalist democracies of Western Europe and America remains to be seen; in newly democratized countries, this crisis is likely to have far more dire consequences.

29. For a discussion based on similar concerns, see Bohman, "Complexity, Pluralism, and the Constitutional State.

30 Bernhard Peters, *Die Integration moderner Gesellschaften* (Frankfurt, Germany: Suhrkamp, 1993), p. 352. For a thoughtful discussion and criticism of this work, see Bohman, "Review of Bernhard Peters, *Die Integration moderner Gesellschaften*," *Constellations*, Vol. I, No. 3 (1995).

31. Peters, *Die Integration moderner Gesellschaften*, p. 329.

32. Ibid., p. 329.

33. Ibid., p. 344.

34. Ibid., p. 351.

35. Ibid., p. 345.

36. Ibid., p. 341.

37. For an interpretation of Mill and Tocqueville along such lines, see Carole Pateman, *Participation and Democratic Theory* (Cambridge: Cambridge University Press, 1970). On the surface, Habermas's use of Peters leaves him with a two-track model resembling Bruce Ackerman's, for whom "normal" democratic politics is substantially less ambitious in scope than "exceptional" political moments when the liberal democratic polity engages in alterations of its fundamental constitutional struc-

ture. But Ackerman is arguably more of a radical democrat than Habermas here: Ackerman may not be willing to accept the "realist" insight that elected democratic legislatures, even during the course of normal liberal-democratic politics, should be satisfied with taking on a secondary role vis-a-vis their administrative brethren. Ackerman, *We the People: Foundations*, vol. I (Cambridge: Harvard University Press, 1991).

38. Habermas, "Zum Begriff der politischen Beteiligung," in his *Kultur und Kritik* (Frankfurt: Suhrkamp, 1973).

39. Ingeborg Maus, *Zur Aufklärung der Demokratietheorie* (Frankfurt, Germany: Suhrkamp, 1992). This is not meant to criticize Habermas's normative defense of civil disobedience; it *is* meant to suggest that the empirical implications of its proliferation may be quite different from those suggested by him.

40. What exactly, for that matter, is a "crisis" in this context?

41. Baynes, "Democracy and *Rechtsstaat*," p. 218.

42. There is a similar ambivalence in Habermas's assorted comments about corporatist decision making here. At times, he repeats a traditional left-wing version of the argument (central to *The Structural Transformation of the Public Sphere*) that corporatist decision making represents a potential threat to popular sovereignty; at other junctures, he seems willing to concede the unavoidability of corporatism. What protections are there against its ills? He says that "[t]here are no easy recipes. In the final instance, only a suspicious, mobile, alert, and informed public . . . serves as a check against the emergence of illegitimate power. . . ." (442). But what if autonomous processes within civil society itself have been undermined by forms of corporatism that privilege the powerful and wealthy?

43. Let me be try to be as clear as possible here: I *do* think that Habermas's idea of law as mediating between communicative and administrative power is fruitful. My concern is merely that he has conceptualized this nexus in such a way so as to generate a series of tensions within his account that arguably could be avoided.

44. Habermas claims that liberal formal law remains imprisoned in the "productivistic" assumptions of industrial capitalism (491). Frankly, this seems to me to be rather too simple. As I have tried to show elsewhere by means of an exegesis of the early Frankfurt school jurists Franz Neumann and Otto Kirchheimer, this view downplays the eminently *democratic* functions of formal law. Scheuerman, *Between the Norm and the Exception: The Frankfurt School and the Rule of Law* (Cambridge: Massachusetts Institute of Technology Press, 1994). Habermas's position here also shares some surprising similarities with free market jurisprudence, which claims that the traditional liberal rule of law can only be preserved if competitive capitalism is maintained, see Scheuerman, "The Rule of Law and the Welfare State: Towards a New Synthesis," *Politics and Society*, Vol. 22 (1994). For a recent empirically minded defense of traditional liberal legal forms, see David Schoenbrod, *Power Without Responsibility: How Congress Abuses the People through Delegation* (New Haven: Yale University Press, 1993).

45. The passage also points out that Habermas sees courts as part of the law making process (see chapter 5). I have bracketed this complex issue here for two reasons: (1) Habermas tends to see courts as playing at most a secondary role in this process and (2) it would raise complicated jurisprudential issues that I simply cannot do justice to here.

46. Interestingly, he admits that this suggestion may imply that "my picture of a democratic 'state of siege' directed against the apparatus of the state" has been rendered inappropriate (531). It seems to me that this argument potentially moderates Habermas's (in my view, unduly harsh) criticisms of authors like Joshua Cohen, who are more willing to accept a far more ambitious democratization of social and political institutions than Habermas tends to (369–373). Cohen, "Deliberation and Democratic Legitimacy," in *The Good Polity*, eds. A. Hamlin and B. Pettit (New York: Oxford University Press, 1989).

47. See also the rather modest reform proposals outlined in *BFN* 442–443: increased possibilities for the exercise of direct democracy as well as the "constitutionalization" of the mass media by means of a set of legal procedures counteracting asymmetries of social power.

II

Historical and
Comparative Perspectives

4

Liberties and Popular Sovereignty: On Jürgen Habermas's Reconstruction of the System of Rights

Ingeborg Maus

The justifications Habermas gives for a system of rights bring together all the central intentions of his theory of law. Chapter 3 of *Between Facts and Norms: Contributions to a Discourse Theory of Law and Democracy* that provides these justifications is devoted in part to developing the underlying tension between "facticity and validity" as the basic structure of law taking the extreme and, for that reason, illuminating aspect of the guarantee of liberty through coercion (83ff.).[1] It also elucidates the motives for reestablishing the centuries-old connection between legal theory and social theory in the context of the most topical social problems. In this chater, I will first present the inner coherence of Habermas's conception of the system of rights and analyze how it reacts to problems that have as yet not been resolved in the historical development of discussions on the theory of law and democracy. This will be followed by critical considerations expounded from the perspective of a more radical notion of popular sovereignty, while examining Habermas's reception of Enlightenment philosophy, especially Immanuel Kant's thought, as well as implications of the justifications given in discourse theory for the relationship between law and morals, or, as the case may be, between positive and suprapositive law.

I

Habermas's reconstruction of rational-law premises in terms of discourse theory conceives of the "system of rights" as one that is juridical from the start, and inconceivable without enactment by a democratic lawmaker (105f.). The classical hierarchy between natural law and positive law is thus transformed into a tension between facticity and validity within the law (106, 83). However, this relationship between facticity and validity is indeed not characterized by the contrast between voluntaristic popular sovereignty, on the one hand, and rights that can be normatively justified, on the other; rather, the tension is located in the system of rights itself, and even within the rights of private autonomy; introducing the principle of popular sovereignty, which is also normative in character, tends to relieve the tension rather than cause it. According to Habermas, this tension, which is heightened to the point of a paradox within the system of rights, is initially characterized by the fact that subjective liberties are equipped with the coercive force of objective law (28). Consequently, the standard for rationality that has to be exhibited by law-making procedure as formulated in Habermas's reconstruction of the popular sovereignty principle in terms of discourse theory is set very high, especially in view of the coercive character of law, even if it is democratically enacted. Indeed, the conception of popular sovereignty must allow for the fact that even fundamental rights can only be established as concrete rights through the democratic enactment of law.

Habermas's extremely complex elaboration of this linkage can be reproduced here only to the extent that it ties into the following discussion. In an historical review, Habermas first examines inadequate resolutions in legal theory of the original paradox of liberties that is typical of subjective private rights (*Privatrechte*). According to Habermas, Savigny's attempt to secure the individualized and coercively protected subjective spheres of liberty morally by introducing the principle of intersubjective recognition between legal subjects loses its plausibility because the bond between private and moral autonomy is eroded in the late nineteenth century (84–85). I would add that the subjectivity of such private rights relates to the dimension of rule over things (*Sachherrschaft*), whereas intersubjectivity refers to the legal relations between subjects with respect to their rule over things. In other words, if this connection merely refers to the view that was elaborated in the same way by both Kant and Marxist legal theory, namely, that legal relations cannot exist directly between legal subjects and things, but only between the subjects themselves with respect to things (much the same way as we try in speech acts to reach an understanding with one another about something in the world), then this intersubjectivity of private law cannot be understood ipso facto as resting on mutual recognition and on the guarantee of equal rights. This structure could be more easily implemented if the norms of private law were generated by a legislative process which, itself, was based on mutual recognition. Consequently, Habermas ties the production of legitimate law, as well as the positive juridification of rights that can be justified in discourse, to the principle of popular sovereignty as reconstructed in terms of discourse theory. Habermas's entire line of argumentation is therefore aimed at explaining the internal link between human rights and popular sovereignty in a system of rights that is based on the equal value and mutual enabling of private and public autonomy. Habermas's conception of a "logical genesis of rights" is explicitly described as a "circular process" in which the liberties of autonomous private individuals and the rights of politically autonomous citizens to participate in the democratic law-making process are constituted *"equiprimordially"* (122). Nonetheless it has been understood by commentators, depending on their point of view, either as subordinating the democratic law-making process to subjective liberties that are simply given in the sense of a classical hierarchy of law,[2] or as one which, conversely, puts these rights at the disposal of a popular sovereignty that has run amok.[3]

The order presented in Habermas's explication of the circular process seems to speak in favor of the first reading. It "begins with the application of the discourse principle to the general right to liberties—a right constitutive for the legal form as such—and ends with the legal institutionalization of conditions for a discursive exercise of political autonomy. By means of this political autonomy, the private autonomy that was at first abstractly posited can retroactively assume an elaborated legal shape" (121). That the principle of law giving popular sovereignty appears to follow upon the subjective liberties of private autonomy would seem at first glance to correspond exactly to the order in which Habermas introduces the justified categories of rights. The first three categories of rights are all assigned to the sphere of private autonomy. They refer to "the right to the greatest measure of equal subjective liberties" (Category 1) and require as necessary correlates rights to equal status as a member in a voluntary association of consociates under law (Category 2), as well as equal rights to individual legal protection (Category 3) (122ff.). "Only with the next step," as Habermas says, "do legal subjects also acquire the role of authors of their legal order, to be exact, through the following: Basic rights to equal chances at participation in the processes of opinion and will-formation in which citizens exercise their political autonomy and through which they make legitimate law"(123).

Because Habermas additionally emphasizes that the first three categories of rights constitute the legal code that democratic lawmakers have to use if they want to enact legitimate law (125, 128), the interpretation of Habermas's system of rights as being based on a "two-tiered legality" that subordinates the democratic lawmaker to a higher law would seem to be airtight.

Habermas's agenda for explaining the "paradox in the emergence of legitimacy from legality" (83 and 130), however, contains an intention that moves in just the opposite direction. In order to preclude any mistake, Habermas notes that in modern law all normative expectations have been shifted onto the laws and explains, "These laws draw their legitimacy from a legislative procedure based for its own part on the principle of popular sovereignty" (83). To the extent that the system of rights is involved here, Habermas expressly emphasizes the fact that the emergence of legitimacy from legality must be explained by means of those rights "that secure for citizens the exercise of their political autonomy" (83). In this passage, the legitimacy of all positive law is not said to depend on the rights in Categories 1 to 3, which guarantee private autonomy and as such constitute the legal code, but exclusively on the political rights of participation in Category 4. Although every legislator and constitutional lawmaker must make use of the legal code because she wants to enact law, this legal code cannot, as Habermas emphasizes, be established *in abstracto* but only by the citizens who first grant one another specific rights by means of democratically enacted laws (125). From this vantage point, there is no question that the principle of democracy has priority. According to Habermas, the principle of democracy must "not only establish a procedure of legitimate law-making, but must also *steer the production of the legal medium itself*" (111). Whereas initially the apodictical motto was that "there is no legitimate law without these rights"—that is, the subjective private rights in Categories 1 to 3 (125), it now turns out that these rights in turn depend on their enactment in the democratic process; in other words, they come after the participatory rights in Category 4.

What at first glance clearly seemed to involve subordinating the legality of democratic legislation to a higher legitimacy justified by a specific hierarchization within the system of rights is decidedly qualified as well by the definition of the discourse principle in *Between Facts and Norms*. Habermas distances himself from a view that remained unproblematic in his work on moral philosophy. Whereas his writings on discourse ethics were characterized by an identification of the discourse principle and the morality principle, in *Between Facts and Norms* Habermas emphasizes the difference between the two with a view to the central object of investigation (108f and 121). Here he introduces the discourse principle as one that is initially neutral vis-à-vis the modern differentiation of law and morality and that only explains the perspective from which action norms, regardless of their nature, can be justified impartially. For this reason, the legitimation of legal norms does not depend directly on their compatibility with the discourse principle, and is certainly not subject to any hierarchy between morality and law. Habermas's formulation that the "discourse principle is intended to assume the shape of a principle of democracy only along the path of legally configured institutionalization, while the principle of democracy for its part confers legitimating force on the process of lawgiving" (121) makes two things clear: Not higher law, but the principle of democracy engenders legitimacy; and the form of law organizes the democratic process, but legitimate law is only possible by virtue of the latter (I shall come back to this "reflexive" structure again). Given this frame, Habermas is able to define the principle of democracy as the "core" of the system of rights and to establish the specific quality of this concept of legitimacy in contrast to competing conceptions: "The law receives its full normative sense neither through its legal *form* per se, nor through an a priori moral *content*, but through a *procedure* of lawmaking that begets legitimacy" (135). With complete justification, Habermas can claim that in his conception the system of rights is not preordained for the democratic lawmaker like a natural law (129). In other words, the reproach that Habermas is still circuitously following the model of "two-tiered legality" that ultimately disavows the democratic lawmaker can be refuted for many reasons. To do so along these lines, however, would ultimately raise the question whether Habermas has not undermined his agenda for explaining the equality and equiprimordiality of liberties and popular sovereignty in a system of rights by coming out in favor of popular sovereignty.

This is the suspicion voiced by Charles Larmore, for example. Although he is very much in agreement with many parts of Habermas's work, Larmore declares the central thesis in *Between Facts and Norms*, namely, that, as enabling conditions of sovereign democratic lawmaking, subjective liberties, cannot at the same time restrict it, to be a scandalous element in Habermas's theory of democracy.[4] He claims that Habermas recognizes democratic autonomy as the "only" and therefore "total" foundation of the modern constitutional state.[5] He also misunderstands the underlying principle that popular sovereignty does not acknowledge any norms other than those that it generates itself to imply random decisionism. Larmore therefore resorts to premodern solutions in the search for a way out. In order to oppose Habermas's "postmetaphysical" understanding of democracy, Larmore brings to bear the dispute between metaphysical and postmetaphysical thought still unresolved in modern society—which is based in fact on the synchronicity of the dissynchronous—and takes a metaphysical position (albeit reluctantly): Democratic lawmaking, he claims, should itself be based on a basic moral principle, namely, that of universal recognition of persons, a principle which, for its part, is prior to all justifications and has necessarily always been presumed to be valid.[6] Thus, as an antidote to the alleged poison of a democracy that in fact knows no higher authority over democratic law-making procedure, a moral principle is mobilized that is introduced in the sense of an "innate idea" and to that extent necessarily points to a "higher authority"—and to its secular administration by judicial experts. Not the moral principle put forward by Larmore, but rather its location beyond the bounds of all innerworldly discourses, invalidates the principle of democracy.

However, the decisive question is whether Larmore's reading of the system of rights, namely, that Habermas merely derives subjective liberties from the concept of popular sovereignty, is at all tenable.[7] Larmore does note in the same connection that this derivation "ultimately proves to be circular"[8]—but without drawing any conclusions from this correct, albeit somewhat pejoratively intended, observation. Habermas's own description of the logical genesis of the system of rights as a "circular process" is, however, absolutely fundamental for an adequate understanding of his conception of the relationship between subjective private liberties and democratic participatory rights (122). With complete justification, Klaus Günther recently called attention to the quasi-dialectical structure of this circular process and criticized from this angle those commentaries that impute a leges hierarchy as well as a range of alleged contradictions to Habermas's conception.[9] From this viewpoint, the fact that in Habermas's work subjective liberties are presented as both the result of, and the prerequisite for, democratic lawmaking is not a contradiction but the "whole point of the argument."[10] Günther shows that in the form of subjective private liberties the legal code preexists for law-making and constitutional law-giving citizens, but only as the "deep grammar" of the language of law that must be transformed into the "surface structure" of the language of law by the speakers themselves in order to be enacted at all.[11] In other words, the legal code and democratic law-making practice are thus posited as equiprimordial elements that become visible on respectively different sides of the circular process.

For Habermas, the primary motive for the "change in perspective," as he calls it, from one side of the circular process to the other was the wish to avoid implying an expertocracy (126): Whereas the circular process of the genesis of rights does not "begin" with the constitution of subjective private liberties though its reconstructive presentation indeed does, the category of democratic participatory rights in the law-making process does not follow from the private liberties, but instead is attributable to the "change in perspective" from the external theoretical line of argumentation to the internal legal practice by the citizens themselves. The order of the presentation simply stems "from the vantage point of the theorist" who deduces those categories of rights—which the citizens "would have to" grant one another if they were to make legitimate law (126)—from the abstract interpenetration of discourse principle and legal form. As a *democratic* theorist, he has to renounce this perspective in favor of the political autonomy of constitutional law-making and law-giving citizens who first develop these rights from their own vantage point, bring them historically to consciousness and to enact them into positive law. This is why Habermas ultimately understands his system of rights as a generalizing reconstruction of the self-understanding on which historically known democratic constitutions and declarations of rights are necessarily based (129). What could easily be interpreted as "validity" kowtowing to the historically contingent "facticity" of constitutional lawmaking is in fact the result of a democratic intention: Having arrived at the democratic side of the circular process, the theorist can no longer explicate to citizens in expertocratic terms what they should rationally decide; rather, conversely, he must reconstruct what is reasonable from their constitutional praxis.—Kant formulated this democratic intention of democratic theory in a more radical and at the same time more paradoxical manner: Not even democracy must be brought to bear against the (as yet unenlightened) will of the people.[12] Much the same applies with regard to rights. In both cases, however, it is normatively assumed that historically established standards are irreversible.

However, there is also another aspect to the circular process, one that contradicts Larmore's extreme fears. Although rights cannot be set by an expertocracy nor guaranteed paternalistically, Habermas is, after all, talking about rights and intentions that "necessarily" form the basis of legitimate democratic constitutions and legislation. In order to explain the status of this necessity and to assess how it can be linked to the principle of democracy, it is important to distinguish clearly the "rights" introduced by Habermas from the rights that are typically contained in the basic rights catalogs of democratic constitutions, and to examine the relationship between legal form and legal code within the circular process.

As to the first problem, it has been objected that Habermas gives a complete program of rights precedence over the democratic lawmaker;[13] he is also criticized for doing just the opposite, namely, for having dispensed with a detailed concretization of his system of rights.[14] The logic behind Habermas's distinction is misunderstood in both cases: The (necessary) rights inscribed in the legal code itself, and without which there can be no legitimate law, are not to be confused with historically known liberal basic rights at all, and are not even on the same level of concretion with them. Rather, they are merely legal principles, "unsaturated placeholders" for basic rights that first have to be developed (*ausgestaltet*) by a concrete lawmaker for a concrete historical and social context (125f). "Categories of rights" and not the rights themselves are grounded in the system of rights—this is a point Habermas duly emphasizes for each category (1–3) of subjective private rights (Categories 1 to 3): In each case basic rights "result from the politically autonomous elaboration *of the right to the greatest possible measure of equal individual liberties*" (122). By deliberately doing without an expertocratic choice of "correct" basic rights from a theorist's position, while conversely referring in definitive terms to "basic rights to equal opportunities at participation in the processes of opinion—and will-formation in which citizens exercise their political autonomy and through which they generate legitimate law" (123), Habermas establishes a hierarchy within the circular process that has nothing more to do with the purposes of presentation. Here, equal participation in the democratic legislative process is given precedence over particular formulations of liberal basic rights.[15] On the other hand, the categories of rights, or the legal principles that constitute the legal code itself, are a prerequisite for the democratic law-

maker, to the extent that he enacts law at all and makes use of the legal code
(126).

That this is not simply a matter of abstract argument, but instead a theory of law and of democracy that articulates practical intentions, emerges in the
contradiction that exists between this theory and the currently prevailing theory and practice of democracy.[16] The latter position, in quite a counter-
Enlightenment vein, believes that it is making a contribution toward coping
with the totalitarian manifestations of this century by villainizing, of all
things, the freedom-protecting principle of popular sovereignty and restricting
democratic processes so extensively through liberal subjective liberties that
even the latter exist at best only in the form of goods administered by the government. By contrast, Habermas construes the relationship between popular
sovereignty and subjective rights in a manner not oriented to restriction but to
mutual optimization. The fact that, according to Habermas, the democratic
legislator and maker of constitutional law has the scope to shape concrete liberal basic rights as he wishes, but is "necessarily" bound by the categorical
definitions of law inscribed in the legal code for the creation of legitimate law,
hinges on this sense of mutual optimization because both elements exhibit the
same normative structure. True democracy is not possible unless it is based on
the right to equal subjective liberties and their correlates: Every attack on this
right violates its own organizational principle, which calls for equal participation because this is the consequence of, and safeguard for, the greatest possible measure of equal subjective liberties.

Justifications for such an interlinkage can only be circular in nature. It is
not—as Albrecht Wellmer explains—a matter of a poor (*schlecht*) theoretical
circle but rather of an "unavoidable practical . . . circle."[17] In other words,
according to a well-known saying, it is not a matter of avoiding the circle but
of entering it at the right place. Contrary to all misunderstandings, the democratic, eighteenth-century theory of natural and of rational law was also not
"two-tiered" but circular in design. The point of entry into the circle was still
formed by the "innate" human rights. They were used by Jean Jacques
Rousseau as well as by Kant to provide a foundation for the principle of popular sovereignty and, conversely, to determine the democratic structure of
lawmaking as a precondition for its "ultimate end," namely, the protection of
human rights, the contents of which, in turn, could only be defined in a democratically structured process and also continuously amended in this concretely defined form.[18] For all of the emphasis on the sovereign, permanent
constitution-giving power of the people, "liberty" and "equality" in the opinion of both theorists were inalienable as such—as was the principle of popular sovereignty itself.[19] The point of entry into the circle was by no means
defined "metaphysically" (to use today's terminology) in this case either. The
"innate" human rights were achieved by theoretical abstraction: In the hypo-

thetical construct of the state of nature, which did not abstract away from ignorance by any means, but quite deliberately from all factual political and social institutions and constraints that had evolved historically, such human rights could be postulated counterfactually that were not recognized anywhere in historico-social reality. In Rousseau as well as in Kant, human rights could indeed only be identified as an a priori that preceded all experience and set out to challenge it.

In Habermas's case, the point of entry into the circle is of a different kind. This is not only attributable to the fact that his theory is formulated at a time when—as he says—it can look back on more than "two hundred years" of development in constitutional law and thus be understood as the "reconstruction" of the rational aspects inherent in that development (129). The point of entry is now the discourse principle; the circle has a new systematic beginning that corresponds to the "linguistic turn" in modern philosophy. However, the discourse principle is also no longer purely an a priori and it is not defined simply in counterfactual terms. It is derived as the principle of impartial examination of action norms from those pragmatic components of speech with which a counterfactual ("ideal") speech situation is presupposed in all factually realized speech—a supposition without which factual speech would not be possible. It is this manner in which everyday communicative practice overtaxes itself with idealizing presuppositions (5, 9ff.), this interpenetration of facticity and validity, which Habermas diagnoses as the basic structure of law as well and at the same time sets into motion at the circle's point of entry: The application of the discourse principle to the legal form gives rise "equiprimordially" (on both sides of the circular process) to the principle of democracy, on the one hand, and individual private rights that are identical to the legal code, on the other (121f). These principles embody the idealistic preconditions for all constitutional practice that lays claim to reason. Regardless of what the actual strategic motivations and interests may be in factual processes of constitutional law-giving and in later constitutional praxis, a critical standard is established in these principles without which the description of reality would be cynical.[20]

Before going into the differences that result from these different presuppositions of the eighteenth-century theory of natural law as opposed to discourse theory, which will be discussed in this chapter, I wish to adumbrate the common structure in the circular justifications of the two. First of all, the circular process corresponds to the "reflexive" structure of modern law (110), which may refer to itself in a variety of internal differentiations between procedural norms and material norms, between law-generating rules and primary rules, or between constitutional norms and legal norms, but without being "self-referential" in a tautological sense.[21] The democratic conception of "self-legislation" as such can also only be given justification in a circular fashion if, in spite of the fact that ideally the persons who are the "free" lawmakers are also the "coerced" legal addressees, the temporal differentiation between lawmaking and application of the law is upheld in every citizen. These internal differentiations of the law, however, already respond to a circumstance that gives the "practical circle" a much more fundamental meaning. Those "deductions" that are still being demanded anachronistically of Habermas's theory have been passé ever since the modern loss of objectively justified certainties.[22] Subjectively or intersubjectively elaborated justifications are necessarily circular if only because they can no longer presuppose common reasons.

Kant captured the essence of this problem when he stated, "This is where we now see philosophy put indeed on a shaky footing which should be solid, regardless of the absence of anything in heaven or on earth on which it depends or on which it is supported."[23] For Habermas, the objective lack of presuppositions in practical philosophy does not constitute as acute a problem as it did for Kant, who radicalized the self-justification of every postmetaphysical practical philosophy by not being able to explain their central principle of liberty as a possible object of experience, but only as a possibility thereby indicating the condition for a future realization of liberty—which was why he had to declare practical philosophy to be the "keeper of its own laws."[24] Habermas, on the other hand, can point to aspects of communicative praxis in which counterfactual idealizations are at least factually assumed, so that philosophy no longer has to rely on its own assumptions, but can take recourse to those of social practice. Nonetheless, Habermas also insists that, aside from the linguistically structured life-forms, there is "neither a higher nor a lower order to which we . . . could appeal" and therefore declares Kant's philosophy, which develops the critique of reason as "its own work" and is based as a whole on a form of "a reason that puts itself on trial" (xli), to be the uncircumventable prerequisite of modernity.

It is essential in respect to the foundation of a democratic constitutional state in which liberties and popular sovereignty are to be equally guaranteed that none of these self-referential, circular structures are tautological. If Kant not only bases a morality free of all substantive standards on the self-legislation of the will,[25] but also entrusts the enactment of law independent of all material natural law to the popular will because the latter "makes decisions on itself,"[26] then the expectation that the results will not be arbitrary is bound up with the presupposition that the respective "self" is no more identical to itself than reason that litigates against "itself." This identity does not mean a split that the respective actors would have to create within themselves such that the moral subject would no longer bear any trace of *homo phaenomenon*, or that the democratic lawmaker would consist simply of citizens who were no longer permitted to have any bourgeois interests, or that philosophy would be locked up in an ivory tower. Such splits could only be oriented to objective certainties which, after all, have precisely been eliminated. Instead, nonidentity is achieved in every case by means of separations in procedure which, in turn, are especially typical of the structure of the law.[27]

The often observed use of legal metaphor, even in Kant's theoretical philosophy, is presented, for example, in the "self-knowledge" of reason that does not simply refer to itself, but is differentiated into two distinct thought processes—the "critique of pure reason" as an independent propaedeutics and the system of pure reason proper.[28] Here, self-knowledge consists of the possibility of applying the first thought process to the second. In other words, thought that refers to thought is not, however, identical with it.[29] Similarly, a differentiated procedure of testing maxims to determine whether they can be universalized also exists for moral self-legislation. For that matter, the Categorical Imperative requires that the form of a (simulated) universal law per se be applied to concrete maxims. Here again, stages of guidelines for action are applied to each other that are precisely not "identical"; instead Kant differentiates between them so rigorously that his moral principle was often misunderstood to involve total asceticism. All that this principle is saying, however, is that the subject of examination must not be contained in the standard of examination: In the Categorical Imperative it is presupposed that we abstract from all aspirations to happiness if we are to be able to use that Imperative as the standard for examining these aspirations (and the latter can definitely pass the test).[30]

Moreover, as far as the structure of modern law itself is concerned, its potentiated possibilities for such differentiation must indeed be regarded as a necessary condition for the institutionalization of liberties and democracy. Kant refers to equal rights and popular sovereignty as first principles of any and every democratic law-making process and construes as their necessary correlate a principle of a separation of powers that strictly subordinates to the democratic lawmaker all government agencies that apply the law.[31] This entire model can be read as a configuration of differentiated, sequentially ordered procedures that are intended to prevent a tautological structure of the said "circle." The highest principles are concretized in the process of constitutional law-making and create the premises for decision making by a democratic law-making process that is otherwise free to shape its own contents. The decisions brought forth by this process in turn form the premises for the subsequent "instances" of constitutional government. Law is also applied to law when examining whether the respectively subsequent procedure did justice to the legal premises of the prior procedure; however, the law applied in this case is not the same law. It is only by means of these procedural differentiations that liberties and popular sovereignty can be guaranteed at all; and, conversely, they prevent the emergence of a state that is identical to itself and generates the law of which it consists, or simply legitimates itself by the law it enacts. Put more concretely: this structure of modern law serves to subsume the state apparatuses under the democratic enactment of law and prevents "totalitarian" solutions that make it possible for administrative and political agencies to program themselves.—If the enactment of all modern law as positive law goes hand in hand with the enlightening realization that all law depends on decision making and that all objective certainties are thus lost, then the structure of this law contains safeguards that compensate for the arbitrary nature of the contents by providing for nonarbitrary procedures.[32]

However, this brings us back to the as yet unresolved question of the function legal form and legal code have in Habermas's circular process of the genesis of rights. An interesting theory maintains that there is a contrast between Kant and Habermas in this respect.[33] Whereas in Kant, the category of law as such is said to be so highly infused with normative contents that he provides justifications for the "exeundum" from a state of nature unregulated by public laws by means of a moral imperative, in Habermas's work, the form of law cannot be derived in discourse-theoretic terms. It is instead only "gleaned historically" (as a product of the disintegration of traditional ethical life) and, from this standpoint, remains "completely contingent."[34] Since Habermas does indeed maintain that the legal form is by no means a principle for which normative justifications can be provided and initially defines the law only in the "functional" terms of its complementing morality,[35] it would seem impossible to counter the proposal of a difference between Kant and Habermas on this point. At second glance, however, one finds that the differences are not that distinct. Kant's "moral" imperative to enter a state of law does not yet refer to morality (in Kant's usage, "ethics") in the narrower sense, but proves explicitly to be a "postulate of public law" itself.[36] In Habermas's theory, on the other hand, the fact that the *legal form* cannot be justified normatively is expressly related to the specific abstractions innate in the law, and indeed he uses this term when referring to them (112). For Habermas, there are clear justifications for the normative intention of the law, albeit in a different respect: To the extent that the legal principle "not only (calls for) the right to subjective liberties as such, but to equal subjective liberties," "the claim to legitimation by positive law comes into play, a claim which we could disregard as long as we considered the formal character of law" (120). It is only with the identical guarantee of subjective freedoms, in other words, that the stage of a "legal code" is reached, without which legitimate lawmaking is not possible. This was why legal form and legal code occupied different positions in the circular process of the genesis of rights. It is only when the principle of discourse is applied to the form of law that the legal code is created "in the shape of *legitimately distributed* rights" (124), and also the principle of democracy, which constitutes the only law-making procedure that allows us to expect an equal distribution of rights.

However, things are much the same in Kant's conception. Kant also does not refer the emphatic postulate of the entry into the state of law to the form of law as such, but refers instead to the legal idea (*Rechtsidee*) of setting up an ideal republic in which the same equal freedom and equal access to law-making are guaranteed. Only such a republic is the "only enduring," the "only constitution consistent with right," whereas prior constitutions of state of some kind (*Staatsverfassungenüberhaupt*) can only be regarded as "provisional."[37] For this reason, Kant calls for entry into an initial state of law with a view to the ideal state of law because the endeavor to realize the republic can only take place within a "constitution of some kind." To that extent, a poor legal and constitutional order is still better than none at all and even law that cannot yet be legitimated as such is indispensable.

The legal form is equally indispensable in Habermas's conception, although discourse-theoretical justifications as such are not given for it. Without the form of law, neither the legal code nor the principle of democracy could take shape. This indispensable quality of the legal form is entirely in line with Habermas's emphasis on the ubiquitousness and immanence of the law and his strong emphasis on the constitutional state. It is not just the legal code, but also the legal form that is the condition enabling democracy; in other words, it is also one of the "necessities" preceding democracy, even if the latter first enacts the former. But not until a legal code (i.e., the legitimate distribution of rights or private autonomy) has been established does that aspect of law exist that forms the basis of Habermas's strong theory of the internal relationship between democracy and the constitutional state.[38]

Inasmuch as Habermas occasionally identifies the reciprocal continuum of private and public autonomy with that of the constitutional state and democracy,[39] it might appear as if he were presupposing a concept of the constitutional state that is exhausted in the negative delineation of a private sphere. However, since according to Habermas we can normatively conceive of a constitutional state only as one that is democratic,[40] its legal configuration simultaneously serves the institutionalization of democracy. In this respect the legal code securing private autonomy is only a necessary but not a sufficient condition for the relationship between constitutional state and democracy. Rather, the actual "hinge between the system of rights and the construction of a democratic constitutional state" is formed by the principle of popular sovereignty, in which the subjective right to democratic participation is combined with the objective-legal institutionalization of democratic procedures (169). However, we shall return to the more precise definition of this concept of popular sovereignty in Habermas, for he states, "The idea of the rule of law sets in motion a spiraling self-application of law, which is supposed to bring the internally unavoidable supposition of political autonomy to bear against the facticity of legally uncontrolled social power that penetrates law *from the outside*" (39). Nevertheless, it is initially unclear whether this self-application of law concurs with Kant's reflexivity of the constitutional procedural order or is distinct from it precisely to the extent that the respective conceptions of popular sovereignty differ from each other.

We must first examine the specific quality of the subjective rights of private autonomy Habermas has introduced in order to fully understand the crucial point of his conception of the reciprocal mediation of rights and popular sovereignty. When Habermas states that "at a conceptual level, rights do not immediately refer to atomistic and estranged individuals who are possessively set against one another" (88), he distances himself from a tradition of perceiving liberal rights guarantees in a way that basically blocks such mediation. In his critique of "abstract right," G.W.F. Hegel had even proceeded from a legal relationship between the isolated owner and his thing (*Sache*),[41] although it remained unclear whether this point of departure for his critique of liberal "atomism" was attributable to an overblown characterization of the opposing party or to the logical development of the concept of law.[42] Karl Marx correctly treats all property relationships as legal relationships between individuals, but understands the latter relationships merely in terms of mutual exclusion and limitation. By declaring in his critique of the human rights catalog of the French revolutionary constitutions that this structure is the character of liberal law per se, he can only qualify human rights en bloc as those "of the egoistic man, Man as removed from his fellow-man and from the community."[43] Thus, he necessarily misunderstands important articles of the French declarations in the sense that in them he sees the "political community . . . reduced to the mere means for the conservation of these so-called rights of man."[44] As already noted, this misunderstanding has persisted up to the current debate between liberals and communitarians. Therefore, if Habermas, by contrast, asserts that both private and political autonomy are guaranteed by one and the same structure of subjective rights, then his positive definition of "negative" liberties is of particular interest.

While subjective private rights were themselves determined by a fundamental ambivalence between freedom and coercion, they exhibit—when exercised by individuals—a further ambivalence that to some extent is elaborated in Habermas's analysis, but also seems to be due in part to an element of indecisiveness in the analysis itself. At first glance, it may appear that Marx's juxtaposition of public sphere and private sphere is merely reformulated in terms of discourse theory when Habermas explains that the private autonomy of a legal subject can be understood "essentially as the negative freedom to withdraw from the public space of reciprocal (*gegenseitiger*) illocutionary obligations" and goes on to add, "Private autonomy extends as far as that the legal subject does not have to give others an account, or give publicly acceptable reasons for her action plans. Legally granted liberties entitle one to *drop out of* communicative action . . ." (120). What Marx termed the *right of stubborn egoism* and juxtaposed to the "polity" would appear in this context to be the private right to irrationality as opposed to the rationality of public discourse.[45] No attempt will be made here to pursue the complex question of whether something that does not follow the logic of discourse hence cannot be justified in discourse theory, and furthermore whether such justifications would moreover subsume private freedom under public freedom.[46] Rather, I will confine myself to examining whether the rights of private autonomy in Habermas's theory remain stripped of normative connotations and, in that respect, are incompatible with political autonomy.

Given that Habermas points up the intrinsic value of "provinces" in relation to universalistic requirements, and also to the intrinsic value of the many "provinces" and subcultures within a pluralistic society vis-à-vis the public discourses of this society, it would have been fitting to deal with subjective private rights not primarily from the standpoint which, unlike public discourse, they permit strategic action. The right to privacy could also shore up private discourses in which justifications can definitely be mutually accepted, but that are protected from being exposed to the requirements of communication in public. The classical intention of religious freedom had this normative aspect, for example. The same issue could be raised from the reverse perspective of the public sphere. As Stephen Holmes has shown, there is a "positive use of negative liberty" or a public use of private liberty when the public sphere is relieved of having to communicate about religious matters.[47] In the process, the refusal to communicate (in both directions) helps to make communication possible. Whereas public communication about the truth of religious contents is already indicative of the refundamentalization of a society, a multicultural society can only be preserved if this discourse in particular is left to the "provinces" of the private sphere and public communication only takes place with regard to the correctness of the way in which the various religious communities deal with one another.

In Habermas's system of rights, insufficient emphasis is placed on this intention, although it is in line with his theory as a whole, because he is aiming for a more emphatic mediation of private and public autonomy than that which underlies the concept of "avoiding" public conflicts. For this very reason, subjective liberties are weak in terms of normative contents. The fact that they cannot be derived by means of discourse theory, as Habermas himself confirms, is apparently only due to their formal legal character (which is linked to abstractions), but not to the rights themselves. Habermas makes not only the legitimate distribution but also the "greatest possible measure of equal subjective liberties" a precondition for enabling the legitimate enactment of law. (122). Thus, according to Habermas, these rights fundamentally appear under a dual aspect. They have a "Janus face" and "can be conceived from a *functionalist* viewpoint as the institutionalizing of a market economy, whereas from a *normative* viewpoint they guarantee individual liberties" (78). Because these rights, in their formal legal character, among other things abstract away from the motivations of the legal subjects, they permit strategic action, although they simultaneously offer rational reasons. It is the structure of these rights that offers legal subjects freedom of choice between the two perspectives that makes them compatible with the principle of popular sovereignty.

In Habermas's theory, however, this compatibility is by no means based on harmony between liberties and democratic rights of participation. As Habermas emphasizes, it is more a matter of rights of different "types": the former presuppose free choice (*Willkürfreiheit*), the latter "autonomy" (33). In other words, the legal subjects of subjective private rights are assigned a free choice that must first be rendered compatible via democratic processes, whereas in the citizen's autonomy, this compatibilization is already presupposed as a motive. In the course of elaborating this argumentation, Habermas transposes the original paradox of subjective private rights onto that of subjective public rights. The latter paradox, in turn, is based on the fact that citizens' rights to participate, as subjective rights, exhibit the same structure as all rights that negatively delineate the spheres of the individual's free choice. The "communicative freedom" of democratic processes of will-formation to which the mutual obligation to provide publicly acceptable justifications corresponds is thus guaranteed in the same way as its opposite, namely withdrawal into the private sphere, whereby the individual is relieved of any obligation to provide such justifications. By securing private and public autonomy both by giving them equal weight, but also by assigning them to the same legal code, the system of rights also leaves it to the discretion of the subjects of democratic rights whether and in what way they wish to make use of their rights to participate (130). Whereas the tension between facticity and validity within subjective private rights resulted from equal freedom being guaranteed by coercive means, the relationship between facticity and validity is reproduced at the level of subjective public law given that the form of subjective rights as such permits strategic behavior, whereas the public dimension of these political civil rights is linked to the insistence on making use of rights to political participation in a consensus-oriented manner (120). The fact that Habermas deviates here from eighteenth-century premises of legal and democratic theory has far-reaching implications that will be dealt with at a later point in this discussion (130). The focus here, however, is on the way in which in Habermas's theory liberties function in light of the dialectics of the public and private spheres that he already delineated in extremely strict terms in *The*

Structural Transformation of the Public Sphere: A critical public is only possible if the private sphere is intact, and vice versa. Negative and positive liberties are mutually enabling.

II

Habermas's mediation of rights and popular sovereignty runs counter to a process that is typical of democratic societies as they exist today. These systems isolate basic rights from the context of democratic will-formation and thus transform genuine civil liberties (*Freiheitsrechte*) into legal goods (*Rechtsgüter*) defined by an expertocracy; these are then rationed and allocated to the subjects (*Untertanen*) as the state apparatus sees fit. Habermas, by contrast, reconstructs the "necessary" connection between liberties and popular sovereignty, via a discussion of historically entrenched misinterpretations and deficient realizations. In so doing, however, he does not simply take up the original conception of this connection as was developed in the eighteenth century. His discourse-theoretical reformulation of the continuum originally justified in terms of natural or rational law rests on innovations that overcome the theoretical inadequacies of Enlightenment philosophy. But the question is still whether a phenomenon well-known from the history of philosophy does not arise here as well: An advance in the provision of theoretical justifications may involve paying a price in terms of substantive or structural options.

However, before this problem can be tackled, given that it is one of theoretical structure and as such is also encumbered with the difficulties innate in reaching an understanding between eighteenth-century and twentieth-century political philosophy, a number of misunderstandings with regard to Habermas's theory must first be dispelled, misunderstandings which, for their part, stem from the extreme discrepancy between Enlightenment thinking and mainstream twentieth-century concepts. The very fact that Habermas's theory maintains a strong relationship to that of the Enlightenment at all is currently a source of irritation in the various camps in the scientific community. Some of the battle lines that have been drawn up stem from an element of the said discrepancy, namely, that the unity of the theory of democracy and the theory of law that existed in the eighteenth century has been dissolved by the division of labor in today's scholarly establishment. Habermas himself points out that his central reconstruction of the "intrinsic" link between the rule of law and democracy is no easy task in view of how self-evidently the constitutional state and democracy are administered by two different disciplines today and thus regarded as completely different subjects. This is one of the difficulties reproduced once more in a number of the critical approaches taken to Habermas's theory.

The critical considerations of Habermas's system of rights I outline in this chapter focus on whether the democratic intentions of Enlightenment theory, and these were still flawed because they were based on a philosophy of the subject, essentially continue to apply in unabbreviated form in Habermas's discourse-theoretical reconstruction. In this investigation, I of course assume that the concrete solutions proposed in the eighteenth century cannot automatically be projected onto the completely changed structures of twentieth-century society. Rather, it is a matter of the current perception of the fundamental democratic and constitutional principles on which those concrete options were based. These principles can be completely refuted today with cynical openness or adapted either in a minimizing manner with a view to current conditions or "translated" into the horizons of current problems by taking their original intention into consideration. These principles, however, may also be so heavily overlaid or suppressed by the contemporary structures of reality that their substance is simply misunderstood.[48]—An indication that even Habermas's theory of law and democracy, which maintains the closest possible contact to the Enlightenment, is not entirely free of such distortions in perception is, for example, that it occasionally underestimates the level of complexity achieved by the eighteenth-century theories. This applies in particular to the present question of the quality of the relationship between rights and popular sovereignty in Rousseau and Kant. It is not just the decisive factor in a problem of reception in the history of philosophy but also helps clarify a specific element in the content of Habermas's theory of law and democracy.

Habermas's theory acts as a successful intermediary between the positions currently taken by the liberals on the one hand and republican communitarians on the other, who either prioritize human rights as the expression of moral self-determination or, conversely, popular sovereignty as the expression of ethical self-realization and in so doing also create structural competition between the two. As Habermas points out,

> The system of rights can be reduced neither to a moral reading of human rights, nor to an ethical reading of popular sovereignty. . . . The equiprimordiality of private and public autonomy first reveals itself when we decipher, in discourse-theoretic terms, the motif of self-legislation according to which the addressees are simultaneously the authors of their rights. The substance of human rights then resides in the formal conditions for the legal institutionalization of those discursive processes of opinion- and will-formation in which the sovereignty of the people assumes a binding character. (104)

Habermas, however, still clings to the abstract juxtapositions of the current controversy to the extent that he allows them to be the frame structuring his retrospective view of the classical thinkers in modern democratic theory. Although he grants that both Jean Jacques Rousseau and Kant attempt to establish a symmetrical interlocking of both principles, he presumes that the outcome is more republican in the case of Rousseau and more liberal in the case of Kant (99f.). However, although these attributions bear out the intuitions of the prevailing history of ideas today, their presuppositions are problematic. The latter refer to the relationship between natural law and positive law, law and morality and, ultimately, between discursive and legislative procedures, attributed respectively to the theorists. In all these respects, the enabling conditions of democracy as securing freedom are affected.

To begin with, as far as the relationship between natural law and positive law in the classics of modern democratic theory is concerned, its definition in Habermas is already linked to the glance he casts on what he believes to be the close connection between law and morality in the work of Rousseau and Kant. According to Habermas, only in the case of Kant do liberties provide the starting point for the attempted mediation of liberties and popular sovereignty. These rights in Kant, moreover, are interpreted as being directly justified in moral terms, which for that reason precede the legislator as something "given" (100f.). Habermas concedes that the institutionalization of the only innate human right of equal liberty first arises in Kant's thought from the logic of the social contract via the enactment of positive law, thus interlocking liberty and popular sovereignty in this respect (93f.). However, Habermas takes the purportedly moral justification of human rights as an opportunity to discuss the alleged opaque relationship between the principles of morality, law, and democracy in Kant. When referring to the citizens' law-making autonomy, the principle of right, Habermas claims, would appear to mediate in Kant's schema between the principle of morality and the principle of democracy, but conceptually the principle of morality and of democracy are mutually enabling, whereas the principle of right merely constitutes the reverse side of the principle of democracy (94). Habermas's objections—from which he derives his hypothesis that in Kant's thought there is an unconceded competitive relationship between human rights and popular sovereignty—can, however, be read like these current references to alleged contradictions in his own reconstruction of the genesis of the system of rights. Kant's mediation of rights and popular sovereignty is necessarily "circular" as well (see the aforementioned discussion): from the point of view of an expert in the theory of natural law, Kant, too, is forced initially to introduce rights at a specific point in the circle before he can make the "change in perspective" to the democratic generation and concretization of these rights by enacting them into positive law. Here, too, the different constellations of the principles in question are defined by the point reached in the circle.

However, as far as the purported moral quality of Kant's liberties (and the concept of law as such) is concerned, the only innate right to equal freedom may be imbued with a moral connotation in the "expert's" mind—but there is no moral justification for it in the philosophy of law elaborated by Kant. This is a point in which Kant and Habermas concur, but that the latter fails to recognize. In fact, as will be shown, Kant upholds a nonmoral starting point of the law in a much more rigorous manner than Habermas himself, and this is also a source of differences between the two authors' concepts of democracy. First of all, as far as the relationship between law and morality in Kant is concerned, Habermas represents the majority opinion in the extended dispute over this aspect, whereas a minority position will be taken here.[49] The latter initially refers to the fact that the thesis (popular above all among legal scholars because it is conducive to the expansion of powers granted to the judiciary) of Kant's derivation of law from morality is due to problems that result from terminological deviations of the *Metaphysik der Sitten* in today's usage: Kant refers to all "laws of freedom" that are in any way a subject of practical philosophy as "moral," contrasting them to laws of physical nature, and subdivides the moral laws into "juridical" and "ethical" laws.[50] Thus, the fact that Kant regards *morality* as a generic term for law and ethics must be borne in mind when he later speaks of a "moral imperative" as a *pflichtgebietenden Satz*, a sentence that imposes an obligation, "from which the capacity to oblige others, i.e. the concept of law, can be developed."[51] The "moral" imperative here is still neutral to the differentiation between law and ethics.[52] The development of the concept of law from this moral imperative, in other words, is only evidence of Kant's equiprimordial justification of law and ethics ("morality" we would call it today) based on the general law of liberty.—If Kant had been able to provide the basis for his theory in a philosophy of language and to introduce the principle of discourse instead of the concept of morality, which is neutral to law and ethics, then we would more clearly see the analogous structure defining the relationship between law and morality in Kant and Habermas.

In the work of both authors, the absence of moral justifications for law certainly does not mean that law is no longer bound to satisfy moral claims (106). Rather, the "autonomy" of law in relation to morality means that moral standards can only be legally enacted in positive law if they can be elaborated and sanctioned by legal means. And, to the extent that they (in contrast to the nonspecificity of moral requirements) can be specified with the "mathematical precision" called for by Kant,[53] they still truly limit the arbitrary power of the state apparatus and by no means unleash it. Kant pinpointed this critical problem in a formulation that again makes his specific use of the language clear: "Politics has little problem accepting morality in the first meaning (as ethics) when it means sacrificing the law of human beings to their rulers: But with that of the second meaning (as jurisprudence), before which it should have to genuflect, it finds it advisable not to make any contract, and instead to dispute its existence, and to interpret all duties on the basis of pure benevolence."[54] The enormous rationality of this consideration on Kant's part and the frightening irrationality of the growing tendency to erode the differentiation between law and morality in today's discourses, even in those of liberal legal theory, can first be fully explored by analyzing the legal structures in twentieth-century totalitarian systems. Despite their highly disparate intentions and respective effects, the clauses of justice and values in both Nazi law and the Stalinist constitution of the Soviet Union, for example, equally appointed the state apparatuses as terrorist administrators of morality, because possession of the state's monopoly on force enabled decisionistic definitions of moral contents, and the "higher value" of (even perverted) moral norms permitted the dissolution of all limitations to the rule of law as were still contained in the coexistent legal norms.[55] Kant, the great admirer and clear-sighted analyst of the French Revolution, was already aware that its potential for liberty was embodied by its democratic constitutions, whereas the state's treatment of "virtue" embodied the terror.[56]—That moral principles can only function benignly as directives of state action after they have been translated into the aggregate state of carefully defined law is a premise that is shared in such equal measure by Kant and Habermas that Habermas's criticism of Kant on this point almost seems like an arbitrary attempt to create a distance between the two.

Thus, Habermas's claim is untenable that Kant's duplication of the law as natural and as positive law perpetuates the leges hierarchy of traditional natural law and indeed rests on the Platonic notion that the positive legal order merely copies and concretizes the ideal order in the world of phenomena (106f). Nonetheless, Habermas emphasizes with the greatest justification that, by taking on the differentiation between positive and suprapositive law, a "burden of debt" was assumed that has "awkward consequences" (105). The current, absolutely prevalent reading of the Enlightenment conception of natural law is indeed the "Platonic" reading. It embarked on its victory march in the wake of twentieth-century developments in Europe that led to the establishment of states that had a dominant judiciary and ultimately counteracted the progressing democratization of lawmaking through the judicial review of legislation. To the extent that the necessity of reviewing "simple" parliamentary laws in terms of a "higher" law—administered by courts and constitutional courts—became the indisputable premise, the formal natural law of the Enlightenment was subject to a resubstantializing interpretation that inverted its original intentions.

However, Kant did not make the correctness of democratic laws depend-ent on whether they corresponded substantively with material norms of natu-ral law but on whether the (democratic) law-making procedure was just. As he puts it, an "external legislation containing only positive laws is conceivable; however, it would have to be preceded by a natural law to ground the legisla-tor's authority . . . " [57] Kant's criterion of legitimacy is no longer geared direct-ly to individual contents of positive law but indirectly oriented to the proce-dural premises of the latter. For this reason, it corresponds precisely to the type of legitimation that Habermas had defined as characteristic of modernity per se: "What is decisive for the legitimacy problems of modernity is . . . that the level of justification has become reflexive. The procedures and preconditions for the process of legitimation are now the legitimating reasons on which the validity of legitimations are based." [58] Far from wanting to reduce the "idea of citizens' self-legislation . . . to the moral self-legislation of individual per-sons," [59] Kant instead develops the democratic model of legitimation as autonomous. Thus, as he sees it, the doctrine of law (*Rechtslehre*) and the doc-trine of virtue (*Tugendlehre*) are differentiated through the "differentness of the legislation," both with regard to the presupposed "motivating force" and also by the fact that in law there is an "external legislator." [60] "Seen in terms of laws of freedom" (which, again, are located beyond the differentiation of law and ethics), the "external legislator" can only be the "united people itself" that decides in a procedure where "every person's decision about everyone and everyone's decision about every person refers to the same thing." [61] Ideally, it is equality of participation and equality before the law that are meant to exclude the use of arbitrary power against any person.

This multidimensional "universal character" of the law is not—as Habermas presumes—a duplicate of the structure of the Categorical Imperative (121). It is true that Kant's criteria for the correctness of the law and for the moral evaluation of maxims for action are all equally free of mate-rial content and defined in purely proceduralist terms. In this sense, they are analogous in structure, but not interchangeable. Kant's distinction, namely, that the law establishes rules directly for the actions but that ethics only gives laws for the maxims for action,[62] makes it clear that the "universal character" in both cases must be developed at completely different levels of abstraction and by means of different procedures. Because the law is directly guiding action in the sense that it sets out certain facts (with corresponding legal con-sequences), it only achieves the degree of abstraction that the "maxim" always already has. For this reason, the process of democratic lawmaking has to establish the universalizability of the specific contents of a specific law, whereas the procedure involved in the Categorical Imperative merely *exam-ines*[63] a maxim with a certain content to determine whether it corresponds with the form of a universal law per se.[64] Since, in the latter case, it is not a matter of lawmaking nor of specific laws, but merely of the criterion of whether something could potentially be law, there is no need here whatsoever for the institutionalization of a procedure on which, conversely, democratic legislation depends as such. For this reason, Kant only deals with the question of autonomous legitimation in connection with this aspect. All of Kant's lines of argumentation are aimed at creating the justifications for a political autonomy of the legislating citizens that is also "autonomous" vis-à-vis morality—but without wanting to contradict it.

If Kant nonetheless adheres to the separation of positive and suprapositive law, this is not because his theory contains a premodern relic, but rather expresses in the extremely specific conception of this relationship a radical democratic intention that has been lost to even the most advanced theories of democracy today. Precisely in keeping the relationship of positive and suprapositive law free of any moral connotations, Kant has laid one of the foundations with which to avoid those "awkward consequences" and regressions that Habermas rightly criticizes in view of the "two-tiered legality" practiced in the twentieth century. Kant's minimalistic core of suprapositive law by contrast, the only "innate" human right of equal freedom (from which the rights treated in "private law" differ in that they must be "acquired" as a matter of principle),[65] is, as a suprapositive right, mediated with the principle of popular sovereignty that Kant also accords a quality of suprapositive law. Whereas in Habermas's theory, the continuum of liberties and popular sovereignty is posited within a system of rights that are juridical from the start, in Kant's theory, by contrast, an endeavor is also made to mediate rights and popular sovereignty outside the legal system. This essential difference between Kant and Habermas has far-reaching implications for the understanding of the rule of law and democracy.

Before this central aspect can be described in more detail, it is necessary to take a closer, if necessarily brief, look at Rousseau, the supposedly republican-communitarian opposite to Kant, in order to dissolve a further communication problem between eighteenth- and twentieth-century theories of democracy. Habermas, who comes closest to doing justice to this most misunderstood and most persecuted theorist of the political history of ideas, and who emphasizes his great affinity with Kant, nonetheless asserts that Rousseau—in diametric opposition to Kant in this respect—advocates that a collective subject described in ethical communitarian terms become independent of the actually intended political autonomy of the citizens (100f.). According to Habermas, Rousseau bases his political conception on a preexisting homogeneous community, and, as a result, his mediation of popular sovereignty and rights, which is more successful than Kant's, is devalued as a whole. However, it is hard to press the claim that this mediation—as Habermas observes—initially proceeds from popular sovereignty and

includes human rights only as a mode of realizing this sovereignty in democratic law-making procedures. Like all contractual theorists, Rousseau
assumes the existence of isolated individuals who must first join together as a
society by means of the highly artificial act of a contract. The first chapter of
the *contrat social* begins with the key principle of any "atomistic" natural
right, namely, that the human being is "born free," declaring that this innate
freedom is an inalienable human right.[66] In addition, it establishes the guarantee of this human right to be the standard of a legitimate political government.[67] It is from this basis that Rousseau then goes on to justify the principle
of popular sovereignty and a legislative procedure, the "final purpose" of
which is freedom and equality because the procedure is based on the free and
equal participation of all legal addressees.[68] Precisely as in the case of Kant,
in Rousseau's thought the innate human right is not only the point of entry
into the "circle," but also has the suprapositive quality of natural law.

By contrast, in Rousseau's theory social homogeneity is not a prerequisite for the political process but the—more or less minimalistic—product
thereof. Morals, customs, and commonly shared values, to which Rousseau
definitely ascribes a high power for social integration,[69] are indeed not "given"
in the strict communitarian sense, but are dependent variables of a very modern function that Rousseau develops in the classical shape, namely, as "public opinion."[70] Far from being leery of cultural heterogeneity, Rousseau
laments the "uniformity" that pervades social patterns of behavior,[71] regarding
it as the negative outcome of an instrumental rationality that has been set free
in the development of arts and sciences. Even the divergence of particularist
social interests (which are as unpopular in Rousseau as they are elsewhere in
the eighteenth century)[72] is not something that he believes should simply give
way to a mystical or substantial *moi commun*, but is instead processed in the
universalization test of the democratic legislative procedure that merely determines the smallest common denominator of the pluralistic society: "The common element in these differing interests forms the social bond, and if there
were not some point in which all interests concide, there could be no such
thing as society. Society must be governed only in accordance with this common interest."[73] The latter statement is to be understood in such a way that
everything that is not held in common remains outside public regulation,
given that Rousseau adheres to the ideal conception widespread in the eighteenth century that a society should manage to get along with as few laws as
possible. Thus, diverging interests are not eliminated, but form a bottleneck
for juridification.

With regard to both Kant and Rousseau, it must be said that it is not so
much the semantic generality of the law—as Habermas stresses (103 and
120)—as above all the democratic generality of the procedure preceding it
that supports the legitimation of the law and the integration of society.

Although Kant and Rousseau are not able to give discourse-theoretical justifications for this procedure, the justifications they provide based on a philosophy of the subject nonetheless do not generate the shortcomings Habermas claims (93 and 102): The political generalizability of interests is not discovered, either via the monologues of moral individuals as in Kant's thought, or through the monologue of an ethical collective subject as in Rousseau's schema. It is intrinsic to the structure of participation in democratic procedures that a political will does not already exist but must first be formed. This explains why Rousseau and Kant alike must resort to discursive elements in this procedure, even if they cannot provide theoretical justifications for them. Thus, Rousseau, who at first glance is inimical to discourse, devotes a great deal of attention to the problems of talking and persuasion in order to distinguish demagogical eloquence in the service of particularist interests from discussions inherent in democratic processes.[74] It is with this latter aspect in mind that Rousseau maintains that the citizen's right to cast a vote must be coupled with another right, namely, "the right to express one's opinion, to make suggestions, to divide and discuss, which the government is always endeavoring to leave exclusively to its members."[75] The fact that Kant's concretization of the principle of publicity in a theory of a critical public sphere goes far beyond Rousseau's allusions need not concern us here.[76] Rather, what is important in the following is the question of what relationships obtain between these early, theoretically as yet unestablished aspects of discursivity and the suprapositive dimension of rights and, in particular, what they mean for a theory of democracy aimed at the principle of popular sovereignty.

Because Kant assigns all rights that concretize the sole "innate" human right of equal freedom the character of natural rights, yet does not consider them to be "given," they form an essential object of the public discourse that is kept going by the "freedom of pen" and by every citizen's free speech.[77] When Kant states that "every human being after all has his inalienable rights, which he cannot give up, even if he wanted to, and on which he is authorized to make *his own judgment*,"[78] then he is upholding both elements that are crucial for the "natural" character of these rights. Here, human rights as such are by definition not at anyone's disposal and they are open in the "postmetaphysical" sense that their contents are decided by the rights-bearers themselves. The apparent paradox of this solution is designed to meet the dilemma innate in every guarantee of freedom, for if the correct contents and use of rights were fixed before the citizens had reached any decision about them, then freedom is already doomed. The reason why human rights are being characterized as natural rights becomes even more evident when it is a matter of instilling them with concrete contents through democratic legislation. In this case, Kant is dealing with a legal positivization of human rights that is nonetheless not intended to eliminate their suprapositive character. As he puts it, liberties are at the same time "principles a priori" on which every state of positive law is grounded[79] and derivatives of the "supreme authority" of the lawmaking people "from whom all rights of the individuals . . . must be derived."[80]—"For all right depends on laws."[81] By expanding the "circular" connection between popular sovereignty and human rights to include the dimension of natural law here, Kant understands rights as positive and suprapositive law, as legal principles of the state and prior to the state. He thus attributes the same structure to them as he does to the principle of popular sovereignty itself. Likewise, according to Kant, as the origin of law, the latter precedes all positive law, and as an authority prior to the state, it even precedes the (fictitious) "original contract."[82] For this reason, popular sovereignty is not constrained by criteria of material correctness, but—once it has been historically established—is itself irrevocable from a normative point of view.[83] On the other hand, popular sovereignty is laid out in the positivized participatory rights of the constitutionally institutionalized or enabled process of opinion—and will-formation, the form in which it exclusively appears in Habermas's work.

Kant's positive-suprapositive doubling up of liberties as well as of popular sovereignty is intended as a democratic allocation of arguments and positions of power, something that cannot be matched in Habermas's discourse-theoretical reconstruction. Whereas the grounding of democratic freedom in terms of natural law focuses on ASYMMETRIES related to the relationship between the grass roots of society and the state apparatus, between the "people" and the political functionaries, between legislation and law enforcement, discourse-theoretical criteria are geared to those SYMMETRIES that are linked to the connotations of the "ideal speech situation."[84] The natural-law theory of democracy accepts the asymmetry of the state's monopoly on force that "disarms" the "people," that is, the sum of nonfunctionaries, and opposes it with the reverse asymmetry of popular sovereignty: The sovereignty of legislation, which precedes all governmental and legal integration, is placed exclusively in the hands of the people (or its immediate representatives) in order to ensure that the state monopoly on force is applied only within the legal directives issued by the grass roots of society. In these asymmetrical allocations of state authority and law-making sovereignty, "above" and "below" are clearly marked and rigidly positioned in corresponding "places" for different functions in the separation of powers. By contrast, the factual antagonism between political functionaries and nonfunctionaries remains underemphasized in the symmetry of democratic communication as justified in terms of a philosophy of language. Although the counterfactual speech situation factually imputed in every real speech situation functions as a normative criterion, and one that shows the real influence of power in actual discourses at that, this criterion itself is not intended as a means of normatively designating "places" and "subjects" for different functions in the fluid process of intersubjective relations.

The allocation of arguments implicit in Kant's dual characterization of liberties as positive and suprapositive law cannot yet develop any links between specific forms of argumentation and various discourses or negotiations.[85] Instead, it is related in turn to the contrast between functionaries and nonfunctionaries: It follows from the character of human rights as existing prior to the state—and, at the same time, those rights are only substantively defined by citizens—that suprapositive law can never serve as an argument for the state apparatuses against individuals. Recourse to suprapositive law is, by contrast, accorded exclusively to those who are not political functionaries, but "only" people. The positive-law character of human rights, on the other hand, is addressed to the state apparatuses that enforce the law. They have to guarantee the basic rights precisely as fixed in the constitution. Any form of activism in a suprapositive interpretation of basic rights by the state apparatuses would destroy the character those basic rights have for the individuals as existing prior to the state and could affect the citizens' monopoly on interpretation in the critical public sphere and democratic lawmaking.

By contrast, according to the criteria of discursive symmetry, in Habermas's project a "community of constitutional interpreters" that pretends that a critical public, parliaments, and all state apparatuses are equal participants in a discourse on basic rights is conceivable (279f.), even if, in actual fact, a constitutional court exists as the authority that has the final say. The fact that Habermas even points to the necessity of judicial review of democratic legislation by a constitutional court—limited, of course, to procedural aspects (162, 168, and 238)—already indicates that his theory leaves the asymmetries of the radical conception of popular sovereignty behind it, according to which all controls can only be exercised "from below": Unjust decisions by a parliament should only be corrected by a critical public and indeed not "from above," by a constitutional court.[86] This simultaneously questions the intuition grounded in natural law thinking that the legally delineated domains of freedom are merely recognized by the state but not constituted by it, and that rights only become inalienable when it is not the powerful but the powerless who decide on the manner in which they make use of their freedom.

The fact that the asymmetrical and symmetrical understanding of democracy move to some extent in opposite directions has a considerable impact on the respective conception of the constitutional state that is to realize democracy. For Kant as well as Habermas, democratic will-formation can only be successful if it binds the state apparatuses to its resolutions by means of a proceduralization that separates the powers—in other words, if the judiciary and the administration are bound by the law.[87] Nonetheless, these observations have different meanings for the two authors. Indeed, as Habermas observes, Kant still has a tremendous "respect for political power as a fact of nature" (138)—but only in the sense that he juxtaposes the equally elementary ("prestate") sovereignty of lawmaking to it and subsumes all activity by the state under the latter. In Habermas's scheme, on the other hand, there is the hope that all of the state's physical coercion (*Gewalt*) can be dissolved in symmetrical relationships by deriving all political power from the communicatively generated power of the citizens (170)—a process in which popular sovereignty itself is transformed into "fluid" communicative power (135).

Although Habermas does not by any means overlook the "threat potential" of all forms of political domination "backed by instruments of force held in reserve" (136), he nonetheless pursues a program for which he seeks in vain to find support in the conception of the democratic constitutional state put forth in Rousseau and Kant. Contrary to Habermas's assertion, their model of a governance of the "rule of law" by no means dares to transform the hard "substance" of political domination itself into a different, aggregate state of governance of the "rule of law" (188f.). The term *rule* here is not related to the domination by the state apparatus in a way that would enable direct processes of transformation between various kinds of power. And this "rule of law" can definitely not also be found on the side of a private autonomy that could be "paternalistically" guaranteed, and for which the principle of popular sovereignty would form the "other hand." [88] In Rousseau and Kant's thought, governance of the "rule of law" was instead identical to popular sovereignty; it always referred to the rule of democratic law and implied the supremacy of the law-making people over all law-enforcing state apparatuses.[89] The dualism of popular sovereignty and the monopoly on force was enshrined precisely in this supremacy, a dualism that Habermas's interpretation seeks to eliminate.

Habermas's criticism of eighteenth-century rational law for not having overcome "the idea of an original antagonism between law and power" [90] makes an issue of something that was never intended. Kant bases the transition from a state of nature to a first state of law "of some kind" on pure violence, from which law first emerges by dint of being arbitrarily posited, and hopes for the historical realization of the ideal legal state of the republic in which the law-giving sovereignty of the people determines all law, which now subjugates violence itself.[91] If Habermas, by contrast, favors the symmetrical conception of an "equiprimordial constitution of law and political power" (142), then "power" in this nexus must be understood in the limited sense in which it was introduced as communicative and jurisgenerative power (146f). With Habermas drawing here on Hannah Arendt's differentiation between (communicative) power and violence, it is easy to see how "power (winds up) on the side of law" in this manner. How the residual risk of violence—as opposed to power—can be eliminated appears more problematic given that the state apparatuses indisputably possess the monopoly on power (and violence), whereas communicative power is characterized by the fact that "no one can actually 'possess' it" (146).

Habermas's reconstruction of the idea of the constitutional state goes hand in hand with a demand that corresponds to the classical options, namely, "to bind the administrative system steered via the power code to the law-making communicative power" (150). However, he weighs the program down with problems that are attributable in part to the symmetry of its own premises, and in part to the perception of factual erosions of the current constitutional state. The internal differentiation of political power by means of which the administrative apparatuses are to be tied to the rule of law also appears in other formulations as the bridge for the transformation of power: "The rule of law regulates . . . the conversion of communicative power into administrative power" (176). This does not yet amount to a contradiction, for law generated by democratic means is not spared the ambivalence of both empowering and limiting state apparatuses through its directives in contents and its formal specificity. What is more problematic in view of this logic of constitutional state law is the fact that Habermas transforms popular sovereignty into fluid communicative power, on the one hand, while insisting on the intrinsic logic of the administrative system, on the other.

As far as the reformulation of the principle of popular sovereignty is concerned, it is directed more against a caricature (widespread in the history of ideas) of the Enlightenment model than against that model per se. The definition of the "place" of popular sovereignty in eighteenth-century theories was not at all, as Habermas assumes, dependent on the incorporation of popular sovereignty into a "visibly identifiable gathering of autonomous citizens" (136). Popular sovereignty could also not be localized "concretistically" in the people (301) because the concept of the people (like that of the nation) was highly abstract in the eighteenth century. It did not refer to ethically, culturally, or socially defined entities, but merely to the sum of those who did not have a position in the state apparatuses, the nonfunctionaries.[92] This abstract notion of the people relating to constitutional law is only understandable in terms of its juxtaposition to the state's monopoly on force. The demand that all sovereignty be concentrated "undivided" in the people is identical to the demand for a separation of powers between the legislative and executive: it is intended to prevent regressions to absolutistic systems in which sovereignty and the monopoly on force would coincide.

Habermas can hardly uphold this unequivocal position if he can only pinpoint popular sovereignty as sublated in the "'subjectless' forms of communication circulating through forums and legislative bodies" (136) or finds that it arises from the "interactions between constitutionally institutionalized will-formation and culturally mobilized publics" (301) or defines it as a quantity that "comes to bear in the power of public discourses" in order to take shape in the parliamentarian legislation (186). Popular sovereignty thus transformed into communicatively generated power becomes nearly ubiquitous; however, it also loses the enforceability that it still had at that "place" that was, as it were, the opposite pole to the monopoly on force. Fluctuating freely, it now only represents a "potential with which the holders of administrative power positions must *reckon*" (147). Constitutionally proceduralized popular sovereignty, on the other hand, had the task of binding the rulers to democratic resolutions by the ruled in a *juridical manner*.[93] From this perspective, by rendering popular sovereignty fluid, Habermas has created a setting more conducive to a form of power generation that also serves administrative power rather than limiting it. In so doing, he has translated the classical French formulation, *Le principe de toute souveraineté réside . . . dans la nation*[94] (The principle of all sovereignty resides in the people) into the German phrase, *Alle Staatsgewalt geht vom Volke aus* (All state authority comes from the people).

On the other hand, Habermas's description of the state administration and its "power code" as systemic would appear to acknowledge a bedrock of original state power that cannot be derived from communicative power. Habermas formulates, "Administrative power should not reproduce itself, but should only be permitted to regenerate from the conversion of communicative power. In the final analysis, this transfer is what the rule of law should regulate, though without meddling with the power code itself and thereby interfering with the self-steering mechanism of the administrative system" (151). The latter aspect would cancel out the radical democratic scheme of the distribution of freedom, according to which only on the grassroots level social spheres of self-will are delineated as free from legislation, whereas all elements of the state apparatuses must be subjected to juridification. Habermas introduces further aspects that underscore the dilemma involved in the reconstruction of the rational meaning of the practice of the rule of law in an historical stage of development that is not favorable to the principles of the rule of law. Not only in state socialist systems, but also in the Western industrialized societies, the extreme increase in the tasks of the state has led to forms of organization that imbue Habermas's fundamental statement with decidedly real contents, namely, that state apparatuses belong to the systemically integrated spheres of action that cannot be open to democratic change without impairing their capacity to function.[95] Habermas finds this latter aspect confirmed by the "bankruptcy of state socialism," [96] but it was rather the intrinsic systemic character of socialist state apparatuses that brought them down. Yet it is more in the sense of this objection that we should understand Habermas's statement that the law should also have to be "constitutive" for the power code of the administrative processes (169). That the law appears both to constitute and destroy central state functions is not so much a contradiction in theory but one that exists in present reality, which is trying to strike a precarious balance between democratic, rule-of-law principles and the pressure of objective problems.

Under these circumstances, Habermas's reconstruction of the principle of the rule of law in the sense of a legally steered transfer of communicative power into administrative power, as well as the asymmetry of classical constitutional procedural arrangements, both have to face up to the harsh resistances of a brittle reality. The *"interpenetration of discursive law-making and communicative power-formation"* (151) as mentioned by Habermas may still come about—it is based on an interplay of critical public sphere and parliament. However, to the extent that the legally codified results of this process can be warded off at the boundaries of administrative systems that have taken on a life of their own, one sees two separate circles, namely, that of communicative power (*Macht*), on the one hand, and that of the state's force (*Gewalt*), as it was still called in the eighteenth century, on the other. In current theories of democracy, the principle of a critical public sphere, which at the time of the Enlightenment was still treated as an independent complement of popular sovereignty tends to take the place of popular sovereignty. The public *judgments* of the citizens have long since been euphemistically referred to as "self-government," whereas political action is left to professional government.[97] What Kant had called for as the minimal necessary condition for freedom even in absolutistic systems,[98] is today treated as the entire "republic" that was once called for.

The asymmetrical sense of the radical-democratic model of the separation of powers on which, at least ideally, parliamentarian systems are also based, did not so much follow a logic of subsumption that would have its point of departure in the semantics of the abstract, general law,[99] but is implied by the procedural conditions of popular sovereignty. It established the one-way street of forming will and control from "below" to "above," but without permitting arbitrary interventions from "below." It was thus possible to unleash the voluntarism of popular sovereignty and at the same time make it binding on all state apparatuses because by creating blinds constitutional procedural differentiation prevents power or interests structurally and in all directions to assert themselves recklessly.[100] Procedures for (ordinary) legislation must be established at the time when the constitution is enacted, without knowing what specific legal projects will have to be decided on its premises in the future. At the next stage of the legislative act itself, it must not be known to which specific case the law will be applied in the future. Conversely, the legal norms that have come into being through the legislative process must not be altered in court proceedings and administrative acts, precisely because here the case is always known. It was for this reason that even radical democratic theorists have denied the "people" the right to meddle in executive and judicial decisions because they are already entitled to legislate. Thus, Rousseau, who has so often been misunderstood, rejected classical Greek democracy because it involved precisely this accumulation of functions in the people; in other words, it dispensed with the separation of powers[101]— instead, he called for a "republic."

In view of the current crisis of the constitutional state in which these structural blinds are no longer upheld, Habermas detects unmistakable trends toward illegitimate power taking on a life of its own and hesitatingly endorses emerging counterstrategies (430). According to them, he suggests offsetting the erosion of legal programming for the state apparatuses by the participation of critical public spheres in concrete decision-making processes (441f.). As much as this project can be understood in Habermas's theory as the insertion of separate "legitimation filters" into segregated agencies, it fails to take into account the risks of arbitrary will that the classical separation of powers sought to avoid. This is particularly true with regard to the judiciary. That court proceedings are not initiated against racist perpetrators of violence because their deeds happen to be "popular" at the time or, conversely, that draconian sentences are meted out because this is "popular," too, would be instances that could precisely not claim to be based on a conception of radical democracy. There is no substitute for the domestification of court decisions either through legal programs or through a predictable culture of precedents that likewise precedes all concrete cases within the process of adjudication.

The more Habermas's reconstruction of the rule of law under current conditions puts the metaphor of "balance" in place of classical asymmetries and makes the transition from the precedence of legislation in the separation-of-powers system to the "equally balanced" distribution of political power (187 f.), the more he allows the constructive principles of parliamentarian democracy to be aligned to those of a presidential system, which follow a different logic. The latter achieves its efficient securing of civil liberty not by means of a one-track vertical control system based on an antagonism in principle between state apparatuses and nonfunctionaries, but by means of the reciprocal horizontal control between antagonistic, partially sovereign state apparatuses (which to a lesser degree are limited by a functional division of labor). For presidential systems, it is not the radical democratic scheme for the separation of powers that is taken as the standard but Montesquieu's division of powers as a principle of constitutionalism. Habermas's dedifferentiating argumentation follows the factual adaptive processes of the still existing parliamentarian systems in the course of European constitutional eclecticism and shares unfavorable heritage. As the failure of the Weimar constitution shows, the explicit attempt to link parliamentarianism and the presidential system— and it was this that was given as the justification for introducing the position of a strong *Reichspresident*[102]—proved to be very costly. The inherently consistent logics of the two systems were invalidated in the process because vertical control and horizontal balancing cut across each other in such a way that, in the end, both procedural structures for guaranteeing freedom were destroyed. The spread of similar constitutional conglomerates, not least of all in the most recently democratized Eastern European countries as well, gives cause to fear that many of these systems will not be able to survive any serious challenge.

The more uncertain the rule-of-law arrangement, the greater the need for additional points of view or functional equivalents. In view of its factual erosion, the separation of powers in Habermas's discourse theory is reconstructed as a "distribution of differential access to various kinds of reasons" (192 and 437f.), which, for example, limits administrations by withdrawing them from own normative reasoning. However, because Habermas emphasizes, and rightly so, that it must be possible to examine compliance with the standards of the rule of law from an observer's point of view, it seems that this aspect can complement rather than substitute for the classical structural guarantees. Thus, in the final analysis, one finds that Habermas is forced to introduce a few further aspects that imply a stronger recourse to morality than was in line with the eighteenth-century understanding of democracy. At first glance, this change seems paradoxical. For, whereas the Enlightenment awareness of the eminently freedom-securing role of the separation between law and morality is gradually waning in the twentieth century, it is to Habermas's credit that he has made this separation the point of departure for his internal differentiation of the principle of discourse.

Nonetheless, at the heart of Habermas's "system of rights," in the mediation of private and public autonomy, we find an essential, moral connotation to the use of public liberty, and it is one that first becomes completely understandable against the background of the current course of debate on the relationship between morality and politics. Habermas himself establishes the following as the result of his discourse-theoretical reconstruction of the system of rights: "On the one side, the burden of legitimating lawmaking shifts from citizens' qualifications to legally institutionalized procedures of discursive opinion- and will-formation. On the other side, the juridification of communicative liberty also means that the law must draw on sources of legitimation that are not at its disposal" (131). In view of the high-minded tone of current discourses on virtue—and they come to the fore to the same degree that the rule-of-law guarantees of rational will-formation collapse—Habermas chooses to accentuate legal procedures. But this procedure is intended to institutionalize the conditions under which moral arguments can unfold. Whereas the complexity of Habermas's mediation of private and public rights consisted in the fact that "freedom of choice" was accorded to the former, "autonomy" to the latter, from which, as a paradox of their connection, the result was that the public use of communicative freedom is guaranteed by the same legal code that also permits recourse to the privatistic, strategic pursuit of interests, Habermas's concept of procedure is not neutral in relation to this ambivalence. Whereas the democratic rights of participation "leave open" the motives for exercising them, "democratic legislative procedure must confront its participants with the normative expectations of an orientation to the common good because this procedure itself can draw its legitimating force only from the process in which citizens *reach an understanding* about the rules for their living together" (83-84). The concept of the common good in Habermas's thought is so drastically stripped of substantive contents that it avoids coming close in any way to current presumptions of virtue; however, legitimation through procedure does not result from the structure of procedure itself, which guarantees the equal right of participation, but in the quality of discursive processes that they make possible.

Here, we see a characteristic difference to the procedural concept of the theory of popular sovereignty, which Habermas quite unjustifiably suggests is weighed down by a surfeit of civic sentiment. Habermas claims that Rousseau places overly great ethical demands on the citizen and Kant makes overly great moral demands of the same and sets his own concept of proceduralization off against it because, in his account, subjective, public rights do not oblige citizens to exercise them in a consensus-oriented manner: they only "suggest" such use (131). A comparison of the procedural concepts themselves, on the other hand, brings us to the opposite conclusion. Both Rousseau and Kant rely so firmly on the rigid strictness of due process of law precisely because nowhere do they presuppose the virtue of the citizens. Rousseau hopes for the virtue of the citizens, but he does not expect it. The radical theory of popular sovereignty also distrusts not only the state apparatuses, but also the "people," and in passing refutes the common theory to be found in the history of political ideas, namely, that democratic theory prerequires a "positive" image of human beings. Rousseau begins with people "the way they are"[103] and not as they could be conceived of in the state of nature in the absence of social deprivation. Rousseau's rejection of classical Greek democracy and his advocacy of the republic based on the separation of powers rests on the argument that democracy (among other things) calls for so much virtue that it is only suitable for a "people of gods."[104] Rousseau calls for a separation of powers because one cannot rely on human virtue.

Kant tests his democratic procedural order from the outset using the borderline case of a "race of devils."[105] The procedure thus has to be created in such a way that it automatically brings about the reciprocal restriction of particular narrow-mindedness and achieves results "as if" its participants were virtuous.[106] This goes hand in hand with Kant's justification of all law, including that of the democratic rights of participation, solely in terms of freedom of choice (*Willkür*), in contrast to Habermas's dichotomy. Kant and Habermas both avoid the elitist contempt for interest-based politics that typically distinguishes conservative theory. However, Habermas's theory of democracy was developed at a time in which one can no longer rely on the automatism of constitutional procedures. For this reason, according to him, procedures must be constituted in such a way that they enable moral argumentation without prejudging them.—The difference between Kant and Habermas is at the same time the difference between their historical situation, pinpointing the span of time that has passed between the rise and fall of a democratic praxis that accords with the rule of law.

Notes

1. All page references in the text are to *Between Facts and Norms Contributions to a Discourse Theory of Law and Democracy* (Cambridge: Massachusetts Institute of Technology Press, 1996). This is a slightly abbreviated version of an essay that appeared in *Carodozo Law Review* 17 (1996): 825–882.

2. An observation most recently made by Thomas Kupka, "Jürgen Habermas's diskurstheoretische Reformulierung des klassischen Vernunftrechts," *Kritische Justiz* 27 (1994) 461ff, 466, and 468f. For a critical reply, cf. Klaus Günther, "A Diskurstheorie des Rechts oder Naturrecht in diskurstheoretischem Gewand," *Kritische Justiz* 27 (1994): 470ff.

3. As viewed, for example, by Charles Larmore, The Foundations of Modern Democracy: Reflections on Jürgen Habermas, in *The Morals of Modernity* (New York: Cambridge University Press, 1996), pp. 205–221.

4. See *BFN*, 128; and Larmore, "Foundations of Modern Democracy," p. 218–219.

5. Larmore, "Foundations of Modern Democracy," 219f.

6. Ibid., pp. 215 and 221.

7 Ibid., p. 219.

8. Ibid.

9. Günther, "Diskurstheorie des Rechts oder Naturrecht in diskurstheoretischem Gewand," 471.

10. Ibid.

11. Ibid., p. 484.

12. Immanuel Kant, *The Metaphysics of Morals*, trans. Mary Gregor (New York: Cambridge University Press, 1991), p. 148.

13. Kupka, "Jürgen Habermas's diskurstheorihiche Reformuliering . . .", p. 467f.

14. Otfried Höffe, "Eine Konversion der kritischen Theorie? Zu Habermas's Rechts- und Staatstheorie," *Rechtshistorisches Journal* 12 (1993): 70ff.

15. Also according to Albrecht Wellmer, "Conditions of a Democratic Culture: Remarks on the Liberal-Communitarian Debate," in *Endgames*, trans. David Midgley (Cambridge: Massachusetts Institute of Technology Press, 1998), p. 44.

16. On this aspect, see Ingeborg Maus, *Zur Aufklärung der Demokratietheorie. Rechts- und demokratietheoretische Überlegungen im Anschluss an Kant* (Frankfurt, Germany: Suhrkamp, 1994).

17. Wellmer, "Conditions of a Democratic Culture," p. 44.

18. Especially clear on this is Jean-Jacques Rousseau, *On the Social Contract* (Indianapolis: Hackett, 1987), Bk I, c. 4, par. 6; Bk I, c. 5, pars. 1 and 2; Bk I, c. 6, pars. 3 and 4; and Kant, *Metaphysics of Morals*, p. 163, 125, and 149f.

19. Rousseau, *On the Social Contract*, Bk I, c. 4, par. 6; Bk II, c. 1, par. 2; Kant, "Theory and Practice," in *Kant's Political Writings*, ed. H. Reiss (New York: Cambridge University Press, 1970), p. 74 and *Metaphysics of Morals*, p. 149f.

20. On the U.S. Constitution, see the analysis, itself in turn controversial for specific interests, by Charles A. Beard, *An Economic Interpretation of the Constitution of the United States* (New York: Macmillan, 1913); for the Basic Law of the Federal Republic of Germany, see Werner Sörgel, *Konsensus und Interessen. Eine Studie zur Entstehung des Grundgesetzes für die Bundesrepublik Deutschland* (Stuttgart, Germany, 1969).

21. See Maus, *Zur Aufklärung*, pp. 249ff.

22. The position taken by Thomas Blanke, "Sanfte Nütigung," *Kritische Justiz* 27 (1994): 439f.

23. Kant, *Grounding of the Metaphysic of Morals*, in *Kant's Ethical Philosophy* (Indianapolis: Hackett, 1983), p. 34.

24. Ibid., p. 55f., 61f., and 34.

25. Ibid., p. 44.

26. Ibid., p. 125.

27. On this, see Maus, *Zur Aufklärung*, pp. 249ff.

28. Kant, *Critique of Pure Reason*, p. 58 (B24), trans. by N. Kemp Smith (New York: St. Martin's, 1965).

29. On this and the following, see Maus, *Zur Aufklärung*, pp. 256f.

30. Kant, *Critique of Practical Reason*, p. 193, trans. L.W. Beck (Indianapolis: Bobbs-Merrill, 1956); "Theory and Practice," p. 64.

31. Kant, *Metaphysics of Morals*, pp. 125 and 128f.

32. On this aspect as a whole, Maus, *Zur Aufklärung*, pp. 249ff, especially, pp. 271ff.

33. In the view of Günther, "Diskurstheorie des Rechts," p. 478.

34. Ibid., p. 473, and 478.

35. See *BFN*, pp. 112 and 117; the latter statement is relativized on p. 118.

36. Kant, *Metaphysics of Morals*, p. 117; see also p. 122 where the "exeundum" from the state of nature is grounded in "all concepts of law" themselves.

37. Kant, *Metaphysics of Morals*, p. 149.

38. Jürgen Habermas, "On the Internal Relationship Between Law and Democracy," in *Studies on the Other* (Cambridge: Massachusetts Institute of Technology Press, 1998).

39. Ibid.

40. Ibid.

41. G. W. F. Hegel, *The Philosophy of Right*, trans. H.B. Nisbett (New York: Cambridge University Press, 1991), sec. 3.

42. See the controversy over "Die Logik der Rechtsphilosophie" in Dieter Henrich and Rolf-Peter Horstmann, Hegels *Philosophie des Rechts* (Stuttgart, Germany, 1982), pp. 225ff.

43. Karl Marx, "On the Jewish Question," in *Early Writings*, trans. R. Livingstone and G. Benton (New York: Penguin, 1975).

44. Ibid.

45. According to Günther, "Diskurstheorie des Rechts," p. 472f.

46. Ibid., p. 474f.

47. Stephen Holmes,"Gag Rules or the Politics of Omission," in *Constitutionalism and Democracy*, eds. J. Elster and R. Slagstad, eds., (New York: Cambridge University Press, 1988), p. 23.

48. On this point, see Maus, *Zur Aufklärung*.

49. Ibid., p. 326ff.

50. Kant, *Metaphysics of Morals*, p. 42.

51. Ibid., p. 64.

52. Ibid., p. 48, speaks of moral imperatives in contrast to technical imperatives in the same general terms as he had previously distinguished moral laws from natural laws—and indeed with a neutrality that overarches law and ethics, as it applies in this chapter on the "Vorbegriffe zur Metaphysik der Sitten."

53. Ibid., p. 58.

54. Kant, "Perpetual Peace," in *Kant's Political Writings*, p. 130.

55. On the Nazi system, see in particular *"Richterbriefe." Dokumente zur Beeinflussung der deutschen Rechtsprechung 1942-1944, Heinz Boberach,* ed. Boppard am Rhein, 1975.—For the former Soviet Union, see the constitution of 1936, for instance Art. 12 or the introductory clauses of the Basic Rights articles, pp. 124ff., in *Staatsverfassungen* ed. Günther Franz, (Darmstadt, Germany, 1975), p. 560ff.

56. Kant, "The Conflict of the Faculties," in *Kant's Political Writings*, pp. 182–183 and *Religion Within the Limits of Reason Alone*, trans. T. Greene and H. Hudson (New York: Harper, Row, 1960).

57. Kant, *Metaphysics of Morals*, p. 51.

58. Habermas, "Legitimation Problems in the Modern State," in *Communication and the Evolution of Society*, trans. T. McCarthy (Boston: Beacon, 1976).

59. However, this is Habermas's view on Kant in *BFN*, 121.

60. Kant, *Metaphysics of Morals*, p. 47f.

61. Ibid., pp. 127 and 125.

62. Ibid., p. 193.

63. Habermas himself points to the difference between making and examining laws in "Morality and Ethical Life: Does Hegel''s Critique of Kant Apply to Discourse Ethics?" in *Moral Consciousness and Communicative Action* (Cambridge: Massachusetts Institute of Technology Press, 1990).

64. Kant, p. 60.

65. Kant, *Metaphysics of Morals*, p. 63.

66. Rousseau, *On the Social Contract*, Bk I, c. 1, par. 1; c. 4, par. 6.

67. Ibid., Bk I, c. 6, pars. 4 and 5.

68. Ibid., Bk II, c. 11, par. 1.

69. Ibid., Bk II, c. 12, par. 5.

70. Ibid., Bk IV. That Rousseau's "censorship" is not a form of geglementation but a mouthpiece of public opinion—which changes in line with "public judgment"— is also clear from pars. 1, 2, and 6.

71. Rousseau, "Discourse on the Sciences and the Arts," in *The Basic Political Writings* (Indianapolis: Hackett, 1987), p. 4.

72. Even the famous "Federalist No. 10" directs its interest exlusively "to break and control the violence of faction"—albeit with means based on the principles of freedom.

73. Rousseau, *On the Social Contract*, Bk II, c. 1, par. 1.

74. Ibid., Bk IV, c. 1, pars. 1-4.

75. Ibid., Bk IV, c. 1, par. 7.

76. Habermas's own remark on this in *The Structural Transformation of the Public Sphere*, trans. T. Berger (Cambridge: Massachusetts Institute of Technology Press, 1989), p. 52.

77. Kant, "Theory and Practice," pp. 84–85.

78. Ibid.

79. Ibid., p. 74; and *Metaphysics of Morals*, p. 63.

80. *Metaphysics of Morals*, p. 149.

81. "Theory and Practice," p. 77.

82. Kant (in *Metaphysics of Morals*, p. 149) calls the law-giving common will the "original foundation of all public contracts" and indeed regards the "original contract" as arising "from the General (united) will of the people" ("Theory and Practice," p. 77). On the prelegal dimension of popular sovereignty in Kant, see Maus, *Zur Aufklärung*.

83. Kant, *Metaphysics of Morals*, p. 149.

84. See, for example, Habermas, "Discourse Ethics," in *Moral Consciousness and Communicative Action*.

85. This is the case in Habermas, *BFN*, 175f.

86. On this point, see Maus, *Zur Aufklärung*, pp. 173ff.

87. Kant, *Metaphysics of Morals*, pp. 125f and 127f.; Habermas, *BFN*, 162, 173, and 188.

88. This is Habermas's view, however, in "The Internal Relationship Between Law and Democracy"; see also, *BFN*, 120, where Habermas takes over the communitarian-republican misunderstanding that there is a contradiction between a "paternalistically" dimensioned "rule of law" and the self-legislation by the people, from Frank Michelman, "Law's Republic," *Yale Law Review* 97 (1988): 1499ff. (Quoted in *BFN*, 99.) The constellation indicated here, however, is to be found in the deficient German constitutional tradition of the nineteenth-century and not in Rousseau or Kant.

89. The legislator—in contrast to the other "powers"—is consistently identified with the sovereignty or, as the case may be, "highest authority." This was already the case in John Locke, *Two Treatises of Government*, ed. P. Laslett (Cambridge: Cambridge University Press, 1960), p. 134; Rousseau, *On the Social Contract*, Bk II, c. 2, pars 1 and 4; and Kant, *Metaphysics of Morals*, p. 125.

90. *BFN*, 146. The empowering resource of sacred law to which Habermas refers for premodern systems (142f.) was thereby negated.

91. Kant, "Reflexion 7947," in *Akademie-Ausgabe* (Berlin, 1900), vol. 19, p. 562; Kant, "Reflexion 8046," p. 592.

92. See Maus, "'Volk' und 'Nation'im Denken der Aufklaerung," *Blätter für deutsche und internationale Politik* 5 (1994): 602ff.

93. Hermann Heller, "Die Souveränität," in Heller, *Gesammelte Schriften*, vol. 2 (Leiden/Tuebingen, 1971), pp. 96 and 98.

94. See "Declaration des Droits de l'Homme et du Citoyen."

95. Habermas, "Further Reflections on the Public Sphere," p. 444, where he is referring to the elaboration of this idea in his *Theory of Communicative Action*.

96. Ibid.

97. In this tradition, for example, see U. Rödel, Günther Frankenberg, and H. Dubiel, *Die demokratische Frage* (Frankfurt, Germany: Suhrkamp, 1989). In Hannah Arendt's Kant interpretation, this reinterpretation is already implicit in the fact that it deals with Kant's *Critique of Judgment* literally in place of Kant's entire work on political philosophy; see Arendt, *Das Urteilen. Texte zu Kants politischer Philosophie* (Zurich, 1985).

98. Kant, "Theory and Practice," p. 85f.

99. This is Habermas's view, however, in BFN, p. 189f.

100. On the following, see Maus, *Zur Aufklärung*, p. 294.

101. In the chapter on "democracy" in *On the Social Contract*, Rousseau comes out in favor of a separation of powers in principle. See also, Bk II, c. 4, par. 5, 6, 9; Bk II, c. 5, par. 5; and Bk II, c. 16, par. 1.

102. Report and minutes of the sessions of the eighth Committee on the drafting of a Constitution for the German Reich, *Berichte der Nationalversammlung* 23 (1920): 231f.

103. Rousseau, *On the Social Contract*, Bk I, c. 4.

104. Ibid., Bk III, c. 4, par. 7.

105. Kant, "Perpetual Peace," p. 112.

106. See, with further references, Maus, *Zur Aufklärung*, pp. 179ff.

5

Habermas, Hegel, and the
Concept of Law

Andrew Buchwalter

Jürgen Habermas prefaces his recently published philosophy of law, *Between Facts and Norms*,[1] by announcing that he will make virtually no reference to G. W. F. Hegel. This acknowledgment is curious, for while Habermas in fact makes scarcely any reference to Hegel, his project reaffirms many components of Hegel's approach to legal and political theory. Like Hegel, Habermas seeks to fashion a philosophy of right, or law, which surmounts the oppositions of empirical and normative considerations—of reason and reality, philosophical right and positive law, and facticity and validity. Like Hegel, he presents right as a principle that cuts across spheres of economic-administrative and political-communicative forms of rationality. Like Hegel, he regards law as a principle—indeed the distinctly modern principle—of societal cohesion and institutionalized public rationality. Like Hegel, Habermas advances an account of solidarity that not only does not ignore modern complexity but builds upon it. And like Hegel, he fashions a concept of law that seeks to surmount many of the dichotomies that traditionally have plagued legal and political theory: for instance, private liberty and public autonomy, liberal constitutionalism and civic self-organization, liberalism and communitarianism, formal governmental institutions and informal sphere of political will-formation, and representative and popular notions of political participation.

For his part, Habermas adduces several reasons for not according Hegel greater attention. Most important is his contention that Hegel's *Philosophy of Right*, like the practical philosophy of his predecessors, rests on the assumptions of a philosophy of consciousness or philosophy of the subject, assumptions that do justice neither to the requirements of a comprehensive theory of law nor the realities of modern social life.[2] Commitment to a philosophy of the subject cedes primacy either to the individual legal subject or to a state-social macrosubject, a state of affairs that eliminates the possibility of reconciling public and private autonomy, the liberty of the ancients, and the liberty of the moderns. Similarly, a philosophy of the subject entails commitment to a view of public life centered in political-state organization, a state of affairs that cannot accommodate a notion of sovereignty that does justice to the diverse forms of social integration characteristic of a differentiated social world. Finally, a philosophy of the subject lays special emphasis on the virtuous sentiment of citizens in accounting for solidarity and social cohesion, a state of affairs that likewise ill accords with the realities of modern life.

Thus to accommodate the requirements of a normative legal philosophy under contemporary conditions, Habermas turns to a discourse-theoretical approach to law, one that scrutinizes the phenomenon of law, not from the standpoint of the individual or communal subject, but in terms of the underlying rules and procedures governing communication and public deliberation. This "retreat into the discursive structure of public communication"[3] is significant because it furnishes a framework that can accommodate an internal relationship of public and private autonomy. Moreover, it allows for a decentered concept of sovereignty, one that does not require identifying the public will with a collective social subject.[4] And by adverting to the integrating power of the "subjectless," "anonymous," or "impersonal" structures that govern the process of deliberation, Habermas's theory accommodates a conception of solidarity and social cohesion that does not overtax the capacity of citizens for public engagement.[5] All these exemplify Habermas's break with the philosophy of consciousness, a break that has rendered unnecessary elaborate consideration of a theory like Hegel's which, whatever its merits, remains hopelessly ensnared by the philosophy of subjectivity.

In what follows I question Habermas's muted reception of Hegel's philosophy of law. My aim, however, is not to dispute Habermas's general characterization of Hegel as a philosopher of the subject, even if he too closely identifies Hegel with the tradition of the philosophy of consciousness flowing from René Descartes to Johann Fichte. Nor is it to defend *in toto* Hegel's philosophy of subjectivity, particularly as it pertains to metaphysical and epistemological issues.[6] I argue instead that Hegel's attention to the subject not only does not have consequences identified by Habermas but that in many respects furnishes tools to achieve, more effectively than may Habermas himself, goals shared equally by the two thinkers. This admittedly broad program can be variously pursued;[7] here I focus principally on Habermas' s idea of social integration, particularly as it bears on the notions of public autonomy and solidarity. Following Hegel, I argue that solidarity cannot be achieved via anonymous, impersonal, or subjectless procedures or structures but must have recourse to forms of subjective sentiment (*Gesinnungen*)—attitudes, orientations, and motivations that give procedures and structures their meaning and validity. Correlatively, I suggest that, while Habermas distinguishes legal-political from sociocultural theory—as he writes, the discourse theory of law from the communicative theory of society[8]—a Hegelian approach rightly insists on their interconnection. I develop this thesis by exploring Hegel's constitutional theory, which, unlike Habermas's, incorporates matters of political sentiment into the conditions for its meaning and validity.

Broadly understood, this chapter has a threefold objective: It seeks to demonstrate the need for a more complete reception on the part of discourse theory of Hegel's philosophy of law; to indicate the continuing value of the concept of subjectivity for legal-political theory; and to reaffirm the continuing value of a dialectical approach to practical philosophy, one which, unlike a dialogic approach, recognizes that procedures and institutions must be addressed not *intentione recta*, but in relation to the forms of subjective sentiment they presuppose.

I

Hegel's account of the role of sentiment in legal theory is traceable to Montesquieu, whose *De l'esprit des lois* identified the social and cultural presuppositions of formal legal and political theory.[9] In the *Philosophy of Right*, Hegel develops Montesquieu's insight along several different tracks.[10] Most important for present purposes is his view of the dependence of a genuine political order on the virtue and public sentiment of its citizens. In asserting this dependence, Hegel, to be sure, does not embrace the republicanism of Rousseau, for whom civic virtue alone is said to forge the bonds of solidarity.[11] His point is rather that the legal-procedural institutions necessary for a modern political order cannot properly function unless they are supplemented by attitudes that evince commitment to uphold and sustain those institutions. This is a central aspect of Hegel's account of the relationship of abstract right and morality to ethical life (*Sittlichkeit*): "The sphere of right and that of morality cannot exist independently; they must have the ethical (*das Sittliche*) as their support and foundation."[12] While asserting the indispensability of general principles of right and duty for a modern political order, Hegel maintains that those principles must be embedded within a public culture characterized by a general willingness on the part of citizens to accept and defend public norms. Without being thus situated general principles are easily manipulated for ends inimical to the public goals they are assumed to serve. Thus in the section on Abstract Right Hegel demonstrates how, in the absence of a commitment to such values as agreement, impartiality, and truthfulness, individuals will commonly enter into contracts that they have no intention of honoring and that they may breach when it is in their interest to do so. Similarly, if legal conventions must be supplemented by a sense of moral duty, duties themselves, in the absence of a corresponding commitment to the value of accepting and honoring obligations, can likewise be manipulated for private advantage. This of course is central to Hegel's discussion of the hypocrisy characteristic of individuals who cloak their conduct in the garb of principles in order to pursue ends that are only too self-serving. In his method of presentation, Hegel considers ethical life only after having first examined right and morality. However, his substantive position, as he often notes, is that principles of right and morality have neither meaning nor reality unless situated in public culture in which individuals exhibit an antecedent commitment to those principles.[13]

As regards Habermas, Hegel's thesis can be stated by considering, in necessarily schematic fashion, their respective treatments of the concept of positive law. In *Between Facts and Norms* Habermas claims uniqueness for his account of positive law, and, while there is much that is genuinely unique to his theory, it is on many points in significant agreement with that of Hegel.[14] Both hold that positive, coercive law plays a central role in any account of valid law. Both develop a theory of positive law in the context of a theory of modernity. Both, that is, claim not only that positive, coercive law emerged with modern, commercial societies, but that it must be invoked once the traditional metaphysical and religious foundations of legal authority had lost their credibility and binding force. In addition, both advance a conception of positive law that is opposed to accounts associated with legal positivism. In particular, both maintain that the validity of coercive law lies neither in the power of an authority to issue commands nor in its authority to enforce compliance. Not unlike H. L. A. Hart, both assert that positive law can successfully command obedience only if it can be rationally accepted by those subject to its authority. The validity of positive law lies not in force but in possible respect for the law. In Habermas's language, positive law claims not only validity (*Geltung*) but legitimacy (*Gültigkeit*) as well. For Hegel, the validity of law is linked to a principle of *Anerkanntsein*,[15] where law is valid only to the extent that those subject to its force can recognize its validity. Finally, both appeal to broader public considerations to account for the legitimacy and acceptability of law. For Habermas this takes the form of an account of the dependence of positive law on a theory of democracy, one in which all those subject to the force of the law ("the addressees of law") can understand themselves as authors of law.[16] For Hegel, the public dimension is of a more mediated character: legitimate law is rooted in a system of justice (*Rechtspflege*) and in a structure of public authority (*Polizei*) committed to the common good.[17] Whatever the differences, both assert that the legitimacy of positive law is bound to some notion of public autonomy.

These similarities notwithstanding, the differences between the two positions are striking. The basic difference concerns the degree to which positive law itself can serve as a basis for a society's commitment to such values as individual freedom and human autonomy. For Habermas there is, at least conceptually, an internal connection between positive law and such values.[18] This follows from his view of the relationship between the rule of law and democratic will-formation, which itself rests on a commitment to liberty and mutual recognition. For Hegel, however, the relationship between law, at least positive law, and these other values is at best contingent. Indeed, given the roots of positive law in modern commercial societies—where the common good is achieved, if it is achieved at all, not directly but as an incidental by-product of individuals pursuing private ends—, positive law for Hegel is compatible with growing injustice, social inequity and what, generally, he calls a *Verlust der Sittlichkeit* (the loss of ethical life). Hegel's *Philosophy of Right* does include institutions of public welfare designed to counteract the injustices associated with an economic construal of positive law. Yet he also notes that these legally sanctioned forms of state intervention into social relations can be counterproductive, as they tend to undermine the very liberties and forms of individual dignity they are intended to protect. In a welfare system, "the needy might be given subsistence directly, not by means of their work, and this would violate the principle of civil society and the feeling of individual independence and self-respect in its individual members."[19] In this regard, Hegel's theory of positive law leads to the forms of legal regulation or juridification (*Verrechtlichung*) that Habermas so astutely analyzed in *The Theory of Communicative Action*,[20] yet seems unwilling to address in his present theory.[21] Whether expressed in market relations or state interventionism, coercive law for Hegel remains in the grip of a dichotomy of universal and particular, public and private, which undermines its pledge to freedom, equality, and mutual recognition.[22]

Thus while Hegel may share Habermas's commitment to the rationality of a system of positive law, he also recognizes that the salutary values associated with such a system cannot be assured via the resources of positive law itself. Instead, positive law, like abstract right and formal morality, must be embedded in a public culture characterized by a commitment on the part of citizens to the principles implied by the rule of law. This is the point of his at once celebrated and infamous supersession of civil society in state. At issue is not the denial of the legal institutions of civil society but rather the accommodation of the attitudes and sentiments needed to sustain those institutions. In the ethical community (*das sittliche Universum*) that defines Hegel's theory of the state, individuals attend to the ends of public life not coincidentally, as in civil society, but directly and deliberately. In this way they are able to defend and nurture those principles of law that are rendered pathological when law is autonomized in the form of markets or the "external" welfare state. The state, Hegel writes, "is the sole precondition of the attainment of particular ends and welfare."[23] For Hegel, the principle of justice implied by civil society is dependent upon a political culture committed to justice as a good. The procedural model of justice entailed by positive law rests on the civic republicanism of an ethical community.[24]

It may seem that we have done Habermas's position a disservice. While he fashions an account of law that is decidedly proceduralist rather than republican, his is a capacious conception of proceduralism, one that does not ignore the ethical considerations that Hegel claims are essential for sustaining positive law and liberal proceduralism. Indeed, he asserts that, via the deliberative politics that conditions its legitimacy, a valid system of positive law is "internally connected" to a lifeworld that it meets halfway (*entgegenkommen*), a political culture characterized by commitment to the values associated with the rule of law.[25] In this respect Habermas asserts that law depends on what, following Albrecht Wellmer, he calls a "democratic Sittlichkeit":[26]

> The democratic procedure of lawmaking relies on citizens making use of their communicative and participatory rights *also* with an orientation toward the common good, an attitude that can indeed be politically called for but not legally compelled. . . . Law can be preserved as legitimate only if enfranchised citizens switch from the role of private legal subjects and take the perspective of participants who are engaged in the process of reaching understanding about the rules for their life in common. To this extent constitutional democracy depends on the motivations of a population *accustomed* to liberty, motivations that cannot be generated by administrative measures. This explains why, in the proceduralist paradigm of law, the structures of a vibrant civil society and an unsubverted political public sphere bear a good portion of the normative expectations. . . . [27]

Yet this appeal to *Sittlichkeit* is problematic for several reasons. On a general level there is something implausible about Habermas's invocation of very *Sittlichkeit*, since, after all, his appeal to the formal structures of law is predicated on his conviction that the modern world has rendered impossible appeal to an ethos as a source of social integration. If law is invoked to counteract the deficiencies of appeal to an ethos, it is difficult to appreciate Habermas's contention that an ethos is also that condition for the legitimacy of the concept of law.[28]

In addition, however much Habermas may wish to situate law within a political culture, he does not follow Hegel in holding that such a culture is part and parcel of the validity of law. On the contrary, Habermas defines the validity of law in a formal-pragmatic manner, through "the rules of discourse and forms of argumentation that borrow their normative content from the validity basis of action oriented to reaching understanding."[29] He makes this point when distinguishing his discourse-theoretical proceduralism from what he takes to be the republicanism of legal scholar Frank Michelman. "[A] discourse-theoretic interpretation insists on the fact that democratic will formation does not draw its legitimizing force from a prior convergence of settled ethical convictions. Rather, the source of legitimacy includes . . . the communicative presuppositions that allow the better arguments to come into play in various forms of deliberation."[30] Here we disregard the question of whether Michelman's position or that of republicanism generally entails commitment to "a previous convergence of settled ethical convictions." It is the case, though, that in Hegel's republicanism law depends for its validity on public sentiment, and not, as Habermas claims, on "the institutionalization of the corresponding procedures and conditions of communication. . . . "[31] While Hegel certainly would not dispute the need for such institutionalization, he would say that the normative content of those procedures and conditions ultimately rests with a culture prepared to sustain them. By contrast, Habermas asserts that "[i]n the final analysis this normative content arises from the structure of linguistic communication and the communicative mode of sociation."[32]

In this regard it seems altogether appropriate that to the extent that Habermas does incorporate an account of public virtue in his theory of law, he does so via the procedural structures themselves. Following Jon Elster, he asserts that in a properly proceduralized order "values of truthfulness, wisdom, reason, justice and other kinds of exceptional moral qualities can be congealed or sedimented in the actual practice of institutions."[33] In this way Habermas demarcates his view from that of Hegel, who maintains that virtue and ethical life generally are not a consequence but enabling condition of a properly functioning procedural order.[34] G. W. F. Hegel, to be sure, also acknowledges the extent to which virtue can be a matter of structure. This is evident on many occasions, notably in his account of civil society, where institutional structures turn self-seeking "into a contribution to the satisfaction of the needs of everyone else."[35] As we have seen, however, the connection between virtue and structure is for Hegel largely contingent, and can, in the absence of corresponding attitudes and commitments, easily undermine the integrative claims made on behalf of institutional structures. According to Charles Taylor, proceduralism—including that of Habermas—holds that "we need structure which, in invisible-hand fashion, behind the backs of the subjects and independent of the forms of motivation, will lead their actions towards certain patterns that preserve freedom."[36] This confidence in procedures is precisely what Hegel disputes.

Habermas's view of the relationship between structure and sentiment thus replicates an interpretation of the relationship between morality and ethical life he asserted prior to *Between Facts and Norms* in writings on discourse ethics. In these writings he maintains that "any universalist morality is dependent upon a form of life that meets it halfway."[37] Such attention to a political culture is needed to allow for the application of principles whose very universality tends to eviscerate the cultural contexts their application requires. Yet this way of phrasing the issue already indicates Habermas's departure from Hegel. For Hegel, a cultural context serves as a condition for the very meaning and validity of moral principles. By contrast, Habermas maintains that cultural contexts are needed simply to accommodate the application of principles whose validity is independently ascertained. In elaborating the relationship between normative principles and cultural values, Habermas writes, "Universalist moralities are dependent on forms of life that are rationalized in that they make possible the prudent application of universal moral insights and support motivations for translating insights into moral action. Only those forms of life that meet universalist moralities halfway in this sense fulfill the conditions necessary to reverse the abstractive achievements of decontextualiation and demotivation."[38] In this way, Habermas advances what Georgia Warnke has called a "top-down" account of the relation of norms to culture, where cultural values are molded to accommodate already justified norms and principles. While he may appropriate certain features of Hegel's *Aufhebung* of *Moralität* in *Sittlichkeit*, he discards the basic principle, one nicely formulated by Warnke (although invoking Taylor rather than Hegel): "cultural values and orientations must be acknowledged not just as elements of the concrete situations to which principles of justice apply but as codeterminers of their meaning."[39]

To be sure, in *Between Facts and Norms* Habermas acknowledges that legal theory, unlike moral theory, must incorporate within its normative framework the values and cultural self-understanding of a particular political community.[40] "Whereas moral rules, aiming at what lies in the equal interest *of all*, express a simply universal will, juridical rules also give expression to the particular wills of members of a determinate legal community."[41] Indeed, given the connection between juridical rules and their enforceability, reference to the collective self-understanding of a legal community is included in the meaning of the validity (*Sinn der Gültigkeit*) of legal norms. Legal norms are justified with reasons that "count as valid relative to the historical, culturally molded identity of a legal community, and hence relative to the value-orientations, the goals and interest positions of its members."[42]

Nonetheless, the fact remains that for Habermas the legitimacy of legal norms must "at least be compatible with moral standards that claim *universal (allgemeine)* validity beyond the legal community."[43] In this sense legal norms must be expressible in terms of the same formal conditions that govern moral discourse. Nor is it clear how it could be otherwise. A more fundamental account of the dependence of legal norms on cultural orientations would question the primacy of a structural-procedural approach to law;[44] it would also call into question aspects of the paradigm shift in legal theory from subjectivity to intersubjectvity.

II

It may seem that with his attention to sentiment Hegel has departed from the very domain of law, jettisoning the question of the norms that citizens adopt to regulate their common life for the ethical-cultural values of a particular community. Ingeborg Maus has argued along these lines when characterizing as "legal nihilism" efforts to "sublate" law in *Sittlichkeit*.[45] Habermas himself levels similar charges against some forms of republicanism. Nor is there any doubt that such charges are warranted when directed at thinkers like J. G. A. Pocock, who, Habermas correctly observes, draws "on the language of classical ethics and politics rather than on a legal vocabulary."[46] But these concerns are unjustified as regards Hegelian republicanism. Here we need not consider in detail how Hegel's republicanism remains distinct from the Aristotelian sort Habermas associates with legal theorist he terms *communitarians*,[47] who construe civic virtue in terms of a commitment to a communal definition of human nature or to a preexisting communal ethos rather than through a defense of modern rights and liberties.[48] What merits special attention here is rather the way in which Hegel redefines the very concept of law to accommodate notions of cultural value and political sentiment.

This expanded approach to law is certainly evident in the subject matter of the *Philosophy of Right*, which comprises not only formal law and political institutions, but the moral principles, ethical values, and indeed historical traditions of a society. "When we speak here of right, we mean not merely civil law, which is what is usually understood by this term, but also morality, ethics and world history."[49] More important, however, is the fact that Hegel incorporates into his very definition of law orientations, attitudes, and other forms of "internal" sentiment. He does not follow Kant, who, he notes, defined right as "the limitation of my will or freedom of choice (*Willkür*) in such a way that it may coexist with the will or free choice of everyone else in accordance with a universal law."[50] Instead, right, or law, is defined by Hegel as the "*Dasein des freien Willens.*"[51] In this way he repudiates Kant's effort—evidently continued in Habermas[52]—to define law in terms of external considerations, be it observable behavior or objective institutions. By focusing on the existence of the moral will rather than free choice, on *Wille* rather than *Willkür*, Hegel announces at the outset that law encompasses internal as well as external considerations.[53] As the "Idea of Freedom"[54]—and, of course, an Idea here connotes the unity of concept and existence—, right denotes a relationship of subjective orientations and objective conditions.[55] Hegel's philosophy of right is indeed a Theory of Objective Spirit.

In the following section I explore Hegel's reconstruction of the idea of law by considering his constitutional theory, itself an effort to reclaim the ethical considerations ignored when law is understood through categories more appropriate to civil society. This analysis will better enable us to pinpoint Hegel's differences with Habermas, for whom constitutional considerations also play a central role in legal philosophy. In addition, it will allow us to better appreciate the extent to which political sentiment, civic virtue, and even patriotism are, for Hegel, central to the meaning and validity of a properly constituted legal order.

I begin with a quick reprise of Habermas's concept of a constitution. Not surprisingly, he proffers a formal-procedural account. His, however, is not the proceduralism of bourgeois-liberal theory, for which constitutionalism, in the service of protecting private liberties, sets limits to state power while regulating social interactions. Although such attention to the claims of private autonomy is certainly not alien to Habermas's theory, his commitment to the internal relationship of private and public autonomy mandates adoption of a position which, more in line with republican accounts, accommodates the activity of citizens collectively deliberating on the ends of public life. At the same time, though, Habermas anchors the public dimension of constitutional theory not in the actual sentiment of individuals but in the formal institutionalization of procedures that secure the conditions of public communication. "[T]he constitution sets down political procedures according to which citizens can, in the exercise of their right to self-determination, successfully pursue the cooperative project of establishing just (i.e., relatively more just) conditions of life." [56]

In certain general respects Hegel's notion of constitutionalism is similar to Habermas's. For Hegel as well, constitutionalism seeks to unite cooperative attention to a common good with a more liberal commitment to institutional limits and to the rule of law. Yet Hegel pursues such goals less through procedural than republican means, by attending again to sentiment rather than to structure. This point can be appreciated if we first consider Hegel's view of the relation of constitutionalism not to political sentiment proper but to those less reflective forms of sentiment expressed in habits, customs, and social practices.[57]

Again with Montesquieu, Hegel claims that a constitution must not be viewed exclusively or even primarily in terms of formal-legal institutions. Such an approach is indeed captured by an account of what Hegel calls the "political constitution," [58] and while such an account is essential to constitutional theory, the constitution itself must accommodate the broader cultural values and practices of a people. A constitution can have binding value for a people only to the extent that it expresses "the customs and consciousness of the individuals who belong to it." [59] Without this specific reference to sentiment, the constitution remains an abstraction (*Gedankending*), and so "will have no meaning or value, even if it is present in an external sense." [60] For a constitution to have constitutive value for a culture, it "must embody the nation's feelings for its rights and conditions." In this regard it is unsurprising that Hegel displays little interest in constitutional theories focused on the best form of *government*, be it aristocracy, monarchy, or democracy. Such questions fail to appreciate that constitutional theory is at least as much a matter of social-cultural theory as legal-political philosophy, that the concept of a constitution, like that of law itself, is defined by the "unity of sentiment and mechanism, internality and externality." [61]

In keeping with this commitment to the centrality and perhaps priority of culture and sentiment, Hegel links his constitutional theory to the idea of a *Volksgeist*, "the spirit of a nation or people." He calls the *Volksgeist* the foundations or "cause" of a nation's constitution, something he intends in a double sense. First, he asserts that the constitution must be in "agreement with the *Volksgeist*." [62] This of course is the thesis that a constitution must express the values of a particular community—what in his 1802–1803 Natural Law he called the living customs present in the nation (*die lebendigen vorhandenen Sitten*).[63] Second, he maintains that a constitution is itself the *Volksgeist*.[64] Here the constitution is conceived as the organizing principle that sustains and indeed constitutes a people, the principle that both expresses and shapes its identity.[65] Our national constitution, he writes in *Natural Law*, is the constituting of the absolute ethical identity" (Konstituierung der absoluten sittlichen Identität) [66]—that principle of collective self-definition or national constitution that animates the laws and institutions of a nation.[67] Both senses of *Volksgeist* are captured in Hegel's claim, advanced in his 1805–1806 *Jena Lectures on the Philosophy of Spirit*, that constitutional theory comprises not only the legal-political domain of societal life but that of absolute spirit as well—art, religion, and philosophy.[68] Not only does a constitution express the broader cultural values of a people—"the spiritual powers which live within the nation and rule over it." [69] Given that the domain of art, religion, and philosophy designates the locus of a people's self-comprehension (its "intuition of itself"), its identification with constitutional theory underscores the role played by collective self-definition in a complete account of a constitution.[70]

In emphasizing the relationship of a constitution to the spirit of a people, Hegel clearly rejects the Enlightenment tendency to regard the constitution as a product of formal political-legislative enactment. As he never tires of arguing, a constitution cannot be regarded as a construction (*ein Gemachtes*). This approach—evidently reaffirmed by Habermas[71]—is ruled out if for no other reason than that it fails to recognize the degree to which a people is always already constituted. The notion that a constitution could be an explicit act of creation is part and parcel of the liberal conviction that, outside formal institutions, individuals are isolated atoms who are related to one another in the formless "shape" of an aggregate (*Haufen*). Yet this view, aside from the injustice it may do to a concept of human nature, misconstrues political action (constitution-making included), which is unintelligible unless individuals are already related to one another in some preconstituted manner.[72]

At the same time, however, denial of the formal constructability of a constitution is not to imply that for Hegel constitutionalism is not linked to an emphatic notion of political action. Hegel's point is not the Burkean one that renders a constitution just a matter of tradition, custom, and historical evolution. Precisely because the constitution is an expression of a public culture, it must, if it is to retain validity, regularly be refashioned to accommodate, and adapt to, changing values and circumstances. While a constitution can never be formally made, it must nonetheless be routinely renewed or rejuvenated (*verjüngert*)[73] if it is to continue to embody adequately and constitute the *spirit* of a people. Indeed, Hegel's constitutional theory in this respect assigns a greater and more demanding role to political action that does the liberal counterpart. In its assumption that a constitution can be the product of self-sufficient individuals who adopt rules to protect their subjective liberties, liberal thought presumes that a constitution is a type of contract, one which, once finalized, acquires a binding force that renders unnecessary further recourse to constitutional politics. By contrast, a more historically sensitive approach to constitutional theory depends on the continued and ongoing involvement on the part of the individuals governed by it. Precisely because a constitution, for Hegel, is never only a legal structure but an organizing principle of an existing people, because it is a principle of collective identity rather than contractual relation,[74] it can retain meaning and validity only inasmuch as it is reconsidered and reappropriated to accord that changes in the conditions of a people's self-definition. If the constitutional language of choice for liberalism is construction (*Machen*), Hegel invokes that of interpretation (A*uslegung*).[75] Understood as a transmitted legacy whose vitality requires renewal, a constitution depends on a community of interpreters who reappropriate and clarify legal traditions, principles, and institutions in light of present realities.[76]

Several important consequences follow from this identification of constitutional validation with the self-interpretive activity of a political community. Here I mention only one: that constitutional theory presupposes an account of patriotism, one in which civic engagement and public virtue play a central role in defining and indeed constituting the constitution. Adapting an expression of Michelman,[77] we might say that Hegel advances a notion of *jurisgenerative* patriotism, one accounting for the very meaning and reality of the constitution. This follows from the fact that a constitution is understood by Hegel not as a fixed and formal construction but as a complex of values and institutions that depends for its continued vitality on the activity of a citizenry prepared to reinterpret and reapply received principles and traditions in light of changing social circumstances. Hegel, to be sure, notes the extent to which patriotism also denotes an attitude of loyalty via-à-vis existing institutions and as such is "merely a consequence of the institutions within the state." [78] Yet the dependence of constitutionalism on interpretive appropriation and revalidation mandates that patriotism also has a constructive role.[79] "Patriotism is the result of the institutions of the state, just as this sentiment is the source through and out of which the state has its activation and its preservation." [80] We find such constitution constitutive patriotism in the participation of individuals in those corporations or intermediate associations whose vitality is central to a constitutional order defined through the unity of legal institutions and the subpolitical domains of family and sociality—those crucibles of civic sentiment termed by Hegel the pillars of public freedom.[81] And it is also discernible in his account of the participation of individuals in public debate, principally in legislative assemblies where the constitution acquires "new and further determination." [82] In both respects civic virtue is essential to the continued meaning and reality of a constitution.

III

In the foregoing I have sought to show how Hegel formulates a constitutional theory that in a systematic way incorporates the structures of political sentiment insufficiently represented in Habermas's procedural account. It may again seem, however, that we have done Habermas an injustice. While his is a procedural account of the constitution, it is one that seeks to accommodate the motives and attitudes of citizens.[83] "The principles of the constitutional state can become the driving force for the dynamic project of actualizing an association of free and equal persons only if they are contextualized in the history of a nation of citizens in such a way that they connect with these citizen's motives and mentalities (*Gesinnungen*)." [84] Moreover, Habermas stresses, as does Hegel, the importance of collective interpretation and reinterpretation for the meaning and even reality of the constitution. "Every constitution is a living project that can *endure* only as an ongoing interpretation continually carried forward at all levels of the production of law." [85] In this respect Habermas distinguishes his constitutional theory from Rawls's constructivist approach, which, like contract theory, binds political will-formation to the requirements of an originary agreement.[86] As he notes in arguing for the co-originality of private and public autonomy, constitutional stipulation regarding basic rights cannot be dissociated from political processes of debate and action.

Furthermore, Habermas underscores the extent to which this dynamic vision of the constitution relies on the public engagement of citizens:

> From this long-term perspective, the constitutional state does not represent a finished structure but a delicate and sensitive—above all, fallible and revisable—enterprise whose purpose is to realize the system of rights *anew* in changing circumstances, that is, to interpret the system of rights better, to institutionalize it more appropriately, and to draw out its contents more radically. This is the perspective of citizens who are actively engaged in realizing the system of rights.[87]

Finally, Habermas follows Hegel in asserting that this form of civic engagement must also be understood as a type of "constitutional patriotism," one that is animated by an effort to interpret and reinterpret basic rights and principles.[88]

Still, the place of collective interpretation and civic engagement in Habermas's constitutional theory remains ambiguous. While he clearly seeks to incorporate such components into his account, he appears to do so at a secondary level. Such activity is necessary for realizing an abstract system of rights whose validity is secured independently—in the analysis of formal pragmatic conditions for discourse. No less sympathetic a critic than Thomas McCarthy has noted the dualism between cultural clarification and normative validation in *Between Facts and Norms*: "Habermas's hermeneutic self-clarification does not function as the basic level of justification in his theory of justice. Rather, it is theoretically subordinate to his derivation of an 'abstract system of basic rights' through an analysis of the presuppositions of democratic self-determination." [89] Indeed, Habermas himself makes this point in the book's 1994 "Postscript," something noted by Rawls in defending himself against Habermas's charges.[90] Not unlike Rawls, with whom his differences, he says, "remain within the bounds of a family dispute," [91] Habermas asserts that the realization of rights is achieved through the institutionalization of rights against the state, not the rights individuals initially cede one another as persons—rights that must be presupposed in subsequent realization processes.[92] At most Habermas appears to argue that a constitution facilitates the process of its realization, but that realization process itself presupposes core principles whose validity is already determined. Nor is it clear how it could be otherwise. Anything else would call into question the basic distinction between justification and application that informs Habermas's practical philosophy—a distinction, he writes, that is no less appropriate for legal than for moral theory.[93] It would also call into question his fundamental distinction between the right and the good as well as his prioritizing the former. If "[u]nlike ethical questions, questions of justice"—and Habermas construes legal norms as matters of justice—"are not related from the outset to a specific collectivity and its form of life,"[94] then efforts at contextualizing rights remain categorially distinct from conditions of their validation.

In this respect, then, Habermas's position remains manifestly distinct from that of Hegel. In Hegel's view, matters of justification cannot be fully demarcated from those of application.[95] Precisely because constitutional principles are inextricably intertwined with the values of a culture, issues of constitutional validation are always linked to their contextualization—just as, conversely, matters of contextualization can never be fully removed from those of justification. Hegel would agree with Michelman who asserts that "[c]onstitutional law is institutional stuff from the word go," and who accordingly accentuates the "substantial-ethical character of originary-justificatory discourse."[96]

It is thus not surprising that Habermas's idea of constitutional patriotism does not assume the jurisgenerative form it has with Hegel. While he follows Hegel in formulating a notion of patriotism based on interpreting basic principles in light of changing circumstance, interpretation remains at the level of the affirmation of principles whose validity can be determined independently of the conditions of their appropriation by a particular community.[97] The efforts of the constitutional patriot, in Habermas's account, remains directed to the "best interpretation of the same basic rights and principles,"[98]—those "equally constitutive (*konstitutiv*) for every body of citizens."[99] His is therefore not Hegel's constitution constitutive patriotism, where republican engagement is part and parcel of an activity through which the meaning and validity of a constitution is shaped and defined.[100]

None of this implies that Hegel conceives constitutional politics merely a feature of popular will. Though Hegel does accentuate the place of legislative activity in constitutional politics,[101] that very fact ensures that the process is governed by constraints—namely the constitutional laws (*Verfassungsgesetze*) that govern ordinary legislation.[102] In addition, any autochtonous notion of parliamentary action is ruled out by the "organic" nature of the constitution. Precisely because a people is always already constituted, any popular change of the constitution itself presupposes the constitution and therefore can occur "only in a constitutional manner."[103] Moreover, commitment to "entrenched" constraints also flows from Hegel's equation of the constitution with the *Volksgeist*. Because a constitution, for Hegel, is understood as the spirit of a people, constitutional change consists in the change in a people's identity. Yet because the object of change is also the source of the change, any act of change is simultaneously an affirmation of principles of constitutional continuity.[104] In this respect, Hegel is as opposed to wholesale transformation as he is to wholesale creation. "Individual components can be changed, but not the whole, which shapes itself gradually."[105] Hegel could well sympathize with Thomas Jefferson's concerns about the dangers to civic life posed by adherence to constitutional structures that no longer express the concerns of the "living," yet his own notion of constitutional renewal is governed by cross-generational constraints whose elimination is neither possible nor desirable.[106]

More generally we can say that any reductionism, be it to precommitments or transformations, misconstrues the nature of constitutionalism itself. Against all one-sided approaches, Hegel again invokes Montesquieu, whose principle of *totality* captured the proper method of constitutional analysis.[107] With Montesquieu he construes the constitutional order as a whole that not only accommodates but presupposes the presence of seeming opposites: formal law and cultural attitudes, norms and values, principles and history, justice and ethical life, the right and the good, justification and application, and—as Michelman would have it—self-rule and law-rule. What distinguishes Hegel from Habermas is not a recognition of such distinctions but the determination to construe them not as rigid polarities but in terms of their mutual implication and interrelationship. Habermas dismisses the value of the principle of totality for contemporary social-political theory. Yet it is arguably this principle that accommodates the dialectic of principled precommitments and their realization that appears to inform his own vision of a dynamic constitutionalism.

IV

A comprehensive defense of an Hegelian approach to constitutional law as well as to constitutional patriotism would have to consider various other matters: It would have to show that, *pace* Habermas, appeal to *Sittlichkeit* and indeed *Volksgeist* in no way binds law to what Habermas calls "the ethos of an already integrated community."[108] It would have to demonstrate why, *pace* Habermas, *Sittlichkeit* is not incompatible with universalist moral principles. And it would also have to consider how anchoring law in the political culture of a particular community is compatible with the pluralism of contemporary societies, a pluralism that, for Habermas, necessitates the turn to proceduralism. These are matters that cannot be addressed in this chapter. What I have attempted here is to indicate why law must be supplemented by an account of ethical life and how, through Hegel's concept of the constitution, such an expanded notion of law might be construed. In addition, by demonstrating how questions of law presuppose a consideration of subjective sentiment, I have sought to indicate the continuing value of dialectical thought for legal-political theory and to question Habermas's thesis of the obsolescence of the philosophy of the subject. At the very least, however, I hope to have made clear that a proper defense of a discourse theory of law cannot be complete without a more thorough and sober reception of its most illustrious dialectical precursor.

Notes

1. Translated by William Rehg (Cambridge: Massachusetts Institute of Technology Press, 1996).

2. In addition, it can be noted that while Hegel relied on a concept of philosophy able to elucidate, by relying on its own resources, the totality of social life, Habermas opts for a methodical pluralism committed to reconstructing knowledge generated by the various human sciences, including jurisprudence, legal sociology, legal history, and moral and social theory. Similarly, while Habermas shares with Hegel a determination to construe the legal-social domain in terms of different logics of normative inquiry—for Hegel, legal, moral, and ethical; for Habermas, legal, moral, ethical, and pragmatic—Habermas cedes to each an independent validity and necessity, while Hegel specifies a supreme discourse to which the others are subordinate. That Habermas may himself chose hierarchy over compatibility and opt for a primary discourse has been suggested by Günther Teubner, "De collisione discursuum," *Frankfurter Rundschau*, November 11, 1992, p. 7.

3. *BFN*, 186.

4. *BFN*, 136 and 298.

5. *BFN*, 136 and 486. Jürgen Habermas accentuates this "structuralist" dimension to his conception of popular sovereignty in his "Reply to Symposium Participants," *Cardozo Law Review* 17, nos. 4–5 (March 1996): 1477–1557.

6. For a critique of Habermas's rejection of the paradigm of subjectivity focusing on epistemological and metaphysical issues, see Peter Dews, "Modernity, Self-Consciousness and the Scope of Philosophy: Jürgen Habermas and Dieter Henrich in Debate," in *The Limits of Disenchantment* (London: Verso, 1995), pp. 169-193.

7. I have done so along different lines in "The Co-Primordiality of Public and Private Autonomy in Hegel and Habermas," American Philosophical Association Colloquium Paper, Chicago, April 1995.

8. *BFN*, 437.

9. *Elements of the Philosophy of Right*, trans. H. B. Nisbet (Cambridge: Cambridge University Press, 1993) [hereafter *PR*], § 3. Unless otherwise noted I use this version of the English translation.

10. For instance, he follows Montesquieu in maintaining that in the legal structures of any particular society can never be understood in a purely autonomous or self-contained manner but always must be related to the communal values and traditions

that give those structures meaning and effectiveness (PR § 3). In addition, the nature and very meaning of a legitimate legal-political order and indeed a genuine state—*sittliche Universum* (*PR*, p. 21)—rests on the balanced relation between formal institutions and the sentiment of individuals—a sentiment based on a individual's appreciation of the congruence between her interests and those of the formal political order (*PR* § 268).

11. Here I follow Habermas's characterization of Jean-Jacques Rousseau. Compare Ingeborg Maus, "Liberties and Popular Sovereignty. On Jürgen Habermas's Reconstruction of the System of Rights," (this volume).

12. *PR* § 141Z.

13. *Encyclopaedia of the Philosophical Sciences*, vol. 3 (Oxford: Clarendon, 1971) [hereafter *Enc.*] § 408.

14. Hegel's concept of positive law, *Recht als Gesetz*, is found principally in *PR* §§ 209–229.

15. *Enc.* § 484.

16. As he writes, there is "no legitimate law without democratic law making by citizens in common who, as free and equal, are entitled to participate in the process." See "Reconciliation through the Public Use of Reason: Remarks on John Rawls' Political Liberalism," *Journal of Philosophy* 92, no. 3 (March 1995): 130.

17. See Wilhelm R. Beyer, "Norm-Probleme in Hegels Rechtsphilosophie," *Archiv für Rechts- und Sozialphilosophie* 56 (1964): 561–580.

18. "On the Internal Relation between Law and Democracy," *European Journal of Philosophy* 3, no. 1 (April 1995): 12–20.

19. *PR* § 245. Here I employ the translation by Knox (Oxford: Clarendon Press, 1967). See Raymond Plant, "Hegel on Identity and Legitimation," in *The State and Civil Society*, ed. Z. A. Pelczynski (Cambridge: Cambridge University Press, 1984), p. 240.

20. *The Theory of Communicative Action*, vol. 2, trans. Thomas McCarthy (Boston: Beacon, 1987), p. 387.

21. In this regard it is perhaps telling that, more so than other contemporary democratic theorists (e.g., Maus), Habermas grants a larger role to the judiciary in preserving and nurturing deliberative democracy. See *BFN*, 280.

22. To be sure, Habermas is aware no less than Hegel of the pathologies that can result when law is subordinated to the exigenices of markets and/or states. Indeed, his discourse theory of law is conceived precisely as an effort to fashion an alternative to paradigms associated with bourgeois and welfare state paradigms of law, neither of which can do justice to the public autonomy central to a democratic approach to legal theory. Still, the differences are significant, since for Hegel the limitations of positive law stem not from its economic or statist construal but from the structure of positive,

coercive law itself. Because positive law does not address matters of sentiment, because it is governed by a formality or lawlikeness (*Gesetzmäßigkeit*) designed only to regulate external behavior (*PR* § 212), it can accommodate and even foster conduct inimical to solidarity. This point has been made by Dews, who with Claus Offe notes the potentially disintegrative dimension of a notion of law that permits anything not actually forbidden. See his "Law, Solidarity and the Tasks of Philosophy" (in this volume).

23. *PR* § 261Z.

24. Charles Taylor has argued along these lines. See "Hegel's Ambiguous Legacy for Modern Liberalism," *Cardozo Law Review* 10, nos. 5–6: 857–870; and "Cross-Purposes: The Liberal-Communitarian Debate," in *Liberalism and the Moral Life* ed. Nancy L. Rosenblum, (Cambridge: Harvard University Press, 1989), pp. 159–182.

25. *BFN*, 302.

26. "Bedingungen einer demokratischen Kultur," in *Gemeinschaft und Gerechtigkeit* eds. Micha Brumlik and Hauke Brunkhorst, (Frankfurt, Germany: Fischer, 1993), pp. 173-196. Richard J. Bernstein has argued similarly from a Deweyean perspective in "The Retrieval of the Democratic Ethos," *Cardozo Law Review* 17, nos. 4–5: 1127–1146.

27. "Postscript to *Faktizität und Geltung*," *Philosophy and Social Criticism* 20, no. 4 (1994): 147. He makes a similar point when positively citing Ulrich Preuss's characterization of a democratic society: "Such society has an interest in the good quality of enfranchised citizens: in their being informed, in their capacity to reflect and to consider the consequences of their political relevant decisions, in their will to formulate and assert their interests in view of the interest of the co-citizens as well as future generations" (*BFN*, 418). See also *BFN*, 358 and "Citizenship and National Identity: Some Reflections on the Future of Europe" (Appendix 2 in *BFN*).

28. Here I repeat an argument astutely made by Dews in the article already cited, "Law, Solidarity and the Tasks of Philosophy" (in this volume).

29. *BFN*, 260.

30. *BFN*, 278.

31. *BFN*, 298.

32. *BFN*, 297, emphasis added.

33. *BFN*, 341.

34. "Postscript," 148.

35. *PR* § 199. He makes a similar point in discussing how formal rules governing professional service render unnecessary appeal to the explicit virtue of civil servants. See Carl K.Y. Shaw, "Hegel's Theory of Modern Bureaucracy," *American Political Science Review* 86, no.2 (June 1992): 381–389.

36. "Hegel's Ambiguous Legacy for Modern Liberalism," p. 863. See also Taylor's "Die Motive einer Verfahrensethik," in *Moralität und Sittlichkeit* ed. Wolfgang Kuhlmann (Frankfurt, Germany: Suhrkamp, 1986), pp. 101–135.

37. "Morality and Ethical Life," in *Moral Consciousness and Communicative Action* (Cambridge: Massachusetts Institute of Technology Press, 1990), p. 207.

38. "Discourse Ethics," in *Moral Consciousness and Communicative Action*, p. 109.

39. "Communicative Rationality and Cultural Values," in *The Cambridge Companion to Habermas*, ed. Stephen K. White (Cambridge: Cambridge University Press, 1995), p. 135.

40. *BFN*, 108.

41. *BFN*, 152.

42. *BFN*, 156.

43. *BFN*, 282, emphasis added.

44. For a critique of Habermas along these lines, see J. M. Bernstein, *Recovering Ethical Life: Jürgen Habermas and the Future of Critical Theory* (London: Routledge, 1995).

45. "Liberties and Popular Sovereignty. On Jürgen Habermas' Reconstruction of the System of Rights," *Cardozo Law Review* 17, nos. 4–5: 829.

46. *BFN*, 268.

47. *BFN*, 267-286.

48. For Hegel's position, see Andrew Buchwalter, "Hegel's Concept of Virtue," *Political Theory* 20, no. 4 (November 1992): 548-583. For Machiavelli and modern political theory, see Quentin Skinner, "On Justice, the Common Good and the Priority of Liberty," in *Dimensions of Radical Democracy*, ed. Chantal Mouffe (London: Verso, 1992), pp. 211–224.

49. *PR* § 33A.

50. *PR* § 29, translation amended.

51. *PR* § 29.

52. It may be noted, however, that in earlier writings Habermas advanced a notion of law that seemed to focus not just on procedural mechanisms but on the "broader political, cultural, and social context" in which "[t]hey are embedded." He called this "law as institution" as opposed to "law as medium."

"By legal institutions I mean legal norms that cannot be sufficiently legitimized through a positivistic reference to procedure. Typical of these are the bases of constitutional law, the principles of criminal law and penal procedure, and all regulation of punishable offenses close to morality (e.g. murder, abortion, rape, etc.). As soon as the validity of *these* norms is questioned in everyday practice, the reference to their legality no longer suffices. They need substantive justification, because they belong to the legitimate orders of the lifeworld itself and, together with informal norms of conduct, form the background of communicative action."

Although Habermas here adopts the type of dyadic approach to law foreign to Hegel's position, his notion of law as institution does capture the sociocultural considerations that for Hegel are part of a comprehensive definition of right. See *The Theory of Communicative Action*, vol. 2, p. 365f.

53. See Miguel Giusti, *Hegels Kritik der modernen Welt* (Würzburg, Germany: Königshausen & Neumann, 1987), pp. 178–185.

54. *PR* § 29.

55. See Bruno Liebrucks, "Recht, Moralität und Sittlichkeit bei Hegel," in *Materialien zu Hegels Rechtsphilosophie* ed. Manfred Riedel, (Frankfurt: Suhrhamp, 1975), 13-51.

56. *BFN*, 263.

57. See also Vincent Descombes, "Is there an Objective Spirit?," in *Philosophy in an Age of Pluralism*, ed. James Tully, (Cambridge: Cambridge University Press, 1994). In this article Descombes seeks to show that, while Hegel's political theory rests on sentiment, this should be understood less as mental representations than habitual dispositions. Inasmuch as he is claiming that objective spirit cannot be exhaustively understood a conscious representations, Descombes is correct. He errs, though, in suggesting that sentiment for Hegel does not also express the explicitly self-conscious experiences of individuals.

58. *PR* § 271; as he also terms it, "the political state proper and its constitution" (*der eigentlich politische Staat und seine Verfassung*) [PR § 267].

59. *PR* § 274.

60. *PR* § 274A.

61. *Vorlesungen über Rechtsphilosophie 1818-1831*, ed. Karl-Heinz Ilting (Stuttgart-Bad Canstatt, Germany: Friedrich Frommann, 1973) [hereafter *Vorlesungen*], 1:326.

62. *Vorlesungen über Naturrecht und Staatswissenschaft*, transcribed by P. Wannenmann, ed. by Claudia Becker et al. (Hamburg, Germany: Meiner, 1983) [hereafter *Wa*] § 134.

63. *Natural Law* (Philadelphia: University of Pennsylvania Press, 1975) [hereafter *NL*], p. 116).

64. *Wa* § 134.

65. See Sheldon S. Wolin, "Collective Identity and Constitutional Power," in *The Presence of the Past: Essays on the State and the Constitution* (Baltimore: Johns Hopkins University Press, 1989), pp. 8–31.

66. *NL*, 116.

67. Heinz Kimmerle, "Die Staatsverfassung als 'Konstitutierung der absoluten sittlichen Identität' in der Jenaer Konzeption des 'Naturrechts,'" in *Hegels Rechtsphilosophie im Zusammenhang der europäischen Verfassungsgeschichte*, eds. Hans-Christian Lucas and Otto Pöggeler, (Stuttgart-Bad Canstatt, Germany: Frommann-Holzborg, 1986), pp. 129–148.

68. *Jenaer Systementwürfe III: Naturphilosophie und Philosophie des Geistes*, ed. Rolf-Peter Horstmann, (Hamburg, Germany: Meiner, 1987), pp. 231–262. In his lectures on the philosophy of history, presented late in his career, Hegel continues to link a constitution with the values of absolute spirit: "political constitutions are not to be separated from religion; realm of inwardness" [*Lectures on the History of Philosophy. Introduction: Reason in History* (Cambridge: Cambridge University Press, 1975), p. 104].

69. *Lectures on the History of Philosophy*, p. 96.

70. For a critique of this expanded understanding of constitutional theory, see Axel Honneth, *The Struggle for Recognition: The Moral Grammar of Social Conflicts*, trans. Joel Anderson (Cambridge: Massachusetts Institute of Technology, 1995), pp. 32f.

71. As he writes; "My reconstruction of the meaning of a legitimate legal order begins with the original resolution (*Entschluß*) that any arbitrary group of persons must take if they want to constitute themselves as a legal community of free and equal members. Intending to legitimately regulate their life henceforth by means of positive law, they enter into a common practice that allows them to frame a constitution." See "Reply to Symposium Participants," p. 1477.

72. *PR* §§ 273f.

73. *Wa* § 134. In arguing that a constitution can and must be renewed, Hegel is obviously ascribing to political action something he denies to philosophy, for which a shape of life that has grown old "cannot be rejuvenated but only known" (*läßt sich nicht verjüngen, sondern nur erkennen*) [22, translation amended].

74. For an overview of different concepts of constitutionalism, see E.-W. Böckenförde, "Geschichtliche Entwicklung und Bedeutungswandel der Verfassung," in *Staat, Verfassung, Demokratie* (Frankfurt, Germany: Suhrkamp, 1991), pp. 29–52.

75. *PR* § 344.

76. For an illuminating discussion of the general relationship between tradition and renewal in constitutional theory, one very similar to Hegel's, see Wolin, "Contract and Birthright," in *The Presence of the Past*, pp. 137–150. Hegel's position also finds rearticulation in the legal hermeneutics of Ronald Dworkin, though Hegel would not

accept, *inter alia*, Dworkin's restriction of the interpretive process to the judiciary. For Habermas's reception of Dworkin's hermeneutic of law, see *BFN*, 205–225.

77. "Law's Republic," *Yale Law Journal* 97 no. 8 (July 1988): 1493–1537.

78. *PR* § 268, translation amended.

79. Cf. Harry Brod, who writes, "Hegel understands patriotism to reflect rather than constitute the political order." See *Hegel's Philosophy of Politics* (Boulder, Colo.: Westview, 1992), p. 121.

80. *Vorlesungen* 4:641.

81. *PR* § 265.

82. *PR* § 298.

83. Such contextualization is also in keeping with his account of the degree to which law is self-referential as regards its own institutionalization.

84. *BFN*, 184.

85. *BFN*, 129. In this Habermas follows Ulrich Preuss: "A society is constituted if it in the proper institutional forms and normatively guided process of accommodation, resistance, and self-corrective is confronted with itself" (*BFN*, 444).

86. See "Reconciliation through the Public Use of Reason," especially p. 126ff. See also Thomas McCarthy, "Constructivism and Reconstructivism," *Ethics* 104, no.1 (October 1994).

87. *BFN*, 384.

88. "Struggles for Recognition in the Constitutional State," in *Multiculturalism*, eds. Charles Taylor et al. (Princeton: Princeton University Press, 1994), p. 144.

89. "Legitimacy and Diversity: Dialectical Reflections and Analytical Distinctions," *Cardozo Law Review* 17, nos. 4–5 (1996): p. 1100.

90. "Reply to Habermas," *Journal of Philosophy* 92, no. 3 (March 1995): 164f.

91. "Reconciliation through the Public Use of Reason," p. 110.

92. "Postscript," p. 43f.

93. "Remarks on Discourse Ethics," *Justification and Application*, trans. Ciaran Cronin (Cambridge: Massachusetts University of Technology Press, 1993), p. 88.

94. *BFN*, 282.

95. An interesting illustration of this point can be found in Hegel's history of philosophy and in particular his account of the transition from Greek to Christian worldview. Though the "Christian" principle of subjectivity makes its conceptual appearance already in Greek thought with the decline of the polis, the relationship of the Greek to the Christian period cannot be understood as merely the historical con-

cretization of an existing principle. Rather, the realization process itself presupposes a process by which the conceptual categories are transformed and revalidated. See Oscar Daniel Brauer, *Dialektik der Zeit*, (Stuttgart: frommann-Holzboog, 1982): pp. 186–191.

96. Frank Michelman, "Family Quarrel," *Cardozo Law Review* 17, nos. 4–5 (1996): 1175.

97. *The New Conservatism: Cultural Criticism and the Historian's Debate* (Cambridge: Massachusetts Institute of Technology Press, 1989), p. 261.

98. "Struggles for Recognition in the Constitutional State," p. 122.

99. *BFN*, 306.

100. In this respect Hegel's notion of civic engagement resembles the "communal democracy" that Wolfgang Kersting juxtaposes to Habermas's idea of constitutional patriotism. What I argue here, though, is that what Kersting champions in opposition to a notion of constitutional patriotism is for Hegel a form of constitutional patriotism itself. See "Verfassungspatriotismus, kommunitäre Demokratie und die politische Vereinigung der Deutschen," in *Universalismus, Nationalismus und die Einheit der Deutschen*, eds. Petra Braitling and Walter Reese-Schäfer, (Frankfurt, Germany: Fischer, 1991); and "Verfassung und kommunitäre Demokratie," Günther Frankenberg, ed., *Auf der Suche nach der gerechten Gesellschaft* (Frankfurt, Germany: Fischer, 1994), pp. 84–102.

101. Here Hegel would clearly disagree with John Rawls, for whom the supreme court exemplifies the "public reason" central to constitutional politics. See *Political Liberalism* (New York: Columbia University Press, 1996), p. 231ff.

102. *Wa* § 131, 146. See Rolf Grawert, "Verfassungsfrage und Gesetzgebung in Preußen. Ein Vergleich der vormärzlichen Staatspraxis mit Hegels rechtsphilosophichen Konzept," in *Hegels Rechtsphilosophie*, eds. Hans-Christian Lucas and Otto Pöggeler, especially p. 294.

103. *PR* § 273.

104. A current version of this thesis has been formulated by Michelman, "Can Constitutional Democrats Be Legal Positivists? Or Why Constitutionalism?" *Constellations* 2, no. 3 (January 1996), especially pp. 298-303.

105. *Wa* § 134.

106. In this regard Hegel would likely agree with Philip Selznick, who has characterized constitutionalism "as a style of decision. It is a way of upholding principles while recognizing the demands of a changing social reality. Constitutionalism provides a perspective of continuity and a resource for the future, but it also insists that each generation be its own master." See "The Ethos of American Law," in *The Americans: 1976*, eds. Irving Kristol and Paul Weaver, (Lexington, Mass.: D.C. Heath, 1976), p. 222.

107. *PR* § 3.

108. *BFN*, 278 and 281.

6

Rawls and Habermas

Hauke Brunkhorst

It seems as if with *A Theory of Justice* John Rawls succeeded in doing what G. W. F. Hegel's philosophy of law failed to do, namely, to put the *membra disjecta* of Aristotelian politics back together again at the level of the eighteenth-century constitutional revolutions—or at least to place the parts in a plausible relationship to one another. In the course of modernity the Aristotelian unity of ethics and politics is not only broken asunder, but the different, deeply transformed, and now autonomous parts also have each withstood modern criticism. So far they have not been wiped off the philosophical agenda. However, depoliticized and deeply alienated from the community as it may be, the Aristotelian ethics of individual self-determination has survived: in the guise of a moral and ethical (and from time to time also "antimoralist") existentialism propagated from Søren Kierkegaard, Martin Heidegger, and Jean-Paul Sartre to Ernst Tugendhat and ultimately taking its cue from Immanuel Kant. And it is thriving, for it is in this form that the classical ethics of autonomy has remained innovative up to the present day. In this connection I would like to speak in terms of Autonomy[1]. Moreover, the underlying idea of Aristotelian politics, that is to say the idea of political self-organization with its clearly republican core, has to date also survived all criticisms. This I will refer to as "Autonomy[2]". This idea of reasonable self-organization by free and equal citizens (which Hannah Arendt accurately identified with the "freedom to rule" or "isonomia") has, of course, just like Autonomy[1], only survived the fire of criticism in the form of what Richard Rorty calls a "radical reinterpretation." Modern individualism, which goes back to the monotheistic heritage of antiquity and, in the form of Autonomy[1], differentiates between morality and ethics, on the one hand, and politics, which corresponds to Autonomy[2], on the other. The latter drastically reinterprets the idea of political reorganization in the light of both Judeo-Christian egalitarianism and the modern division—once again prompted by Kant—between public freedom and private happiness.

Hegel did not feel comfortable with either. This was why he developed a philosophy of right (*Recht*) which degrades the modern form of individualism to the admittedly inevitable accidence of an essentially ethical life and sublates egalitarianism in the hierarchy of a rationally ordered state body. In fact, Hegel's attempt amounts to a vision of society, which Rawls, in his essay on "The Law of Peoples," calls a "well-ordered hierarchical society." [1] In that sense, Hegel's attempt succeeds, but to the extent that it does, it falls short of precisely the normative core of an understanding of the constitution as is upheld by all Western democracies and that is based on the political ideals of 1789.

The latter is an understanding of the constitution as "egalitarian liberalism." [2] As distinct from the "well-ordered hierarchical societies," Rawls refers to these states today as "well-ordered egalitarian societies." Rawls regards the two types of society as players of equal status in the project of an inter- and supragovernmental legal setting. Rawls has developed the idea of a well-ordered egalitarian society in *A Theory of Justice*. I thus view this theory as an attempt to link the dissected body of Aristotelian politics—that is, an egalitarian and procedural understanding of political self-organization on the one hand, and an individualistic understanding of self-determination on the other, that is, Autonomy[1] and Autonomy[2],—with each other in such a way that the intrinsic independence and inherent logic of both aspects is preserved.

A Theory of Justice sketches a blueprint of a constitutional order based on reason. It contains a contractualist justification for "justice as fairness" and the institutional sketch of the "basic structure" of a "well-ordered egalitarian society." This idea of egalitarian political self-organization is essentially an idea based on rights. It is aimed at that which can be expected of everybody, independently of the motives behind their actions, as an external legal responsibility. The "constraints" of the "original position" are intended to make the arbitrary will of the one person compatible with that of all the others in all instances "according to a general law of freedom," as stated by Kant. "The idea of the original position is to set up a fair procedure so that any principles agreed to will be just." This makes the concept of "pure procedural justice" the basis of the theory.[3] The "constraints," and they function externally as pure procedural principles to which our arbitrary will is subject in the "original position," "must be constituted in such a way" that the same principles of justice are always chosen. The "veil of ignorance" is the "key condition" for this.[4] Anyone who takes the "original position" steps behind the veil of ignorance, and is thereby forced "to evaluate principles solely on the basis of general considerations." [5] The procedure of veiling that can be reconstructed hypothetically at any time has the purpose of nullifying the partiality of self-interested players: "Whatever his temporal position, each is forced to choose for everyone."[6] In this way, everyone arrives at the same principles of equal freedom for all and of the same value of freedom for every individual ("difference principle"). This roughly corresponds to Habermas's "system of rights" as put forward in *Between Facts and Norms: Contributions to a Discourse Theory of Law and Democracy* or the historically oriented typology of basic rights given by T. H. Marshall.[7] Such a system of principles of justice in the sense of human rights must be presupposed by the citizens in order to be able in a constitutional assembly to oblige a concrete legal cooperative to uphold just institutions, namely, the social "basic structure." From the perspective of his theory, Rawls now devises an "ideal legislative procedure." In sharp distinction from the economic and (interest-)pluralistic theories of democracy from the late Joseph Schumpeter all the way to the early and middle writings of Robert Dahl, Rawls construes this as an imperfect procedure geared toward the idea of just laws: "Each rational legislator is to vote his opinion as to which laws and policies best conform to principles of justice."[8] The principles of justice in the theory of the social contract are teleologically prescribed as an external standard for the rational legislator. In this respect, Rawls's idea of legislation corresponds precisely to the paradigm of imperfect procedural justice in a law court.[9] It is obvious (even if this need not necessarily be the case owing to the imperfect state of the legislative procedure) that we expect an ideal constitutional legislation will spawn a constitutional democracy with a strong social-welfare state ("fair and equal opportunity" and "distributive justice"). Indeed, Rawls also outlines the institutions of such in *A Theory of Justice.*

In *A Theory of Justice* Rawls develops a modern, procedural and egalitarian idea of political self-organization, whereby he assumes that law and morality, what is right and what is good, are separate domains. Rawls also turns to address the question of individual self-determination. The goals, sentiments, and conceptions of justice bound up with to the politically neutralized rational life plans must fit the theory and the corresponding institutions of political self-organization. The theory of the individually good, which is closely linked to the decidedly bourgeois model of the liberty of rational life-planning has a weakness. It does not take sufficient account of the indisputable factual cultural pluralism of modern societies. Even at the level of models of liberty that are typical of modernity, there are competing "comprehensive doctrines" that are inspired, above all, by various strands of Romanticism.[10] The competitors in the bourgeois planning model of liberty involve the doctrines of liberty of an aesthetic experimentalism (from John Stuart Mill to Jacques Derrida and Adorno) or an authentic individual life (from Kierkegaard to early Heidegger) and that of authentic community life (from Herder to Charles Taylor).[11] The conflict between such "reasonable comprehensive doctrines" is solved by the later Rawls with the help of the theory of a public "overlapping consensus." [12] Here, autonomous persons with different, deep-seated mutually incompatible convictions on which consensus cannot be reached come to public agreement in respect of a core area of conceptions of justice. These conceptions of justice, of the autonomous person and of reasonable cooperation follow from the respective "comprehensive doctrines," or are compatible with them and can be recognized to the same degree by all.

In other words, at the heart of Rawls's later theory, which reacts to the "fact of pluralism," there is a specific idea of the public sphere. This idea brings him closer to Habermas's thought, yet at the same time puts a greater distance between the two men. What must now fit together and have to be mutually assimilated via a reciprocal corrective learning process ("reflective equilibrium") are first the "basic structure" of just institutions that establishes a rational legislator by applying the two principles of justice to a certain society, and, second, the "overlapping consensus" resulting from the "reasonable comprehensive doctrines" of reasonable citizens on the other.

So, how do the public sphere and democracy fit together in this model of an egalitarian liberalism, and what is the role of the principle of democracy or that of political self-organization in the procedure of reasonable will-formation and just legislation? How is ideal, rational legislation connected to democracy and how are the principles of justice connected to popular sovereignty?—This is highly unclear in Rawls. What is clear, however, is that for Rawls the connection between justice and democracy—and between private and public autonomy—is by no means intrinsic to the theory or a necessary consequence of the social contract. In contrast, the philosophy of law that Habermas published in 1992 hinges on the assertion of an internal and necessary connection between popular sovereignty and human rights (principles of justice). Habermas always speaks in terms of "equiprimordiality." In a later essay from 1993, he states, "Private and public autonomy are cooriginal and of equal weight." [13] The difference and the concurrence between the two theories, that is, those of Rawls and Habermas, are closely associated in this quote (much as they are in the concept of the "public sphere"). Rawls is also concerned with an "equal weight" between "private" and "public autonomy." That is precisely what he calls a "reflective equilibrium." The public principles of justice must fit to our private sense of justice. But unlike Habermas, he does not define "public autonomy" (Autonomy^2) by the principle of democracy (or a "principle of discourse" preceding it), but instead by means of a theory of the "original position" and an "ideal legislator." Rawls orients himself throughout toward the paradigm of scientific methodology, namely, that of a theory applied to an object domain. Learning processes result from the reciprocal correction of theory and experience. The goal is to produce coherence ("reflective equilibrium") between the observable, singular evaluations of justice in the object domain of the theory and the abstract principles of justice constructed by the theory. The evaluations of justice in the object domain of the theory are summarized in *A Theory of Justice* under the concept, closely related to experience, of rational life plans. These stem from the "private autonomy" (Autonomy[1]) of individual citizens as if possible under the conditions of negative civil rights. In this sense, the 1971 theory is a matter of "equal weight" between "private" and "public autonomy."

However, democracy still has no place in this methodological position of the theory. The principles of justice can be created by someone on her own purely by adopting a hypothetical procedure. That is tantamount to the perspective of the theorist as a singular subject. And in a constitutional assembly, even the rational legislator must be willing to accept the consensus of many opinions that converge to form a common will, if only for instrumental reasons. Because there is no perfect procedure, the method of revisable majority-formation through discussion is the best known means of coming as close as possible to a just result that has been targeted as a goal. In the ideal procedure, every discussion is superfluous; if anything, it would merely distort the result through partiality, given that the opinions are "influenced by the course of the discussion," which in turn jeopardizes the independence and impartiality of the decisions taken.[14] This is one of Jean-Jacques Rousseau's key arguments, which he develops via cultural critique in the "First Discourse on the Sciences and Arts" and later transformed in his *Social Contract* into the procedural proposal to ascertain the general will by communicatively isolating the citizens from one another. "If the citizens had no contact with one another whatsoever, the large number of small differences would, if the people decided on the basis of being well-informed, always give rise to the common will and the decision would always be good."[15] This is Rousseau's version of the "veil of ignorance" argument. Discussion is ambivalent. It can make our opinion just as dependent on that of others as it can help to correct our own prejudices through confrontation with the other's point of view. Be that as it may, it is quite simply superfluous in the ideal procedure, where "the veil of ignorance means that the legislators are already impartial."[16] Only in an imperfect procedure is there a compensatory role for discussion: "The benefits of discussion lie in the fact that even representative legislators are limited in knowledge and the ability to reason." In this case, discussion is "a way of continuing information and enlarging the range of arguments. At least in the course of time, the effects of common deliberation seem bound to improve matters."[17]

In the last sentence, Rawls and Habermas concur with Peirce: "In the long run," given a halfway uninhibited and open discussion, a reasonable consensus is more likely than any other result. The difference, however, lies in the concept of reason. For Rawls, consensus in uninhibited discussion is only a methodological means by which to approximate as closely as possible, even under overly complex conditions, a previously established ideal of justice that has been specified, without discussion, through purely hypothetical construction ("original position"). This ideal is reason, the actual Logos. Rawls's understanding of reason remains Platonic and teleological because it does not manage to shake off the ideal of scientistic methodology, namely, that theory and experience must correspond or at least be coherent with each other.

Habermas and Apel see things differently. They proceed from an intersubjective and performative understanding of reason, according to which there are no reasonable goals that lie outside the procedure of uninhibited discussion itself and are recognizable or at least constructable from the outside. Here, Logos lies in the discursive consensus itself, so to speak, and in the possibility of continuing the discussion if necessary, of coming back to it and casting any factual consensus into question. And it is this question that is the actual hub of a scrutinizing reason (*vernehmende Vernunft*). Habermas and Apel have very consistently completed the paradigm shift "from eye to ear" as called for by Dewey in *The Public and Its Problems*. "Logic," John Dewey writes there, "in its fulfillment recurs to the primitive sense of the word: dialogue. Ideas which are not communicated, shared and reborn in expression are but soliloquy, and soliloquy is but broken and imperfect thought." [18] Only consensus that can be criticized freely is reasonable.

If, in agreement with Apel and Habermas, one proceeds from an intersubjective concept of reason, then this has the advantage of assigning a place to democracy at the center of the theory of justice, making it possible, by the same token, to remove the residues of Platonism latent in the empiricist concept of the theory and in Rawls's teleological understanding of reason. The merely hypothetical and monological "original position" is replaced by an open, factual "community of critics" [19] that can be expanded across all borders, for everything that counts as argument in a given case. The theory of justice becomes a theory of radical democracy in the very first step. And factual discourses that differ from one another only in terms of the kind of questions the validity of which is being debated take the place of the theoretical construction of principles. The external mutual confrontation between theory and experience becomes unnecessary because the theory has become superfluous and the factual process of common will-formation is all that remains. The "constraints" of the "original position" are now the conditions for validity and equality of the respective discourses, whereby these serve as filters for that part of our respective "comprehensive doctrines" that holds up under public criticism. What passes through the filters corresponds to the Rawlsian "overlapping consensus," only it is not a matter of a consensus that can be identified once and for all from the outside, from the bird's-eye view of the theorist, but of an agreement reached through active debate by the participating citizens themselves. And in the ideal legislative procedure, the "system of rights" then takes the place of those "constraints" of the discourse the sole purpose of which is to make reasonable will-formation possible. Anything can therefore be poured through the instruments of the various filters of legal discourse, in other words anything the citizens affected in each case bring with them in terms of ethical, moral, and aesthetic convictions as a result of the private autonomy in their motives. But only that which passes through the filter can lay claim to having democratic legitimation on its side when it is enacted into law. As a law that henceforth applies only to "external actions," irrespective of the motives, it can be enforced in cases of doubt. Only as authors of the law can the actively participating citizens realize their public autonomy, as addressees; however, they only owe obedience to the laws (in the rational model) which do not violate their private autonomy. For, without private autonomy—having demonstrated this is certainly one of the great merits of *Between Facts and Norms*[20]—there can be no public laws and thus no laws that deserve our respect. Only in this way is it apparently possible to link the political self-organization of a body of citizens and the freedom of individual self-determination, without destroying difference and merging the one into the other.

For Habermas private autonomy is given as a mere fact of the evolution of right. It belongs to the historical facticity of modern positive law. All law is positive law. There is no higher law before positive law. As a fact "the rule of law" does not need any justification by practical philosophy or a theory of justice. Problems of justification only emerge on the side of the concerned participants of a concrete community of law. They have to decide what to do with the fact of the state of law, into which they are already born. If they want to realize their full private and public autonomy in the process of organizing their lives by positive laws, they need something like "principles of justice" or a "system of rights." But there is no further moral argument for living in a state of law. Rawls neglects this important difference between law and morality. He is always trying to give a moral justification of the legal basic structure of a well-ordered society. But if justice is prior to law, then all law is only an application of prepolitical justice or—in his later theory—of a prepolitical, always already constituted overlapping consensus, which is only reinforced by education and public discourse.

In my view Rawls nullifies the difference between a *Rechtsperson*, which is constituted by the very form of right, and moral persons with a number of "moral powers." If we start with that distinction, moral powers only come into play in the process of democratic law giving and the public discussions between free and equal people, which are the very basis of democratic law giving. But no simple law and no constitutional right can be justified, measured, or deduced outside this process of public will-formation. It has—as any cooperative practice—some more or less ideal presuppositions, but these are completely internal to this process. Finally, it is only a sociological hypothesis that links the legitimating force of a legal will-formation excluding nobody concerned with the validity of positive law. If positive law needs such "legitimation through legality" it depends on the manifestation of a "legitimation crisis." In the final analysis this crisis is the only proof for a theory of radical democracy.

Notes

1. In *On Human Rights*, eds. Stephen Shule and Susan Hurley (New York: Basic, 1993), pp. 41–82.

2. See John Rawls, *Political Liberalism*, (New York: Columbia University Press, 1993), p. 6.

3. Rawls, *A Theory of Justice* (Cambridge: Harvard University Press, 1971), p. 136.

4. Ibid., p. 139.

5. Ibid., p. 137.

6. Ibid., p. 140.

7. Jürgen Habermas, *Between Facts and Norms: Contributions to a Discourse Theory of Law and Democracy* (Cambridge: Massachusetts Institute of Technology Press, 1996), chapter 3; and T. H. Marshall, *Citizenship and Social Class* (New York: Cambridge University Press, 1950).

8. Rawls, *A Theory of Justice*, p. 361.

9. Ibid., p. 107.

10. On these different conservative-communitarian and aesthetic modernist versions of Romanticism, see H. Brunkhorst, "Romanticism and Cultural Criticism," *Praxis International*, 6, no. 4 (1987): pp. 397–415; also "Romanticism, Rationality and Alienation—The Triple-H-Theory Revisited," in *History of European Ideas*, vol. 2 (1989), pp. 831-839.

11. Also see C. Menke, "Liberalismus im Konflikt," in *Gemeinschaft und Gerechtigkeit*, eds. M. Brumlik and H. Brunkhorst, (Frankfurt, Germany: Campus Verlag, 1993), pp. 218–243.

12. See most recently *Political Liberalism*.

13. Habermas, "Human Rights and Popular Sovereignty: The Liberal and Republican Versions," *Ratio Juris*, 7 (1994): p. 13.

14. Rawls, *A Theory of Justice*, p. 358.

15. Jean-Jacques Rousseau, *On the Social Contract* (Indianapolis: Hackett, 1987), Bk II, c. 3.

16. Rawls, *A Theory of Justice*, p. 358.

17. Ibid., p. 359.

18. John Dewey, *The Public and Its Problems* (Chicago: Henry Holt, 1927), p. 218.

19. Also see H. Putnam, *The Many Faces of Realism* (La Salle, Ill: Open Court, 1987), p. 53f.

20. Much the same case is made by I. Maus, *Zur Aufklärung der Demokratietheorie* (Frankfurt, Germany: Suhrkamp, 1992), sec. 10.

III

Further Assessments and Wider Implications

7

Law, Solidarity, and the Tasks of Philosophy

Peter Dews

Between Facts and Norms: Contributions to a Discourse Theory of Law and Democracy marks a major development in Jürgen Habermas's thinking in a number of respects, not least—of course—in his conception of the status and social function of law itself. In *The Theory of Communicative Action* Habermas had highlighted a "parodoxical structure" of the advancing juridification of the social world, whereby the application of legal norms both makes possible the dismantling of inherited, authoritarian power relations, but also produces an effect of "deworlding," by disrupting the delicate fabric of lifeworld communication, and the social identities, that this sustains.[1] In *Between Facts and Norms*, however, Habermas reaches the conclusion that this paradox is not inevitable. For he contends that when all citizens, including oppressed and marginalized groups, can participate equally in the shaping of law, bringing forth their own interpretations of their needs, they are able to determine for themselves the appropriate point of equilibrium between a formal and a material intepretation of law. They can strike an appropriate balance between the paternalistic restriction of freedom that social-welfare legislation often brings with it, and the limitation of freedom that results from the application of the same legal rule to materially different cases.[2]

It becomes clear on closer inspection, however, that the dilemma that Habermas describes in *Between Facts and Norms*, one that results from the "ambivalence of guaranteeing freedom and taking it away,"[3] is no longer precisely the same as that explored in *The Theory of Communicative Action*. For in the earlier book the negative side of juridification was not revealed merely by the restrictions on individuals' freedom of choice, through regulations such as those governing the workplace, living conditions, or intrafamilial relations, or even through the imposition of an objectifying form of control on citizens, who are treated as cases to be legally processed. Rather it also involved a "disintegration" of those life contexts that are intrinsically dependent on social integration, obliging individuals to take up the depersonalizing and instrumentalizing attitude of juridical subjects toward each other.[4] Furthermore, this disruption was not simply the result of the fact that the juridical reshaping of ever more social domains is driven by the aim of opening them up to the imperatives of profit and administrative manipulation. Habermas also stressed that the legal medium was simply "dysfunctional" for "domains of life which, from a functional viewpoint, are necessarily dependent on a social integration via values, norms, and processes of reaching understanding."[5]

Of course, Habermas emphasizes throughout *Between Facts and Norms* that neither a productive market economy nor an effective public administration are sufficient to hold together a complex modern society: "The resources which primarily require protective handling are an exhausted natural environment and a social solidarity which is in the process of disintegrating."[6] However, Habermas will not allow that the continual extension of the legal medium might itself play a role in the etiology of the second of these problems. It is indeed central to Habermas's perspective on law that the function of law in modern society is to expand, albeit in a controlled and ultimately consensual way, the scope for individual instrumental action. But he maintains that the development of legal regulation must be seen as a response to the erosion of traditional *Sittlichkeit*, and not as a causal factor in its decay. It is modern societies, and in particular the autonomous dynamic of their economies, which requires an ever-increasing number of "socio-structurally indispensible strategic interactions,"[7] giving rise to the need for a form of regulation of such interactions that can be understood as ultimately grounded in consensus, without depending directly on the solidarity or discursively attained agreement of participants.

However, there is a wide range of evidence that suggests that processes of juridification do indeed weaken a solidaristic sense of responsibility. For example, in an essay on the problems of fostering "intelligent self-limitation," Claus Offe cites the case of legally backed pollution controls, which may—counter-productively—encourage the view that everything that is not explicitly forbidden is allowed. Indeed, Offe suggests, individuals and organizations may come to assume a "right to pollute" below the technically established threshold, or even to include the possibility of legal sanctions itself in the calculation of risks and benefits.[8] In *The Theory of Communicative Action* Habermas himself cites a range of evidence suggesting that juridical intervention in areas such as wefare, intrafamilial relations, and the school system, leads to counterproductive consequences. He argues, for example, that

> the protection of pupils' and parents' rights against educational measures (such as promotion or nonpromotion, examinations and

tests, and so forth) or from acts of the school or the department of education that restrict basic rights (disciplinary penalties), is gained at the cost of a judicialization and bureaucratization that penetrates deep into the teaching and learning process. For one thing, responsibility for problems of educational policy and school law overburdens government agencies, just as responsibility for the child's welfare overburdens the wardship courts. For another, the medium of law comes into collision with the form of educational activity. Socialization through the school is fragmented into a mosaic of legally contestable administrative acts.[9]

One of the reasons why Habermas, just over a decade later, no longer takes this problem so seriously, may perhaps be found in his current conception of the relation between justice and solidarity. In an essay on Lawrence Kohlberg, Habermas has suggested that, because morality is concerned with the vulnerability of individuals, it must also entail a concern for the communities to which they belong, since "the integrity of individuals cannot be preserved without the integrity of their common lifeworld, which makes possible shared, interpersonal connections and relationships." [10] From this perspective, justice and solidarity are the two coequal dimensions of a postconventional morality, emerging from the same fundamental form of consciousness. Accordingly, Habermas also suggests that "every demand for universalization would remain powerless if an awareness of unrenounceable solidarity, the certainty of belonging together in a common life context did not also spring from the consciousness of belonging to an ideal community of communication." [11]

This account of the relation between justice and solidarity seems far too harmonistic, however. For it could be argued that, far from springing from "consciousness of belonging to an ideal community of communication," solidarity, in the form of relations of trust and concern for the well-being of others with whom we belong in a concrete community, is a precondition for such consciousness to have any effective moral reality. There may be situations where even though, as an individual, I can see what course of action would be in the best interests of everyone, I feel justified in not carrying it out because I have no confidence that others will do the same.

In his impressive study *Autonomie und Anerkennung: Hegels Moralitätskitik im Lichte seiner Fichte Rezeption*, Andreas Wildt has explored this problem in the course of a reconstruction of Hegel's critique of Kant's moral philosophy. The core of Hegel's critique, according to Wildt, is not—as is often supposed—that the validity of moral principles must be relativized in some historicist sense, but rather that there can be situations of "hopelessly destroyed *Sittlichkeit*" where it is no longer reasonable to expect individuals to behave morally. In order to accommodate this possibility, Wildt suggests, we need to distinguish between what is morally right and what is practically right. We can then acknowledge that there may be circumstances "in which it is no longer plausible to adopt a moral standpoint, and thus in which the knowledge that one is morally obliged to do something is no longer a sufficient reason so to act." [12] By contrast, Kant's assumption that moral rightness is unconditional "categorical" rightness presupposes an overindividualistic concept of autonomy that misleadingly abstracts from the concrete context of motivation. [13]

Interestingly, in *Between Facts and Norms* his account of the breakdown of moral motivation is part of Habermas's explanation for the emergence and extension of modern law. He stresses that one of the functions of law is to relieve the excessive burden that modernity places on moral consciousness, and that has three important aspects. First, the complexity of the situations to be morally assessed often overstretches the cognitive powers of the individual; second, the organizational resources required to fulfill certain duties are beyond the capacities of the individual; and—most importantly for our purposes—the abstraction of postconventional morality from concrete forms of life weakens its motivational force, as does the breakdown of expectations that others will follow the same moral norm. But significantly, Habermas does not seem to consider this breakdown of the ethical mediation of morality as in any sense a socially pathological condition. There are, I would suggest, two contradictory reasons for this. On the one hand, Habermas misleadingly equates acceptance by individuals of the "nonrecoverable" (i.e., morally unenforceable) obligations of trust, benevolence, and concern with the subsistence of an intact traditional *Sittlichkeit*. [14] From such a perspective, modern moral consciousness will inevitably suffer from an intrinsic lack of motivational force. As Habermas puts it, "every post-traditional morality requires a distanciation from the self-evidence of unproblematically habitual life-forms. Moral insights which are disconnected from the concrete *Sittlichkeit* of everyday life no longer automatically have the motivating force which allows judgements to become practically effective." [15] Yet on the other hand, as we have just seen, Habermas also implies that a commitment to the common good—presumably in a degree sufficient to sustain the moral authority of law as a form of collective self-regulation, even when law supplants individual moral consciousness—is built into the idealizing play of intersubjective role-taking that he considers essential to the normative infrastructure of communication in general.

If one combines these two—apparently incompatible—assumptions, then the transfer of moral responsibilities to the sphere of legal regulation will appear unproblematic. Habermas speaks of an "interlacing" of law and morality in modern society: "This comes about through the fact that in constitutional states the means of positive law are employed to distribute burdens of argument and to institutionalize forms of justification which are open for moral argumentation."[16] Presumably, on this account, the "solidarity" that is the complement of justice will also be injected into the sphere of law, and indeed, at the beginning of *Between Facts and Norms*, Habermas writes of solidarity being "preserved" in "legal structures."[17] Yet if the weakness of moral consciousness itself in part derives from a deficiency in forms of collective trust and concern that cannot be legally enforced or required, then the transfer from morality to law will do nothing to address this problem—and indeed, as just suggested, may even aggravate it, perhaps to the extent of triggering a degenerative spiral.

Habermas does stress throughout *Between Facts and Norms* that the good design of procedures for the making and implementation of law in effect only solves half the problem: "The rational quality of political legislation depends not only on how elected majorities and protected minorities within parliament operate. It also depends on the level of participation and education, on the level of information and the sharpness of articulation of contested issues, in short on the discursive character of the non-institutionalized formation of opinion in the political public sphere."[18] In this sense he shares those anxieties which, in the absence of any vivid public commitment to democratic ideals, the *Rechtsstaat* may become an oppressively hollow shell, which—as Charles Taylor has recently reminded us—are least as old as Alexis de Tocqueville.[19] However, Habermas has little to say, from the standpoint of a philosophically informed social theory, about kinds of solidarity that would encourage such participation. He prefers instead to put his trust in the spontaneous potential of civil society and social movements to respond to the dangers posed by the autonomous dynamic of social systems.[20]

This lack of explicit discussion of the problem of solidarity in *Between Facts and Norms* becomes more curious when one observes that sensitivity to the "structural dilemma" that Habermas identified in *The Theory of Communicative Action*, in the context of his discussion of juridification, has not entirely disappeared from his current work. If anything, this dilemma has been identified at a more general level, in the form of an "ambiguous process of individualization" that Habermas takes to be characteristic of contemporary society. Formerly, as we have seen, Habermas had tended to assume that modern society generated more or less spontaneously the forms of consciousness that could underpin and motivate a universalistic morality.[21] Now, however, influenced by the work of Ulrich Beck, he acknowledges the negative aspect of individualization, namely, the process of "singularization" in which the individual increasingly becomes an isolated rational decision-making unit, understanding herself objectivistically as consumer, taxpayer, voter, and so on, engaged in interaction with a range of social systems.[22] In the light of this more pessimistic account of the consequences of modernization, Habermas's concept of the lifeworld has lost some of its originally protective and defensive coloring. For part of the answer to the problem of singularization, Habermas suggests, is that individuals must learn "to create socially integrated life-forms themselves."[23] Yet, in his discussions of this issue, Habermas has little to say about the conditions under which such life-forms could be achieved, other than to suggest that individuals must "recognize each other as autonomous subjects capable of action."[24] But although this may be necessary, it is certainly not a sufficient condition for the creation and sustaining of new, nonregressive but solidaristic forms of life, since it omits any consideration of the need for a common ethical orientation that is implied by Habermas's own account of solidarity as grounded in the awareness of sharing a form of life.

II

The theory of recognition developed by Axel Honneth is his recent book *The Struggle for Recognition* can, in one sense, be seen as an attempt to deal with problems of normativity and identity that Habermas's current emphasis on law leaves unaddressed. Recovering and developing a tripartite schema that he finds both in Hegel and in George Herbert Mead, Honneth argues that it is possible to distinguish three qualitatively distinct forms of recogition that must all be in play if the individual is to acquire the "external and internal freedom, upon which the process of articulating and realizing individual life-goals without coercion depends."[25] The first form of recognition, which Honneth refers to as "love," is initially experienced in the balance of separation and fusion that characterizes the relationship between the small child and its primary carer. Honneth contends that the fundamental self-confidence that this "symbiosis refracted by recognition" provides functions as the basis for the development of more complex social relationships: "this fundamental level of emotional confidence—not only in experience of needs and feelings, but also in their expression— . . . constitutes the psychological precondition for the development of all further attitudes of self-respect."[26]

By contrast with the affect-laden relation of love, Honneth interprets modern law as involving "an achievement of purely cognitive understanding" in which individuals are acknowledged as autonomous and morally responsible subjects, a recognition that gives rise to the basic feeling of self-respect.[27] However, perhaps the most innovative aspect of Honneth's study is to be found in his discussion of the third form of recognition, "solidarity." For here Honneth emphasizes that the preconditions for the individual's self-understanding as an autonomous and individuated being, and for the capacity to identify with his or her own aims and wishes, include not just the recognition of all social members as of equal dignity in the eyes of the law, but also an appreciation of the specific concrete contribution of individuals to the general well-being of society: "Persons can feel themselves to be 'valuable' only when they know themselves to be recognized for the achievements which they precisely do not share in an undifferentiated manner with others."[28] However, "esteem" in this sense, as the third form of recognition, can only become a reality if there is "a social medium . . . able to express the characteristic differences among human subjects in a general—that is, an intersubjectively binding—way. This task of mediation is performed, at the societal level, by a symbolically articulated—yet always open and porous—framework of orientation, in which those ethical values and goals are formulated that, taken together, comprise the cultural self-understanding of a society."[29]

The difference between Honneth's perspective and that of Habermas emerges clearly if one considers the latter's discussion of contemporary feminist critiques of welfarist legal intervention in *Between Facts and Norms*.[30] For what is at issue here is not simply whether such intervention restricts the freedom of women, but rather the fact that it treats them as anomalies, and does not reflect an appropriate, nonandrocentric valuing of their gender-specific contributions of society. Habermas's solution to this problem is that women, like other groups, should constitute discussion forums within the general space of the public sphere that could articulate their specific feelings, needs, and aspirations, and feed them into the formal law-making process. From Honneth's perspective, however, this in itself would be insufficient to compensate for a sense of lack of worth, if not accompanied by a transformation in the values that organize the distribution of social esteem. Furthermore, as is well-known, in the case of large discrepancies between legal recognition and social value, the effectiveness of law can be seriously undermined.

Such examples seem to confirm Honneth's advocacy of the need for what he terms a posttraditional *Sittlichkeit* that would provide individuals with a sense of worth through acknowledgment of their concrete contributions to the general social welfare. However, Honneth does not believe that a philosophically informed social theory can say anything concrete about the character of such a *Sittlichkeit*, apart from stipulating that it must integrate all three levels of recognition, and be compatible with modern notions of juridical equality.[31] Yet at this point an important asymmetry between the practical function of the philosophical explication of the "moral point of view," that Habermas's discourse ethics undertakes, and that of the philosophical definition of the form of a functioning "posttraditional *Sittlichkeit*" comes to light. For although, in demonstrating the possibility of the moral point of view, one can defuse moral skepticism, and to this extent produce a practical effect without advocating any specific moral perspective, it is not possible in the same way to encourage a general social commitment to fostering solidarity, merely by providing a philosophical analysis of *Sittlichkeit*. For no one wonders whether social solidarity is possible—merely what expressions of it, if any, are desirable. In concluding *The Struggle for Recognition* Honneth suggests that a future "posttraditional solidarity" could be organized around a variety of value schemes, from "political republicanism" or an "ecologically based asceticism" to a "collective existentialism." But, in tune with a certain Marxist tradition of skepticism about moral desiderata, he hands over the future predominance of one of these schemes to the outcome of social struggles.[32]

Yet even if Honneth has succeeded in demonstrating that human integrity and well-being presuppose a society and culture that incorporate his three forms of recognition, his agnosticism may well be self-defeating if it requires the philosopher simply to stand back and observe while a variety of socioethical conceptions clash with one another intellectually and politically. To be effective, such a demonstration must surely also be accompanied by other forms of philosophical exploration and argument, intended to discover how well—and to what extent—fundamental human concerns and aspirations are articulated by various value schemes, and whether such schemes, or elements of them, can be combined or reconciled with others, which foreground different dimensions of human existence.

This point naturally raises the question of why Honneth strives to restrict his description of *Sittlichkeit* to a "formal" level. The obvious answer is that he wishes to avoid the imputation that culturally specific values and assumptions have implicitly shaped his general account of the good (social) life, thereby vitiating its universality. But this answer raises two separate sets of difficulties. On the one hand, it seems very unlikely that the material that Honneth uses to substantiate his argument—for example, studies of child development drawn from the object-relations tradition in psychoanalysis—has not itself been shaped by culturally specific presuppositions. Honneth tries to avoid this problem by stressing the empirical dimension of the enquiries he draws on—indeed, he describes his method, in a somewhat puzzling phrase, as an "empirically controlled phenomenology."[33] But this description surely begs the question. For as the history of the social sciences, with its range of competing paradigms, amply demonstrates, the fact that the accounts of recognition on which Honneth relies can find empirical support does nothing to overcome their potential relativity. In this sense, even the supposedly "formal" concept of *Sittlichkeit* that Honneth wants to provide runs a high risk of resting on material presuppositions, and therefore being ab initio nonneutral between competing conceptions of the good (social) life.

On the other hand, even if one accepts, as seems only fair, that Honneth's account of the "good life" achieves a high level of generality, albeit not pure formality, the range of contents that it can accommodate is still severely restricted by the key-concepts around which it is organized. Honneth's three forms of recognition are described as preconditions of autonomy and self-realization, or what Honneth calls the "unforced articulation and realisation of individual lifegoals." Yet one can easily imagine other positions, even within the spectrum of contemporary ethics, such as those of Taylor or Emmanuel Levinas, in which the subordination of individual life-goals to the "the Other who dominates me in his transcendence," in Levinas's phrase, or to the choosing of goals that respond to the claims that an ultimate, divine source of goodness makes upon me, claims that may thwart my personal aspirations, might be considered more important than self-realization understood in terms of individual fulfillment.[34]

Thus, once the deceptive methodological patina is stripped away, it becomes clear that Honneth's work takes a specific ethical perspective on human subjects and their integrity and well-being, and argues this through by drawing both on philosophical reflection and empirical forms of inquiry. This is not to say that the resulting conception is arbitrary, of course—merely that its formality can only be a matter of degree. Accordingly, there seems to be no reason of principle why the claims could not be made even more specific, in ther course of an attempt to assess and render compatible insights drawn from a variety of ethical and political traditions and orientations. Naturally, social-scientific, psychoanalytic, and other forms of evidence would play a major role in such explorations—there could be no question of a purely philosophical "deduction" of a picture of the good life. Nevertheless, the question of the ethical texture of the society that we inhabit, and should aspire to inhabit, could then once more become an explicit object of philosophical reflection, in a way that has fallen into disrepute in the Critical Theory tradition ever since Adorno's *Minima Moralia*. The counterargument that the answer to such a question will always be historically relative does not seem to me to be decisive. For one can fully admit this relativity, while nevertheless insisting that it cannot be total, and that the answer should therefore be informed by an awareness of the constant, fundamental features of human existence.

III

It is interesting to note, in this context, that Habermas does not deprive philosophy any capacity whatsoever to engage with questions of the structure and integrity of forms of life. On the contrary, his current metaphilosophy distinguishes emphatically between two fundamental functions of philosophy, which he describes as those of "stand-in" and "interpreter." As stand-in, philosophy holds open the space for, and acts as a collaborator with, reconstructive theories in the human sciences, which spell out the implicit knowledge mobilized by certain very general human competencies, and thereby helps to provide the underpinning for universalistic theories of morality and law. In its interpretive function, however, philosophy explores, and may help to correct, the reifications that ensue from the excessive predominance of one rationality complex within the lifeworld, and helps to bring the cognitive and moral resources developed within the institionally specialized rationality spheres back into its domain—the only place where they can be put democratically to work.[35] According to Habermas, philosophy, in this interpretive role, is a culturally specific activity—it can only help to illuminate a determinate lifeworld, a particular totality of background assumptions, but cannot offer an account of the totality of the world as a whole, the "object" of traditional metaphysics. As a consequence, philosophy in its role as interpreter is also debarred from producing qualitative rankings of different cultural totalities.

However, a paradox seems to result from this philosophical division of labor between reconstructive and interpretive tasks. On the one hand, Habermas attributes the cognitive progress of modernity to the differentiation of the three value spheres of "truth," "rightness," and "authenticity." It is only when cognitive claims, for example, can be filtered out from the symbolic and ethical contexts in which they were formerly embedded, and thematized with the aid of specific, institutionalized forms of inquiry, that the epistemic takeoff of modern science becomes possible. Similarly, modern moral universalism implies the existence of a sphere within which questions of justice can be treated by legal and other experts who are skilled in isolating normative issues. At the same time, however, Habermas stresses that— within the lifeworld—the three dimensions of validity continue to be intrinsically interwoven. Yet, if this is the case, a question arises concerning which "ontology" should be taken to be more fundamental. As Martin Seel has expressed the issue: does the lifeworld exhibit an illusory integration of rationality dimensions, which is exposed as such by their modern institutional separation, or is it rather the integration of the lifeworld that reveals the illusory separation of rationality dimensions characteristic of specialized cultures of expertise?[36] To put this in another way: the problem with Habermas's conception is that natural-scientific knowledge—to take this example—is universal in its scope, but can only be produced through a process of cognitive abstraction on the part of subjects who remain existentially embedded in the lifeworld. Such knowledge therefore remains epistemically derivative in relation to this context. On the other hand, the lifeworld, which then appears as existentially more fundamental in terms of its formal fusion of validity claims, will always appear as particular and relative in terms of the content that these validity-claims articulate.

Habermas, in his reply to Seel, appears not to appreciate the force of this objection. He states that each specialized form of argumentation can indeed, under the pressure of problems encountered, be abandoned in favor of another form, and that judgment will play an important role in deciding if and how this takes place. In this way a coherence and interdependence of the forms of argumentation is acknowledged, while at the same time allowing Habermas to claim that "every discourse stands, so to speak, equally close to God."[37] Habermas goes on to suggest that this is not surprising, since "communicative action encounters in the different types of argumentation only its own reflected forms." But this reply omits to consider that the types of argumentation also have ontological implications: that discourse within the cognitive-instrumental rationality complex, for example, implies a world of normatively neutral facts, while discourse in the legal-moral sphere, as Habermas conceives it, presupposes the existence of a source of normativity which is logically independent of any specific states of affairs. This splitting of ontological domains is incompatible with the fusion of truth, rightness, and aesthetic appeal that characterizes our experience of, and ways of assessing, the everyday human world that we inhabit. So the question arises: which ontology is more fundamental? Are the fusions of fact and value typical of the lifeworld projections that veil an essentially value-neutral reality or not?

In itself, this may appear to be a relatively minor problem for Habermas's position. But it takes on greater importance as soon as one tries to locate philosophy on one side or the other of the divide between the lifeworld and the specialized spheres. In its role of placeholder, philosophy is located unambiguously by Habermas within the institutions of systematic research. But he also stresses that philosophy would betray its age-old inheritance if it were to understand itself merely as one specialized discipline among others. In the form of interpretation, philosophy is both closely allied—and radically opposed—to everyday understanding. It moves within - and is related to—the nonobjectifiable totality of a lifeworld, in a manner similar to that of common sense, yet at the same time its critical and reflective stance opposes it to everything that is taken for granted.[38] We already know that philosophy, in its function as stand-in, is expected to meet the same fallibilistic criteria of truth as any other specialized science. But now the difficulty arises that these expectations will require philosophy to satisfy a standard that is itself abstracted from the lifeworld whose integrity philosophical interpretation seeks to explore and sustain.

Habermas himself appears to sense this problem when he remarks that "this mediating task [of interpretation] is not devoid of a certain paradox, because in the expert cultures knowledge is always treated under individual aspects of validity, whereas in everyday practice all functions of language and aspects of validity encroach on each other, constitute a syndrome."[39] Although Habermas does not say so directly, the task of mediation appears "paradoxical" because the philosophical language that translates specialized validity claims back into the terms of the lifeworld must itself fuse the various dimensions of validity, and in this case will not be susceptible to any straightforward assessment of its "cognitive" truth. According to Habermas's own account, the philosophical task of interpretation embodies "the interest of the lifeworld in the totality of functions and structures which are bundled and joined together in communicative action. However it sustains this relation to the totality with a degree of reflexivity which is lacking in the background of the lifeworld, which is only intutively present."⁴⁰ But there is no obvious reason why the introduction of reflexivity as such need disrupt the interfusion of validity dimensions that this account implies—there are, after all, forms of reflexivity other than the cognitive, such as those that we find in works of art.

Yet despite his awareness of this paradox, Habermas, in some of his recent writings, seeks to maintain that philosophy must now satisfy the specialized criteria of cognitive truth. Against the historical background of the institutionalized separation of validity spheres, he argues that "Today, philosophy could establish its own distinct criteria of validity—in the name of genealogy, of recollection (*Andenken*), of elucidating *Existenz*, of philosophical faith, of deconstruction, etc.—only at the price of falling short of a level of differentiation and justification that has already been reached, i.e. at the price of surrendering its own credibility [*Glaubwürdigkeit*]."⁴¹ Curiously, it does not occur to Habermas to consider the types of philosophical activity that he lists here as primarily concerned not to evade a specialized treatment of truth-claims, but rather to perform the interpretive task that he immediately goes on to describe as "an enlightening promotion of lifeworld processes of achieving self-understanding, processes that are related to totality', and which is necessary because 'the lifeworld must be defended against extreme alienation at the hands of the objectivating, the moralizing, and the aestheticizing interventions of expert cultures."⁴² This dismissal of the major modalities of contemporary philosophy becomes even more surprising when one recalls that Habermas himself has stressed the necessarily "multilingual" character of philosophy in its role of interpretive mediator between science, art, and the lifeworld.⁴³ For what can these multiple languages be, if not precisely the genealogical, hermeneutical, phenomenological, and deconstructive currents of twentieth-century philosophy? What other discourses are available that weave between validity-dimensions, reflecting upon the textures of the lifeworld as a whole, and thus simultaneously confirming and disrupting them? To suggest that such discourses are not credible (*glaubwürdig*) seems a clumsy accusation at best, since they clearly do not aspire to provide "knowledge" in the modern, specialized sense. This is not to suggest, of course, that they need be simply taken at face value.⁴⁴

It would seem that the difficulties in which Habermas finds himself here arise from the fact that, on the one hand, he wishes to restrict the status of the claims of philosophy to the validity sphere of cognitive truth. Partly in consequence of this, he then restricts the scope of the claims of philosophy as interpretation to specific lifeworlds, since it does not appear that the evaluative claims of philosophy could aspire to the strict, transcultural universality typical of successful truth-claims. Indeed, Habermas currently limits the role of philosophy as interpreter primarily to the task of explicating lifeworld intuitions, and defending the force of these intuitions against the invasive movement of technology and science. This already represents a certain defiant reversal of direction in the traffic between the lifeworld and the differentiated spheres of expertise, compared with Habermas's former account of interpretation as the translation of specialized insights into the dedifferentiated context of an "impoverished" lifeworld.[45] Nevertheless, it still remains implausible in its attempt to constrain the universalistic aspirations of philosophical discourse.

IV

I would now like to retrace the argument so far. We have found that, in *Between Facts and Norms*, Habermas downplays the possibilities for conflict between law and solidarity, arguing rather that law can be understood as a remote but nonetheless still identifiable distillate of solidarity. Habermas does indeed acknowledge that a sense of collective belonging is a necessary though endangered resource in contemporary society, but he proposes no philosophically informed analysis of this situation. By contrast, Honneth's recent work, particularly *The Struggle for Recognition: The Moral Grammar of Social Conflicts*, develops a theory of solidarity as a third essential dimension of recognition, alongside love and law. But Honneth seeks—not entirely convincingly—to limit himself to a formal account of the good life and to avoid assessing the relative merits of different structures of value and of social projects that entail different distributions of social esteem. In this respect Habermas's notion of philosophy as "interpreter," although underdeveloped, could be seen as filling a lacuna in Honneth's work. Habermas himself, of course, insists that philosophy in its interpretive role is always bound to the horizons of particular traditions, and cannot make claims, even by negation, about the good life in general. Yet, as we have seen, this attempt to restrain the scope of philosophy leads to inconsistencies.

Fundamentally, what is at stake here is the sense in which Habermas's theory can still be regarded as emancipatory—as expressing a viewpoint that is "anchored extratheoretically in an empirical interest or moral experience," as Honneth puts it,[46] and in this sense as continuing the tradition of Critical Theory. Habermas himself is clear that an emancipatory process involves the conjunction of moral and ethical reflection: "If in posing 'ethical' questions we would like to get clear about who we are and who we would like to be, and if in posing 'moral' questions we would like to know what is equally good for all, then an emancipatory transformation of consciousness combines moral insight with a new ethical self-understanding. We recognize who we are because we have also learned to see ourselves differently in relation to others." [47] Yet while he affirms that philosophy, by reconstructing the normative presuppositions of communication in general, can provide a justification of morality and democracy, Habermas sees no role for philosophy in ethical discourses, the responsibility for which must—he insists—be left to the participants in discussion themselves.

However, this restriction seems to be dictated by Habermas's assumption that the contribution of philosophy to ethical discussion could only consist in the imperious handing down of a priori insights. He affirms, for example, "I do not at all correspond to the traditional image of the "philosopher," who explains the world with one thesis." [48] Such a perspective fails to recognize that we can be forced into a philosophical investigation of our deep tacit assumptions and presuppositions precisely by ethical tension and conflict. An outstanding recent example of such investigation would be Taylor's critical analysis of the internal contradictions of our modern "ethics of authenticity." [49] Habermas might reply, of course, that there is no reason to describe such investigations as "philosophical" rather than reflectively "ethical," but such a reply would in turn highlight the difficulties of his attempt to restrain the claims of evaluative discourses within the confines of specific traditions.

In his general account of "evaluative" discourse in *The Theory of Commnicative Action*, where he takes aesthetic critique as his main exemplar, Habermas suggests that the claim raised by such discourse is the relative one of the "appropriateness of standards":[50] "Above all," Habermas argues,

> the type of validity-claims with which cultural values appear do not transcend local bounds in the same way as claims to truth or rightness. Cultural values do not count as universal. . . . Values can only be made plausible in the context of a specific life-form. For this reason, the critique of value-standards presupposes a common pre-understanding of those who participate in argumentation, which is not at their disposal, but which simultaneously constitutes and limits the domain of the thematized validity-claims.[51]

As an account of "aesthetic critique," this description must already be considered tendentious, since such critique undoubedly strives for universality, even while being aware that this is far harder to achieve than in the case of cognitive claims. Furthermore, in cases where the aesthetic standards at the basis of the discussion are themselves problematized by the fact of disagreement, the specifically philosophical issue of the appropriateness of these standards, assessed in the light of what is essential to a work of art as such, cannot help but be raised. Aesthetic critique, and indeed therapeutic critique in many of its modes, and a fortiori philosophical interpretation of the ethical sphere, cannot help but address the question of the relation between our culturally embedded standards and values and the ultimate or true nature of the relevant phenomena.

This point could be made in another way by pointing out that Habermas lacks (and indeed must lack, given his current assumptions) a "philosophy of culture." Despite the centrality of the concept of tradition to his account of interpretation, and indeed to his theory of "ethical discourse," Habermas gives no account of what culture itself might be, as a fundamental human phenomenon, other than an ultimately contingent constellation of assumptions and values that varies from one society to another. Yet there exists an powerful tradition of thought, prominently represented in Germany, which has plausibly claimed that the varied forms of human culture can be viewed as a repertoire of responses to certain fundamental dilemmas of human existence and self-awareness.[52] This is the perspective of what Maurice Merleau-Ponty termed *vertical history*[53]—as opposed to the horizontal relativity of cultures. Consideration of this dimension might have allowed Habermas to break through the rather shallow linguisticality of his conception of the lifeworld, and to accept that no genuine self-exploration of a culture can ultimately avoid confronting the basic questions of human existence as such.

Of course, it is always easy and tempting to be skeptical about the possibility of transcending our cultural and linguistic confines, in the manner currently exemplified by Richard Rorty, who nonchalantly claims that "we have no prelinguistic consciousness to which language needs to be adequate, no deep sense of how things are which it is the duty of philosophers to spell out in language."[54] However, such a position overlooks the fact that the linguistically disclosed lifeworld is not simply a world, but also the world: there is no neutral space in which it could be situated as one self-enclosed world among others, since the only neutrality on offer, that of naturalism or physicalism, cannot accommodate lifeworlds conceptually at all. Thus the assumptions and values that structure the lifeworld are not projections onto the screen on an independent reality, but rather perspectival ways of experiencing the world as such. Implicitly Habermas recognizes this, since he is highly critical of Rorty's celebration of "the final victory of metaphors of self-creation over metaphors of discovery,"[55] insisting that frames of world-disclosure shift in reponse to the resistance of what they disclose. Yet by describing the task of interpretation as a rendering explicit of the intuitions of a particular lifeworld, Habermas fails to acknowledge that philosophical thought, in its interpretive dimension, cannot help but weave back and forth in the field of tension between a cuturally-sedimented interpretation of the world, and the experience of the world *tout court*.[56]

Without this depth dimension, Critical Theory would begin to lose its emancipatory point. The vibrant ethical and political culture that Habermas regards as necessary to complement and sustain the formal structures of the Rechtsstaat must surely include—albeit as a modest component—philosophical explorations and assessments of our fundamental values and existential orientations. Interpretation without reconstruction may be morally blind, but reconstruction without interpretation is surely empty. Furthermore, interpretation cannot be merely an elucidation of the internal structure of a lifeworld. It must appraise the claims and assumptions made by our culture in the light of a conception of human existence and its place in the world as such, since such claims and assumptions are bound to be multiple and conflictual, and cannot be evaluated simply by appealing to traditions that are themselves susceptible to multiple interpretations.

The reluctance of Critical Theory to take on this task will not result in ethical discourses and struggles for recognition untainted by the uncomfortably absolutist claims philosophy, as Habermas often seems to imagine. The current influence of a certain philosophical tradition, running from Friedrich Nietzsche to Foucault and Jacques Derrida, in providing the vocabulary for the politics of identity and difference, the pervasiveness of its terminology as the medium of articulation for the self-understanding of oppressed and marginalized groups, suggests that, if Critical Theory abandons the field, then other philosophical resources will inevitably be drawn upon. Such resources often lack the commitment to a thoroughgoing reflexive elucidation of their own genesis in historical experience that is characteristic of the Critical Theory tradition. They can often be insensitive to their own pretheoretical roots in contemporary social developments and for this reason may generate categories whose inappropriateness can harbor moral and political confusions—perhaps even dangers. Thus a conjoining of the defense, a democratic understanding of law, as one of the essential frameworks for emancipation, with the articulation of a philosophical self-understanding that could play a role in fostering new forms of social solidarity, and thus help to impede the overextension of law, should not be discouraged out of an exaggerated fear of succumbing to metaphysical foundationalism. For different, though related, reasons both Honneth and Habermas consider themselves to have moved unequivocally onto a "postmetaphysical" terrain. But, as Herbert Schnädelbach has pertinently enquired, "Does not the post-metaphysical age truly begin when, inundated by the media and other tranquillizers, we simply no longer ask certain questions?"[57]

Notes

1. Cf. Jürgen Habermas, *The Theory of Communicative Action*, vol. 2, *Lifeworld and System: A Critique of Functionalist Reason*, trans. Thomas McCarthy, Cambridge: Massachusetts Institute of Technology Press 1987, pp. 361-373.

2. *BFN*, 417.

3. *BFN*, 416.

4. *The Theory of Communicative Action*, vol. 2, pp. 362 and 369.

5. Ibid., pp. 372–373 (translation amended).

6. *BFN*, 445.

7. *BFN*, 26.

8. Claus Offe, 'Bindung, Fessel, Bremse: moralische und institutionelle Aspekte "intelligenter Selbstbeschränkung,"' in *Zwischenbetrachtungen: Im Prozess der Aufklärung*, eds. Honneth et al., (Frankfurt: Suhrkamp 1989), pp. 767–768. Cf. Günther Teubner's argument that juridification finds itself confronted with a "regulatory trilemma": if legal norms do not trangress the boundaries of social domains that have their own internal steering mechanisms, they will remain ineffectual; however, in overstepping these limits they risk triggering consequences that will have "disintegrative effects" either on the intergrity of law itself, or on the integrity of the relevant social domain. (Teubner, "Verrechtlichung—Begriffe, Merkmale, Grenzen, Auswege," in *Verrechtlichung von Wirtschaft, Arbeit und sozialer Solidarität*, ed. Friedrich Kübler, (Baden-Baden: Nomos Verlagsgesellschaft, 1984), especially pp. 313–325.)

9. *The Theory of Communicative Action*, vol. 2, p. 371 (translation amended).

10. Habermas, "Justice and Solidarity: On the Discussion of 'Stage 6'" in *Hermeneutics and Critical Theory in Ethics and Politics*, ed. Michael Kelly (Cambridge: Massachusetts Institute of Technology Press, 1990), p. 46.

11. Ibid., p. 48.

12. Andreas Wildt, *Autonomie und Anerkennung: Hegels Moralitätskritik im Lichte seiner Fichte-Rezeption* (Stuttgart, Germany: Klett-Cotta 1982) p. 153.

13. Ibid., p. 176.

14. Axel Honneth has recently pointed out, in a critique of Ulrich Beck, that "detraditionalization" should not be automatically equated with processes of the loss of community. Cf Honneth, *Disintegration: Bruchstücke einer soziologischen Zeitdiagnose* (Frankfurt, Germany: Suhrkamp, 1994), p. 25.

15. Habermas, "Law and Morality," in *The Tanner Lectures on Human Values*, trans. by K. Baynes (Salt Lake City: University of Utah Press, 1987), p. 245.

16. Ibid., p. 246.

17. *BFN*, xlii.

18. "Law and Morality," p. 248.

19. Cf. Charles Taylor, *The Ethics of Authenticity* (Cambridge: Harvard University Press, 1992), p. 76.

20. Habermas claims that "One can at least affirm that, to the extent that a rationalized lifeworld encourages the formation of a public sphere with a strong basis in civil society, then the authority of public attitudes in the context of escalating public controversies is strengthened" (*BFN*, 382).

21. On this see Claus Offe, "Bindung, Fessel, Bremse," p. 137.

22. Cf. Habermas, "Edmund Husserl über Lebenswelt, Philosophie und Wissenschaft," in *Texte und Kontexte* (Frankfurt, Germany: Suhrkamp, 1991), p. 48. Cf. Ulrich Beck, *Risk Society* (London: Sage, 1992).

23. "Edmund Husserl über Lebenswelt, Philosophie und Wissenschaft," p. 48.

24. Ibid.

25. Honneth, *The Struggle for Recognition: The Moral Grammar of Social Conflicts*, trans. Joel Anderson (Cambridge: Polity Press 1995), p. 174.

26. Ibid., pp. 106–107.

27. Cf. Ibid., pp. 107-111.

28. Ibid., p. 125.

29. Ibid., p. 122 (translation amended).

30. *BFN*, 419–427.

31. Cf. *Struggle for Recognition*, chapter 9.

32. Cf. Ibid., p. 179.

33. Ibid., p. 227.

34. Cf. Emmanuel Levinas, *Totality and Infinity*, trans. Alphonso Lingis (Pittsburgh: Duquesne University Press (n.d.), and Taylor, *The Sources of the Self* (Cambridge: Harvard University Press, 1989). The Levinas phrase cited is from p. 215.

35. Cf Habermas, "Philosophy as Stand-In and Interpreter," in, *After Philosophy: End or Transformation?* eds. Kenneth Baynes, James Bohman, and Thomas McCarthy (Cambridge: Massachusetts Institute of Technology Press, 1987).

36. Martin Seel, "The Two Meanings of Communicative Rationality," in *Communicative Action*, eds. Axel Honneth and Hans Joas (Cambridge: Polity Press, 1991), pp. 36–48.

37. *"denn jeder Diskurs ist sozusagen unmittelbar zu Gott"* (Habermas, "A Reply," in *Communicative Action*, p. 226).

38. "Edmund Husserl über Lebenswelt, Philosophie und Wissenschaft," p. 34.

39. Habermas, "Exkurs: Transzendenz von innen, Transzendenz ins Diesseits," in *Texte und Kontexte*, p. 38 (Frankfurt: Suhrkamp, 1991).

40. Habermas, *The Philosophical Discourse of Modernity*, trans. Fred Lawrence (Cambridge: Massachusetts Institute of Technology Press, 1987), p. 300.

41. Habermas, "Metaphysics after Kant," in *Postmetaphysical Thinking*, trans. William Mark Hohengarten (Cambridge: Massachusetts Institute of Technology Press, 1992), p. 17.

42. Ibid.

43. "Edmund Husserl über Lebenswelt, Philosophie und Wissenschaft," p. 41.

44. An important criterion of assessment for such discourses would be the extent to which they merely "express" a particular constellation of attitudes, or social mood, as opposed to also taking a reflective distance on the lifeworld context from which they derive.

45. Cf. "Philosophy as Placeholder and Interpreter," p. 314.

46. Honneth, "The Social Dynamics of Disrespect: On the Location of Critical Theory Today" *Constellations* 1 (October 1994): 255.

47. Habermas, *The Past as Future*, trans. Max Pensky (Lincoln: University of Nebraska Press, 1994), pp. 103-4.

48. Ibid., p. 113.

49. Cf. *Ethics of Authenticity*, passim.

50. Habermas, *The Theory of Communicative Action*, vol. 1, trans. Thomas McCarthy (Boston: Beacon, 1981), p. 39.

51. Ibid., p. 42.

52. Continuing this tradition, which includes such figures as Wilhelm Dilthey, Max Weber, and Max Scheler, Dieter Henrich has suggested, for example, that "there is a continuity between the fundamental constitution of conscious life and the cultural process of humanity which is in no sense identical with socialization, and collective self-preservation and need-satisfaction. Of course it is intertwined with these, but in such a way that it co-determines the forms in which this self-preservation is organized." (Henrich, *Fluchtlinien* [Frankfurt, Germany: Suhrkamp 1982], p. 92).

53. Cf. Maurice Merleau-Ponty, "Working Notes," in *The Visible and the Invisible* (Evanston, Ill.: Northwestern University Press 1968), p. 186.

54. Richard Rorty, *Contingency, Irony and Solidarity* (New York: Cambridge University Press, 1989), p. 21.

55. "Philosophy as Placeholder and Interpreter," p. 308.

56. Habermas writes that "Instead of grounding the lifeworld in the primal founding of an acting subjectivity or in the event of a world-interpretation which prejudices everything, philosophy can concentrate on the task of reconstructing the background knowledge which is connected with our grammatical intuitions. The goal of such an analysis is less the tracking of hidden foundations than the explication of what we always already know and can do" ("Edmund Husserl über Lebenswelt, Philosophie und Wissenschaft," p. 41). However, this account overlooks that fact that the recourse to an absolute subject or to the Heideggerian sending of Being (*Seinsgeschick*) must be seen as attempts, albeit unsatisfactory, to account for the relation between the lifeworld and its source in a way that does not leave "grammatical intuitions" hanging question-beggingly in the air.

57. Herbert Schnädelbach, "Metaphysik und Religion heute," in *Zur Rehabilitierung des animal rationale*. (Frankfurt: Suhrkamp, 1992), p. 138.

8

Rational Politics? An Exploration of the Fruitfulness of the Discursive Concept of Democracy

Geert Munnichs

The central thesis of *Between Facts and Norms: Contributions to a Discourse Theory of Law and Democracy* is that the modern constitutional state cannot be maintained without "radical democracy" (xlii). In this chapter I will try to develop a better understanding of the meaning of this radical democracy. After a brief reconstruction of the two steps in which Jürgen Habermas elaborates his central thesis, I will consider the fruitfulness of his discursive concept of democracy in more detail.

In the first step of his thesis, Habermas maintains that the legal order and the political system of decision-making presuppose one another. The functioning of the legal order rests upon its ability to use coercive power in order to force compliance with the law, as well as upon a voluntary acceptance by the people. The legal order by itself, however, is not able to produce its normatively binding force. The legitimacy of the order does not follow from its legality, but is dependent on the way in which the legal norms are produced by the political system of decision making. In turn, the political process depends for its legitimacy on the correct use of the democratic procedures (e.g., free elections and majority rule), which must in turn be legally institutionalized.

The legitimacy of the democratic process, however, cannot be reduced to its procedural correctness. Also on the level of political decision making, legitimacy does not follow from legality (*Legitimation durch Verfahren*). Instead, the democratic procedures must be conceived of as institutionalizing a discursive process of opinion and will formation. This means that the legitimacy of the legal norms ultimately rests on the communicative quality of the democratic process. Thus Habermas applies his discursive concept of normative validity to the democratic process.[1]

This discursive interpretation of the political process of decision making brings us to the second step of Habermas's central thesis. The communicative quality of the political process is dependent on the extent to which the process satisfies the communicative requirements for a free and unconstrained discussion, in order that all relevant arguments will be heard. Unlike the formal, legally institutionalized requirements for democratic decision making, however, the extent to which the political process meets these communicative requirements cannot be judged from an objective 'observer'—perspective, but asks for judgment from a performative 'participant'-perspective. Only those involved in a certain political decision can judge whether all relevant arguments are indeed heard and, consequently, whether the decision at stake deserves to be recognized as legitimate.

Habermas is well aware of the fact that the process of political decision making generally fails to meet the communicative requirements. Apart from the massive influence of "power politics," which I will address hereafter, the continuous pressure of time places a heavy burden on the political process and the confined social space of representative legislative bodies impose severe restrictions on the discursive nature of political decision making. As a consequence, the results of the political process can claim at best a presumption of reasonableness (*Vermutung der Vernünftlichkeit*). The latter restriction, however, which results from the exclusionary character of participation in legislative political decision making can be compensated for, at least to a certain degree, by an openness and sensitivity of the political process to the communicative flows of the public sphere.[2] Conceived of as a network of more or less spontaneously organized public spaces of communication, the public sphere can be thought of as a critical forum in which the communicative quality of the process of decision making is checked by discussing the given political argumentations. Thus the legitimacy of the decision making is dependent on the—argumentative—persuasiveness of its public justification.

The public sphere is only able to play this critical role to the extent that the possibility of spontaneously organizing communicative public spaces is guaranteed by a legal protection of fundamental democratic rights, such as the freedom of organization or the freedom of expression. These rights are constitutive for the public sphere.[3] The political system and the public sphere, therefore, presuppose the proper functioning of one another. In short, besides resting on the legal enforcement of its decisions, the social-integrative force of the political system rests on its public justification, a justification to which the political system is compelled by the possibility of a free and unfettered public contestation of the rightfulness of its policies. Because this possibility of public contestation is warranted by the political system itself, one could say that in a democracy the political system creates the opportunities to distrust its own performance.

The required openness of the political process to the public sphere, however, does not mean that the public forum is the ultimate authority with regard to the legitimacy of the process of decision making. The communicative flows of the public sphere, because of their noninstitutionalized, "anarchic" nature, run the risk of being determined by the existing relations of social power. Therefore, these communicative flows have to be "filtered" by the democratic procedures, in order to test to what extent these public flows articulate generalizable interests. Thus, the presumption of reasonableness is ultimately dependent on an "interplay" between the formal, institutionalized process of decision making on the one hand, and the informal, noninstitutionalized flows of the public sphere at the other.

In this chapter I will focus on the second step of Habermas's central thesis, in which the democratic process of decision making is linked to the communicative structures of the public sphere. In a sympathetic reading of *Between Facts and Norms*, I will first explore the significance of the discursive concept of democracy by discussing some critical objections with regard to the fruitfulness of the discursive perspective. I will then try to develop a further interpretation of the discursive perspective by considering the growing "gap" between politics and citizens, currently much discussed in Western countries. In doing so, I will take a closer look at the role of political parties, which almost wholly is neglected in *Between Facts and Norms*.

I

The most obvious objection to the discursive understanding of democracy is that it overlooks the dominant influence of what could be referred to as "power politics." From a power perspective the political process should not be understood as a "struggle" for the best argument (*Meinungsstreit*) among all persons involved, but as a struggle for power and political influence among political parties and major interest groups. These parties and interest groups are not primarily concerned about the communicative quality of the process of decision making, but are instead mainly interested in gaining office, or realizing—particularistic—interests. In this view, political opinions and arguments merely have an instrumental meaning. Accordingly, political decisions should be interpreted as compromises that reflect the actual, political or societal balance of power. In their classics *Capitalism, Socialism, and Democracy* and *A Preface to Democratic Theory*, Joseph Schumpeter and—the early—Robert

Dahl have developed the theoretical framework for such a strategic, "empirical" account of democracy.

If Schumpeter and Dahl are right, the discursive perspective could easily be rejected as idealistic or utopian. However, one of the central claims posed by Habermas in *Between Facts and Norms* is that the democratic institutions embody "particles" and "fragments" of an "existing reason" in the discursive sense (287), and that the "empirical" accounts of democracy misrepresent political reality because of their one-sidedness. I think Habermas is right in his criticism of the one-sidedness of the power perspective. The following argument indicates the shortcomings of a strategic account of democracy, and lends a certain plausibility to a discursive understanding.

The importance of a basic normative agreement for the functioning of a democratic political system seems to be underestimated from the power perspective. To be sure, both Schumpeter and Dahl recognize the need for a fundamental democratic or "polyarchal" consensus. So Schumpeter states; "I have emphasized that democracy can not be expected to function satisfactorily unless the vast majority of the people in all classes are resolved to abide by the rules of the democratic game and that this in turn implies that they are substantially agreed on the fundamentals of their institutional structure" (Schumpeter, 1952, p. 301).

Similarly, Dahl stresses the fact that the existence of a democratic political order rests on a general acceptance by the people of what he calls "polyarchal" norms (Dahl, 1956, pp. 74–81). However, neither of them is sufficiently aware of the normative restrictions that such a democratic consensus necessarily imposes on "the incessant competitive struggle" for political power. The restrictive nature of a basic democratic consensus can be clarified by means of the specific social-integrative problem that is characteristic for binding collective decisions. Because the results of collective decisions usually benefit some groups more than, or even at the expense of, others, acceptance of the results by the "losing" groups can only be reasonably expected if these groups voluntarily agree on the rules basic to the process of collective decision making. Voluntary acceptance of these rules, however, can only be expected to the extent that they can claim—at least to a certain degree—to embody impartiality and, consequently, to restrict the possibilities of powerful groups to instrumentalize the process of decision making for their own purposes. The conditions necessary to attain a "fair" compromise, highlighted by Habermas in his criticism of a strategic understanding of the democratic process, are one example of the need for a normative agreement on basic rules.

This "moral dimension" of democracy can also be illustrated by the fundamental political rights (e.g., freedom of association, speech, and press) that are constitutive for the democratic process, and that cannot be violated without violating the democratic process itself. In his book *Democracy and Its Critics*, Dahl explicitly recognizes this moral dimension:

> If a majority were to deprive a minority, or even itself, of any of its primary political rights, then in the very act of doing so it would violate the democratic process. . . . Of course the majority might have the power or strength to deprive a minority of its political rights. . . . The question is whether a majority may rightly use its primary political rights to deprive a minority of its primary political rights. The answer is clearly no. (Dahl, 1989, p. 171)

Of course this normative understanding of democracy does not imply a denial of the possibility of a strategic use of the democratic rights and rules. The reconstruction by Dahl (in his later work) and Habermas of a normative understanding of democracy is precisely motivated by concerns for the dominant influence of power politics. The central thesis of *Between Facts and Norms*, though, could be reformulated by stating that in the long run a dominant strategic use of democratic rights and procedures will undermine the social-integrative force of the constitutional state. I will return to this subject below.

On the empirical level of political argumentation, the "moral dimension" of democracy can be recognized in the vocabulary used by the political actors (including politicians, political parties, and interest groups) when they publicly try to gain support for their policies or demands. In order to succeed in gaining support, the political actors feel obliged to formulate their politics in terms of "common interests" or in terms of necessary prerequisites for the realization of generally recognized, fundamental rights. A strategic understanding of democracy cannot satisfactorily explain why political actors feel the necessity to use such vocabulary, and why it is not sufficient merely to state that they are only concerned with their own self-interest—which is evidently not the case.

Again, this does not mean that political actors cannot make use of this vocabulary in a strategic way and try to endow their demands with legitimacy by presenting their—particular—interests as if they were in "our" common interest. But as long as the political actors feel obliged to justify their policies and demands in terms of common interests and fundamental rights, the discursive concept of democracy seems to have a mooring in reality.

In sum, I think Habermas is right in criticizing the power perspective on democracy as defective. This does not mean, however, that we can reach an adequate understanding of the democratic process by merely taking its moral or discursive dimension into account. The discursive model does not simply reflect reality. The influence of power politics—as described, for instance, by

Schumpeter or the early Dahl—is usually intertwined with the communicative requirements of the discursive model. Thus, the functioning of democratic political systems can only be adequately understood by taking both the power perspective and the discursive perspective into account.[4]

A second objection to the discursive concept of democracy is of a more conceptual nature. It questions the basic discursive presupposition that the validity of norms ultimately rests on the possibility of reaching a rational agreement on controversial normative questions—implying, for example, that the voluntary acceptance of the rules of political decision making by the people relies on such rational consensus.[5] In my opinion, this objection can be put forward with renewed strength in the light of the recent, rather far-reaching change in Habermas's discursive understanding of normative validity. In the latest version of "discourse ethics," developed in *Justification and Application* and applied in *Between Facts and Norms*, he makes a distinction between different forms of practical reason and corresponding forms of practical discourse. For my purposes it will suffice to focus on the distinction between "moral" and "ethical-political" discourse.

As before, the moral-practical discourse serves as a test for the generalizable content of norms in the light of the principle of universalization (*Universalisierungsgrundsatz*). The domain of universal moral claims, however, is now explicitly restricted to the abstract content of metanorms such as universal human rights or the democratic principle of the equal consideration of interests. From this abstract, universalist level Habermas now distinguishes a second, more concrete level of norms, which are at issue in ethical-political discourses. Ethical norms give expression to conceptions of "the good life" that are shared by the members of a social community. The validity of these norms, therefore, is restricted to those who recognize themselves in the "politicocultural self-understanding of a historical community" (BFN, 160). Political-ethical discourses serve to acquire a better understanding of "who we are" and "who we want to be." In these discourses arguments that elucidate the self-understanding of our traditional life-forms are decisive.[6]

The main difficulty that troubles the notion of ethical-political discourse lies in the unclear status of arguments in such "discourse." Because ethical issues include volitive elements—as Habermas recognizes—the question arises whether it is possible to rationally decide on issues concerning our collective self-understanding. Habermas's statement that ethical arguments have "a relative validity, one that depends on context" (156), merely expresses the problem. How should we deal with the (sub)cultural conflicts between *adverse* conceptions of our self-understanding that are characteristic for our pluralist, multicultural societies?

This question has possibly far-reaching consequences for the significance of a discursive account of democracy. Not only do political decisions consist to a large degree of matters of ethical substance, but also the meaning of universal rights is characterized by an ethical dimension. To address the latter aspect first: the relationship between moral and ethical "discourse" is not unambiguously hierarchical, but twofold. On the one hand, universal rights and principles have priority above conceptions of the good life, and, consequently, the latter must be compatible or "consonant" with acknowledged universal norms. On the other hand, however, universal norms only become meaningful when they are interpreted "within the horizon of a specific form of life imbued within particular value constellations" (283). Thus, even our understanding of universal rights is inevitably also determined by volitive elements.

In my opinion, though, this need for a contextual interpretation does not necessarily lead to relativist conclusions. Although universal rights allow for different articulations (see, e.g., the rather different constitutions of Western democracies), they do not permit *contrary* interpretations.

Ethical issues, however, do allow for adverse opinions. In contrast to moral issues, they cannot be decided upon only by the "force" of the better argument. This does not mean, however, that argumentation plays no role whatsoever: argumentation makes it possible to reflect on our cultural traditions and to enlighten our self-understanding. One could say that in ethical discourse argumentation plays a *mediating* role rather than a decisive one: the extent to which we *recognize* ourselves in an argumentation becomes decisive. We could judge our self-understanding as being more or less rational to the extent that these—mediating—argumentations can be qualified as reasonable. The very moment of recognition, however, seems to be beyond the reach of argumentation. Consequently, dealing with ethical-political issues that are relevant for the society as a whole presupposes the existence of a basis of shared substantial norms and values. Then the question arises whether this presupposed, substantial communality is in fact not strongly at odds with the pluralist reality of the modern, Western society.[7]

Although the discursive concept does not offer a clear-cut answer to the question of how to settle controversial ethical issues, the strength of this concept consists of the perspective it opens with regard to the *mode of dealing* with such controversies. In contrast to the republican concept that presupposes an already existing ethical consensus on the one hand and, on the other, the liberal concept which, because of its controversial nature, defines ethical questions as private, the discursive concept states that only on the basis of argumentation can we find out which issues we can agree on and, consequently, where the limits of reaching consensus lie. We cannot conclude whether a specific matter is beyond the reach of consensus beforehand. Moreover, paralleling Joshua Cohen's interpretation of political preferences as—partly—formed in the process of political deliberation (Cohen, 1989), one could say that only

by expressing and discussing our self-understanding in a process of deliberation can we develop a genuine understanding of "who we are" and "who we
want to be."

II

As just mentioned, the central thesis of *Between Facts and Norms* is that
the legitimacy of the democratic process of decision making is dependent on
an interplay between the formal democratic procedures on the one hand, and
the communicative flows of the public sphere on the other. Consequently, a
proper functioning of the democratic process requires a vital public sphere,
which in turn presupposes the existence of a liberal political culture and a
"civil society" that rests on the initiatives of "a population *accustomed* to
freedom" (130). Thus Habermas has sketched a discursive interpretation of
the classic democratic idea of self-legislation (*Selbstgesetzgebung*)—according to which the political power of the state springs from the community of
free and equal citizens.

Following from the first part of my chapter, to understand the functioning of the democratic order adequately, one has to take both its normative
dimension and the dimension of "power politics" into account. Although
Habermas recognizes the intertwinement of both dimensions, it remains
unclear in *Between Facts and Norms* how the power perspective connects
with the required discursive interplay. Apart from his considerations with
regard to the functioning of the mass media,[8] Habermas confines his analysis
to a rather abstract contrasting of the "official" cycle of power—that corresponds to the normative idea of self-legislation—with the "unofficial" counter
cycle (*Gegenkreislauf*) of power—according to which the political process of
decision making and the functioning of the state apparatus are largely uncou-
pled from the force of legitimation. This uncoupling amounts to a "neutralization" of the possibilities for political participation of the citizens, implying
a reduction of their political role to merely going to the polls.[9]

How these cycles of power are interrelated, however, remains unclear.
One of the main questions that remains unanswered is what implications the
discursive concept has for the functioning of the political parties. Although
Habermas recognizes the crucial role political parties play with regard to the
required interplay between the legislative bodies and the public sphere, he
does not consider this role in any detail. Similar to his dualistic sketch of the
two cycles of power, he characterizes the role of political parties ambivalently.
On the one hand, Habermas suggests that the—bureaucratized—political parties have largely become part of the state; on the other hand he stresses that

the discursive interplay requires a mediating role of the political parties (434 and 442). The latter would imply that the political parties, instead of being *part* of the state, stand *between* the citizens and the state.

In order to say something more about the political "mechanisms" that are basic to the functioning of the political parties and to their different roles, I will discuss the disputed phenomenon of public "discontentment" with politics, and, in my opinion, the related phenomenon of the vote-maximizing "catch-all party." In addition, by doing so, I will attempt to explore the empirical usefulness of the discursive concept of democracy: what new light does the discursive concept throw on an empirical phenomenon like public discontentment, for example?

In most West European countries, the natural authority of the democratic political system nowadays is challenged by a growing distance between the citizens and the political "establishment." This distance results in feelings of political alienation and apathy on the part of the citizens. In the Netherlands this phenomenon is referred to as the "gap" between voters and political representatives, in Germany it is referred to by the term *Politikverdrossenheit* (Knapen, 1992; Von Weizsäcker, 1992).[10] Public opinion research indicates that the discontentment of the citizens with the functioning of their political institutions does not primarily concern the democratic political system itself—in which the people generally (still) do have great confidence. Apparently something is considered wrong with the way in which political parties and politicians actually make use of the democratic rules and procedures.

From a historical perspective, the phenomenon of the gap between voters and representatives can be accounted for with reference to social processes such as the decreasing persuasiveness of traditional political ideologies, together with the increasing independence and political awareness of citizens, leading to the disintegration of the traditional grassroots support, and to the rise of "the floating voter." These processes have led to a transformation of the political parties. Deprived of their traditional electoral support, the political parties are forced to struggle competitively for the voters' favors. Consequently, the traditional mass party, whose natural persuasiveness and social binding force were ensured by its ideological identity, has increasingly been replaced by the vote-maximizing "catch-all party." The latter is generally thought to be prototypical for the modern, de-ideologized political party (Kirchheimer 1966; Koole, 1990).

Otto Kirchheimer characterizes the catch-all party by a drastically reduced ideological 'baggage' that is loose enough to appeal to a heterogeneous electorate, and to a search for electoral support via interest group intercession. Because it cannot count on permanent electoral loyalty—as the traditional party did—it has to secure its mass support by satisfying a variety of interest groups, who provide "mass reservoirs" of readily accessible voters. Furthermore, the catch-all party is characterized by a centralized party organization, which is required to maintain a continuous presence on the political market. This centralizing tendency leads to the strengthening of top leadership groups, and goes hand in hand with a downgraded role for individual party members. These characteristics must enable the catch-all party to attract a maximum of voters and to realize the "immediate electoral goal" of obtaining government office (Kirchheimer, 1966, pp. 185-193).[11] Kirchheimer further describes the catch-all party as "an ingenious and useful political instrument" that could function "as one of the many interrelated structures by which (the citizen) achieves a rational participation in his surrounding world" (p. 199). Thus, he stresses the ability of the catch-all party "to provide a clear-cut basis of legitimacy" (p. 199).

Assuming that the dominant postwar type of political party can indeed be sketched by Kirchheimer's concept of the catch-all party, the question arises—how we should interpret this phenomenon of public discontentment with politics. The public discontentment seems to contradict Kirchheimer's appraisal of the catch-all party's ability to provide a satisfactory basis of legitimacy. This assumption is confirmed by Claus Offe's analysis of the modern competitive party (*Konkurrenzpartei*) which strongly resembles Kirchheimer's catch-all party. This analysis even suggests that the catch-all party has strongly *contributed* to the phenomenon of public discontentment. Offe argues that the vote-maximizing attitude of the catch-all party, in combination with its preoccupation with obtaining political power, leads to political alienation of the citizens. In order to attract a maximum number of votes, the catch-all party is forced to adjust its program to the expediencies of the electoral market (Offe, 1984). Paradoxically, however, the adjustment to this "public opinion" implies a neutralization of the citizen's will, namely, the only thing that matters for the party is whether people *do* vote for it, not *who* votes, or *why*. Thus, the citizen's will is reduced to a merely calculative contribution to the party's goal of obtaining office. According to Offe, this neutral attitude toward the citizen's will leads to a "destruction" of the citizen's identity, because it ignores that the will of the citizen is inextricably bound up with the context of the citizen's form of life (Offe, 1980).

More light can be thrown upon the neutralizing effect of the vote-maximizing tendency of the catch-all party from the discursive perspective. The neutral attitude toward the citizen's will can be more specifically interpreted as a neutral attitude toward the argumentative content of political opinions. Precisely this neutral, indifferent handling of political views widens the scope to adjust the policies to the opportunities of the political market. It goes together with a mode of political decision making that is determined by the parliamentary distribution of power and by the current opinion poll rates, rather than by the quality of political argument. The neutralizing effect implies that counter arguments of opposing politicians and involved interest or citizen groups are not taken seriously. However, this lack of attention for argument can become a source of massive political frustration and alienation, resulting, for example, in phenomena such as public discontentment.

Whether this indeed happens, depends, among other things, on the extent to which a—potential—dissatisfaction with the way in which political decisions are made can be compensated for by a share in the societal wealth.[12] As long as one's demands are being fulfilled by the process of decision making, agreement with the political motivations underlying the policy at stake is less important. Thus, creation of mass loyalty is possible by satisfying a multitude of diverse demands and concerns. Such policies of "appeasement"[13] were successful during the postwar period, which was characterized by a—seemingly—endless growth of economic productivity and societal wealth.[14] Under different circumstances, however, as in the eighties and nineties, in a period of economic stagnation and drastic reductions on governmental expenditures, the possibilities for a compensatory politics of appeasement become exhausted. Under these changed circumstances, the neutralizing effect of vote-maximizing can become a serious problem. Although, as just mentioned, a lack of political argument is less important as long as one's demands are being fulfilled, it does matter considerably when one is *impaired* on the basis of a defective reasoning—or, using a phrase of Habermas, on the basis of a decision that lacks the "presumption of reasonableness." There is little that affects the *basis for trust* characteristic of the relationship between voter and political representative more than the feeling that one is *wrongfully* harmed by a political decision. This is aptly expressed by Habermas in his summary of Cass Sunstein's observations: "For the citizens themselves, it makes a difference, in normative terms, whether the legitimate policies and goals that may require them to accept disadvantages are the outcome of a legitimating, deliberative process or whether, on the contrary, they merely emerge as side effects of programs and processes motivated by other, private concerns unfit for the purposes of public justification" (*BFN*, 276).

Although the catch-all party generally has been rather successful in gaining mass support,[15] the public discontentment seems to indicate that the public becomes more and more aware of the fragile legitimacy of the catch-all party, whose primarily concern is not the interests of the citizens, but striving for political power. The catch-all party seems to be unable to renew—under postmetaphysical conditions—the persuasiveness that characterized the traditional mass party. From the discursive perspective, this incapacity can be explained with reference to its indifference to political argument. The catch-all party lacks the capability of justifying political decisions that run counter to the interests of its electorate.

The thesis can now be formulated that the modern competitive party, in order to restore its public credibility, has to qualify its striving for government office and develop a "communicative sensitivity." Following Offe, a "new type" of political party is needed that refrains from striving for the fifty-one percent norm, and that instead focuses on the bonds of loyalty that enable the party to channel the "energies" originating from social conflicts (Offe, 1980, pp. 41–42). Moreover, a more serious consideration of political argument is needed in order to meet the required communicative sensitivity. Within the organizational apparatus of the political parties more space should be created for open, public discussion. This requires an "upgrading" of the role of individual party members and a kind of "internal democracy" that runs counter to the centralizing tendency of the catch-all party. Thus, the extent to which the political parties become forums for public discussion seems to be determinative for the parties' ability to restore their function as intermediate between the citizens and the state.[16]

The "debureaucratization" of the political parties, however, deals with only one factor, however important, concerning the required interplay between the citizens and the legislative bodies. Habermas's emphasis on the interrelatedness of a proper functioning of the democratic process with a vital, public sphere—which in turn rests on the commitment of the people to freedom and justice—implies that "radical democracy" not only presupposes a "new type" of political party, but also a "discursive" kind of citizenship. Moreover, this interrelatedness suggests that the way in which political parties function and the existing form(s) of citizenship must be conceived of as *two sides of the same coin*. As a consequence, it would be too one-sided to interpret the phenomenon of public discontentment as merely a criticism of the actual functioning of the political parties. The criticism could also be reversed, implying a criticism of the political behavior of the public itself. Thus, the recent appeals made by various Dutch politicians for a stronger "civic virtue"—though often far too moralistic[17]—could be understood as a mirror image of the public discontentment with politics.

In *Between Facts and Norms*, however, neither the functioning of the political parties, nor the question of citizenship is considered in any detail (see Baynes, in this volume). In this chapter I have attempted to throw some more light on the role of political parties with respect to the intertwinement of the discursive and the power perspective. The discursive concept of democracy, however, is still in need of further interpretation, both with regard to the specific conditions for a "new type" of political party, and with regard to the presupposed type of citizenship. Only such elaboration could show whether our political reality can indeed be characterized by "particles" of an "existing reason," and whether a discursive perspective can clarify the possibilities for a further democratization of the liberal, Western democracy.

Notes

1. See Habermas (1990 and 1993) for his discursive concept of normative validity.

2. Habermas restricts this need for an openness and sensitivity of the political process to questions of moral and political-ethical substance, which he distinguishes from questions concerning interest representation (*BFN*, 182–183). In my opinion, this distinction makes no sense: since the social space of legislative decision making is structurally confined, I see no reason why this exclusiveness could not also affect the latter. This means that also in the case of interest representation a sensitivity is needed toward a possible neglect of certain interests, which would violate an equal consideration of interests.

3. Compare Cohen and Arato (1992).

4. Compare Munnichs (1994).

5. Contrary to the discursive concept of democracy, John Rawls's notion of "overlapping consensus" implies that the basic structure of a modern constitutional democracy does not require a rational consensus (Rawls, 1985). H. R. van Gunsteren, et al (1992) go even further by stating that agreement on "the rules of the game" is impossible as well as undesirable in the light of the pluralism of modern life-forms.

6. "[In ethical discourses] the outcome turns on arguments based on a hermeneutic explication of the self-understanding of our historically transmitted form of life. Such arguments weigh value decisions in this context with a view toward an authentic conduct of life, a goal that is absolute for us" (*BFN*, 161).

7. Compare Habermas's own similar criticism of the presumptions of the republican concept of democracy: "Of course, the ethical particularism characteristic of an unproblematic background consensus does not sit well with the conditions of cultural and societal pluralism that distinguish modern societies" (*BFN*, 279).

8. See *BFN*, 359–387.

9. Compare Habermas (1987, pp. 346-347).

10. In the Netherlands even a parliamentary commission (the Commission Deetman—named after the chair of the Second Chamber) has been appointed to examine the ins and outs of the "gap" between citizens and politics.

11. Similarly, Dahl (1956) has conceived of the postwar democratic political system as "interest group democracy," in which the political parties gain electoral support by "appeasing" a variety of interest groups.

12. The possibility of compensating the lack of attention to (political) argument is easily overlooked from the discursive perspective. Compare McCarthy (1978, p. 383).

13. See Dahl (1956, p. 146). Compare note 12.

14. Compare Isaac (1988, p. 141).

15. In the Netherlands, for example, during the last decades, the turnout at the elections fluctuated around 80 percent of the electorate.

16. Compare Kalma (1982).

17. Compare Van Gunsteren (1992).

References

Jean Cohen and Andrew Arato. 1992. *Civil Society and Political Theory*. Cambridge: Massachusetts Institute of Technology Press.

Joshua Cohen. 1989. "Deliberation and Democratic Legitimacy." in *The Good Polity*, edited by Hamlin, A. Pettit, B. Oxford: Basil Blackwell.

R. A. Dahl. 1956. *A Preface to Democratic Theory*. Chicago and London: University of Chicago Press.

―――. 1989. *Democracy and Its Critics*. New Haven and London: Yale University Press.

H. R. van Gunsteren, ed. 1992. *Eigentijds burgerschap* (Contemporary citizenship). Den Haag, Sdu uitgeverij.

J. Habermas. 1987. *The Theory of Communicative Action*. Vol. 2. Boston: Beacon.

―――. 1990. "Discourse Ethics: Notes on a Program of Justification." In *Moral Consciousness and Communicative Action*. Cambridge: Massachusetts Institute of Technology Press.

―――. 1993. *Justification and Application*. Cambridge: Massachusetts Institute of Technology Press.

―――. 1996. *Between Facts and Norms: Contributions to a Discourse Theory of Law and Democracy*. Cambridge: Massachusetts Institute of Technology Press.

J. C. Isaac. 1988. "Dilemmas of Democratic Theory." In *Power, Inequality, and Democratic Politics*, edited by I. Shapiro and G. Reeher. Boulder and London: Westview Press.

P. Kalma. 1982. De illusie van de "democratische staat" ('The illusion of the 'democratic state"). Deventer, Netherlands: Kluwer.

O. Kirchheimer. 1966. "The Transformation of the Western European Party Systems." In *Political Parties and Political Development*, edited by J. LaPalombara and M. Weiner. Princeton: Princeton University Press.

B. Knapen. 1992. "Het publieke ongenoegen" (Public discontentment). *NRC Handelsblad* 12, no. 9.

R. A. Koole, J.Th.J. van den Berg. 1990. De veranderende rol van politieke partijen (The changing role of political parties). *Beleid & Maatschappij* 17: 1–42.

Thomas McCarthy. 1978. *The Critical Theory of Jürgen Habermas*. Cambridge: Massachusetts Institute of Technology Press.

G. Munnichs. 1994. "Demokratie, Macht und Legitimität" in *Mythos Wertfreiheit? Neue Beiträge zur Objektivität in den Human- und Kulturwissenschaften*, edited by K. O. Apel and M. Kettner, Frankfurt, Germany: Campus.

C. Offe. 1980. "Konkurrenzpartei und kollektive politische Identität," in *Parlamentarisches Ritual und politische Alternativen*, edited by R. Roth. Frankfurt, and New York: Campus.

———. 1984. "Competitive Party Democracy and the Keynesian Welfare State" in *Contradictions of the Welfare State*, edited by C. Offe. Cambridge: Massachusetts Institute of Technology Press.

John Rawls. 1985. "Justice as Fairness: Political not Metaphysical." *Philosophy and Public Affairs* 14: 223–251.

J. Schumpeter. 1952 (1943). *Capitalism, Socialism, and Democracy*. London: George Allen & Unwin.

R. von Weizsäcker. 1992. *Richard von Weizsäcker im Gespräch mit Günter Hofmann und Werner A. Perger*. Frankfurt, Germany: Eichborn.

9

The Disappearance of Discourse Ethics in Habermas's *Between Facts and Norms*

Matthias Kettner

Introduction

Jürgen Habermas's recent book *Between Facts and Norms* (*BFN*) makes so many important points and draws on such a wealth of different conceptual resources that it is hard to extricate from its rich texture of normative politico-legal analysis the few operative arguments that provide its distinctively "discourse theoretical" deep structure. It is highly rewarding in its own right to follow Habermas's thoughtful discussion of concepts such as deliberative democracy, civil society, and the public sphere, and to see him endorse the momentous thesis (which many readers, this author included, will embrace) of an essential link between the modern constitutional state and radical democracy. However, this enthusiam must not obscure the somewhat disturbing fact that there are only scant methodological remarks in *BFN* on what it is for a theory of x, for instance, a theory of modern law, to be a "discourse theory" of x. Certainly, a discourse theory of x (as distinct from other sorts of theories of x) will characteristically look at relevant features of x (e.g., functions of x) in terms of forms of communication and potentials of reasons.[1] But the very idea of a discourse theory (of law, of democracy, of morality, and of whatever else a discourse theory is possible)—its theoretical aims, its explanatory or justificational scope, its basic conceptual structure, and its rational status—remains in *BFN* in a strange twilight.

To be sure, anyone familiar with Habermas's *The Theory of Communicative Action* and his writings on discourse ethics during the last decade will have a rich understanding of the nuts and bolts of Habermasian "formal pragmatics" that underwrites all his discourse-theoretical deliberations. *BFN* is not an occasional piece. Yet *BFN* should provide a self-sufficient explication of its argumentative deep structure. This is all the more important because there is not only continuity with previous work but also some startling innovations and discontinuities between *BFN* and previous Habermasian theorizing—discontinuities that may be extensions, revisions, corrections, or shifts. Two salient discontinuities are (1) the relaxation of constraints on the concept of a discourse, and (2) the diversification of the taxonomy of basic types of discourse. I comment on these discontinuities in turn.

1. *The relaxation of constraints on the concept of a discourse.* The very idea of a discourse gets respecified in *BFN* via the introduction of a generic *discourse principle* (D). Habermas wants D to have "normative content" yet be "neutral" with regard to, and thus be "more abstract" than, both morality and law.[2] I take this to mean that D's normative content (whatever that content may be) cannot be equated with normative content of principles that we recognize as principles of a normative moral theory nor with those recognizably belonging to a normative theory of law. To be sure, principle D could be neutral with respect to principles of law and of ethics without being more abstract than those principles, if law and ethics happen to share a normative principle. But Habermas does not conceive of D as a normative principle that both domains have in common.

Why does Habermas make D "more abstract" than he did in previous writings when D denoted what Habermas used to refer to as "the principle of discourse ethics"? Habermas is eager to avoid reductionism. He wants to avoid giving the impression of theoretically reducing the legal to the moral sphere; of reducing (the discourse theory of) law to a branch of discourse ethics. Hence, D as such is supposed to be neither a moral nor a legal principle. Instead, D is supposed to yield both the (discourse theoretical) "principle of morality" as well as the (discourse theoretical) "principle of democracy"[3] on the strength of an argumentative operation that Habermas adumbrates as "specification." How is this specification supposed to work?

2. *The diversification of basic types of discourse.* Habermas's initial dual typology of "theoretical" versus "practical discourse" proved already in *The Theory of Communicative Action* to be too restrictive and thus had to be broadened in order to countenance some other important types of discourse.[4] This typology is replaced in *BFN* by a complicated "vertically" and "horizontally" differentiated matrix of basic types of discourse. The discursive matrix now comprises justificatory discourses (*Begründungsdiskurse*) and application discourses (*Anwendungsdiskurse*) in the vertical dimension and a tripartite distinction of moral (*moralische Diskurse*), ethical (*ethisch-existentielle Diskurse* and *ethisch-politische Diskurse*), and pragmatic discourses (*pragmatische Diskurse*).

These two innovations involve a substantial amount of theoretical change. The conceptual deep structures in a piece of theorizing determine, among other things, its specific validity claims and, correspondingly, the distribution of overt and covert burdens of proof. For example, Habermas's derivation of a system of basic rights in the core of *BFN* certainly is a new and persuasive device for introducing a number of familiar elements of legal thought and normative political theory in a cogent sequence. But if it is more than an expository device—and surely it must be more than that—what is the exact nature of the claim inherent in the derivation of "the" system of rights? Abstract and formal as such questions may appear, they need to be answered if we are ever to arrive at an assessment of the rational strength and originality of *BFN*. Therefore my remarks will focus on what might be called "questions of Habermas's architectonics." Within the confines of this chapter I will mainly trace what I take to be difficulties, unclarities, non sequiturs, and unresolved burdens of proof. That is, my task is mainly negative and critical, with one major exception: I propose a constructive reading of the discourse principle that goes beyond Habermas's own most recent explication of it.

The Discourse Principle, Old D and New D_{FN}

Two principles define Habermasian discourse ethics. The first is a principle of universalizability that takes contested action norms as *universalizanda* and takes generalizable self-interest[5] as a *criterion* by which a contested action norm N gets tested for its distributive compatibility within the set of all persons whose interests are affected:

(U) "*All* affected can accept the consequences and the side effects its [=the norm's] *general* observance can be anticipated to have for the satisfaction of *everyone's* interests (and these consequences are preferred to those of known alternative possibilities for regulation)."[6]

The second principle Habermas used to refer to as "the distinctive idea of an ethics of discourse." He formulates this principle as follows:

(D) "Only those norms can claim to be valid that meet (or could meet) with the approval of all affected in their capacity *as participants in a practical discourse*."[7]

According to D the conjunction of two properties make my (or anyone else's) practical deliberations a necessary factor in the intersubjective product that constitutes the validity of a norm N. The first property is that whether N *in praxi* enjoys the status of a valid norm or not is a difference that makes a difference to my interests such that this difference is sufficiently important for me to care about it. The second property is that I participate in practical discourse, that is, in the uncoerced argumentative practice of scrutinizing, testing, and constructing justifying reasons for or against statements that judge some action norm as valid. To judge N as valid is of course to do something prescriptive.[8] Habermas refers to D as a moral principle and to U as a principle of argumentation. Conducting practical discourse on principle U, Habermas maintained, is sufficient for making rationally convincing ("cognitive") normative solutions possible whenever a targeted practical problem is such that it is presumed that what counts as a normative solution to it is constrained by what is equally in the interest of all whose interests the respective problem, and its solution, might affect.[9]

The new version of the initial principle D, D_{FN}, reads:[10]

D_{FN}: "Action norms are valid if and only if all possibly affected people could assent to them as participants in rational discourses."[11]

As a matter-of-fact Habermas's comments at this argumentatively crucial juncture in *BFN* are disappointingly vague. Piecing together his scant remarks yields the following view whose inherent problems I will point out as I go along.

The Meaning of D_{FN}

As it stands, D_{FN} formulates a definition of validity. It defines a generic notion of validity—generic in the sense of being attributable to *any kind of action norm*, where any behavior that people in fact expect to be the same across varying times, across varying actors, and across varying social circumstances, is to count as an action norm. This is a sociologically descriptive use of the term *action norm*.[12] However, D_{FN} is not a descriptive use of the term *valid*. Habermas offers D_{FN} neither as a description of how people do in fact think, nor as a suggestion as to how people may choose to think, about the validity of action norms. Rather, Habermas offers D_{FN} as a correct account of what constitutes validity of action norms. D_{FN} thus gives the way in which rational people *should* think about the validity of action norms. More precisely, D_{FN} specifies what Habermas thinks it is rationally required to think about the validity of action norms, at least on a "postconventional level of justification."[13] An action norm N satisfying D_{FN} is a valid action norm. For N to be valid requires that it can be claimed that N ought to be followed and that there are reasons that could be marshaled in order to show that claim to be justified if it is doubted that it is justified. In this sense, the concept of a *valid* action norm is a normative concept (i.e., it can be the source of prescriptive force in suitable utterances) whereas the concept of an action norm is a purely descriptive concept.

How do we get from the nonnormative concept of action norm to the normative concept of valid action norm? The quick answer is: via D_{FN}. D_{FN} captures the property that bestows validity on all norms that have it and renders invalid all norms that lack it.

The Rational Authority of D_{FN}

Why should anyone accept D_{FN} as the sole adjudicator of validity for action norms? Surely not for some incidental reason, for instance, because D_{FN} renders all those action norms valid that one strongly likes to uphold (e.g., action norms of peaceful conflict resolution), and renders invalid all those that one would like to see go down (e.g., patriarchal marriage norms)? Why should *we all* accept D_{FN} as *rationally required*? As long as this question remains unanswered the status of Habermas's derivation of "the" system of rights in *BFN* as an extended argument remains obscure. One even wonders what kind of account is required for an answer. Surely neither a genealogy, nor a history of ideas, nor a sociological reconstruction of the constitutional democratic project as we (French, Americans, Dutch, Germans, and a handful of other Western nation states) understand it will do. Habermas posits D_{FN} in a completely general way. This is consistent with D_{FN}'s completely general content. Nonetheless D_{FN} is but a posit. On which grounds then does Habermas's posit merit universal rational assent? Owing to the general level of this question one might have expected some foundational arguments of a scope that commonly goes by the name of philosophy. There are hints of a somewhat transcendental background argument. Yet Habermas's aversion to recognizably transcendental arguments prevents him from elaborating these hints.[14] As a result, the introduction of D_{FN} in BFN is only backed by a thin chain of explicatory remarks of notions pertaining to D_{FN}.[15] In the next section I examine the notions that carry the argumentative weight in Habermas's explicatory remarks.

The Postconventional Level of Justification and Its Discontents

"Postconventional level of justification" is a concept that *describes* historically a change in our justificatory practices. Roughly, this is the change from social conditions where people could call into question or ask for justifying reasons concerning only a few action norms to (modern) social conditions where the demand for justification becomes unlimited and at the same time the justificatory force of traditional sources for justification such as religious beliefs, customs, or mores, tends to disappear.[16] Besides its descriptive component, Habermas contends that the concept of a "postconventional level of justification" also has *normative* content; its normative content is the normative content that is articulated in D_{FN}. Now is this normative content (if D_{FN} has any) justifiable by a self-contained string of reasoning, that is, independent from a *narrative* (however sociologically enriched) about the "intrusion of reflection" on the occidental lifeworld since the eighteenth century?[17] If it is not possible to distinguish grand narrative and argument—and Habermas, eschewing the completely general and self-referential level of argument that would be consistent with his argumentative aim of introducing a general normative definition of rationality or rational validity respectively, says nothing to dispel this impression—then D_{FN} has the normative content it has because western history has been what it was. This invites Foucault-type skepticism and, worse perhaps, lands Habermas in exactly the cultural relativism that he scorns Rawls for having fallen prey to.[18]

What, exactly, is D_{FN}'s normative content? D_{FN}'s normative content is supposed to consist in the "the sense of impartiality of practical judgments" that Habermas takes D_{FN} to express.[19] In the next section I unpack the notion of a practical judgment in D_{FN}; I will then scrutinize the corresponding idea of impartiality.

Practical Judgments, Action Norms, and Valid Action Norms

The term *practical judgment* contained in the crucial formulation just quoted that specifies D_{FN}'s normative content is far from clear. Nor does Habermas specify the "sense of impartiality" that goes with them or with our attempts at justifying practical judgments—*any* practical judgments—we make. Are singular judgments at which I arrive when deliberating about what I ought to do here and now in this situation (given that such and such holds) practical judgments? Or does the format of a practical judgment require nonindexical situation types and, perhaps, generality ("we" and "everyone with the property p") at the subject position?

From what was just cited about the action norms which, ultimately, must apply to or in practical judgments, I surmise that practical judgments are deontic judgments. That is, they are judgments people make when they express action requirements and their rational attitudes toward such requirements. Rational attitudes are those based on the evaluation of reasons; they are reflected in people's judgments concerning whether, given certain reasons, certain requirements do or do not hold. A deontic judgment (*dj*) is a judgment that under certain circumstances certain types of action are required, in some qualified sense of a deontic modality, of certain agents. A *dj* makes a certain way of acting a norm for certain people.[20] For a person to sincerely accept (or "endorse") a *dj* (that S under circumstances C ought to do X) is to think of the person who is the logical subject of the *dj* as someone who ought to do what according to the intentional content of the *dj* someone is to do.[21]

What takes us from the nonnormative sociological concept of action norm to the normative concept of valid action norm then is the fact that on the postconventional level of justification action norms (and the ways of acting that are expressive of them) are objects of practical judgments (i.e., *dj*s) which require justifying reasons and thus link up with all of our generally recognized discursive practices of reason giving and taking.

The Neutrality of D_{FN}

What has been said so far helps to throw into relief Habermas's claim, puzzling at first, that the normative content of D_{FN} is "still neutral" vis-à-vis the distinction of law versus morality.[22] Action norms and corresponding deontic judgments rationalizing their authority usually fall into a matrix of recognizably different domains of authority. This sociological fact is reflected in the semantic fact that the expression for the deontic modality in deontic judgments (standardly by constructions using the word *ought*) is adverbially qualified so as to indicate domains of authority to which the respective *djs* pertain. Hence we say things like "it is *legally permitted* to smoke in here but you *ought prudentially* to abstain from it (because it is bad for your health); however, *morally* there *ought* to be a law against it anyhow (because it affects nonconsenting others for ill)." The speaker if pressed for justifications of her diverse deontic judgments will marshal juridical, scientific, and moral reasons respectively in support of her judgments. So the neutrality claimed for D_{FN} can be taken to mean that there is an unqualified sense of ought in deontic judgments such that it is possible to judge action norms as valid no matter to which domain of authority they pertain. An action norm N is valid (in this unqualified sense of ought) if a deontic judgment that N *simply* ought to be followed can be backed by justifying reasons R that are conclusive for all whose interests are affected by N and who appreciate R in contexts of "rational discourse."[23]

However, this reading of D_{FN}'s neutrality would seem vacuous. To put no constraints on the kinds of reasons in virtue of which N satisfies D_{FN} leaves us with no kind of reasons in particular but with *all* kinds of reasons. Why should we call action norms valid if all affected judge them valid for all kinds of reasons? On the face of it this move would land us in an inflationary use of the predicate "valid."

This objection to D_{FN} can be blocked if one takes the expression "rational discourses" in D_{FN} not as denoting the generic public space of uncoerced argumentation,[24] but as a placeholder for particular formations of discourse each of which qualifies as rational in virtue of how well it enables us to handle specific ranges of problems. This second reading of D_{FN} coheres much better with the idea, introduced at a later point in *BFN*, that it is useful to distinguish pragmatic, ethical, and moral discourses as three particular types of discourse.[25] In the next section I highlight two problems inherent in these distinctions.

Dubious Distinctions of Discourse

According to Habermas, as three particular types of rational discourse, "pragmatic," "ethical," and "moral" discourses are each rational in their own way, that is, relative to the task of determining good reasoning with regard to pragmatic, ethical, or moral questions, respectively.

I have argued elsewhere at length that this taxonomy of discourses does not support Habermas's claim to have articulated rationally authoritative divisions within practical reason.[26] In particular, to stipulate that all and only questions of justice (justice being understood as what is in the interest of everyone alike) be labeled *moral* and that all and only questions of self-realization (self-realization understood as the appropriate realization of an authenticated idea of the good, both individually and collectively)[27] be labeled "ethical" amounts to little more than semantic politics by terminological *fiat*.[28] It presents disputable predilections of a particular theory of morality as an insight into practical reason itself. This cryptodogmatism unnecessarily tends to obscure the profoundly important insight, contained in the proffered distinctions, that self-realization and Kantian self-determination, contemporary society being what it is, are *conflictive* dimensions of normative significance.[29] That is, it can be the case that there are reasons why R1 made good by convincing considerations of self-realization in favor of some policy, intention, or action x, and that there are reasons why R2 against x made good by convincing considerations of Kantian self-determination, and that R2 and R1 mutually have no bearing on each other, and there is no other recognizably convincing consideration available to decide the issue.

Moreover, there is what might be termed the *problem-sorting problem*: The taxonomy of "pragmatic," "ethical," and "moral" discourses, though heuristically useful, has no rational credentials to offer to parties who may want to employ it in a dispute whenever the dispute already concerns the way to sort the problem, or to sort subproblems within an agreed common ground of a problem area. Unfortunately, this applies to most practical problems of some moment.[30] There is no neutral and overarching metadiscourse for discerning "true natures" of complex practical problems. The right way to sort a problem may already be part of its solution; it may also be part of the problem. The rhetoric of terms like *the logic of a problem* borrows its evidence from undisputably simple cases where it is in order. However, it loses all force in the face of notoriously disputed problems. Practical problems have no uninterpreted natures waiting to be discovered;[31] and to interpret a practical problem as having a particular nature is an abductive activity (of problem sorting) for which a theory of discourse types can be useful but in no way foundational.

I do not want to deny the feasibility of an illuminating discourse theoretical interpretation of the logic of practical questions, where "logic" is shorthand for topic-related reasonable patterns of discussion. What I deny is that such a theory will be able to assign questions to problems when part of the problem is which questions should be asked.

The Abstract Impartiality of D_{FN}

I now examine the claim that impartiality is the nonmoral normative content of D_{FN}. D_{FN}'s normative content is supposed to consist in "the sense of impartiality of practical judgments." However, the point of view from which action norms can be *impartially grounded* is not identical with the moral point of view. This is readily apparent from the fact that the latter, according to Habermas, consists in

a. equal respect for everyone,

b. equal consideration for the interests of all.[32]

Both a and b strike a note of impartiality. For all persons, if S is a person and if persons ought to be respected then S ought to be respected; this rules out that that S be respected but not another person S and thus characterizes a type of impartiality. And if persons ought to have their interests considered then (b) rules out that someone's interests are considered more than someone else's—again, impartiality. Impartiality, however, neither dictates that persons must be respected nor that anyone's interests must be anyone else's concern. That is why the moral point of view—(a) and (b)—cannot be exhausted by impartiality.

Impartiality is only a necessary, not a sufficient, condition of acting morally. Unfortunately, Habermas does not explain what he means by impartiality. Let us assume that what he means does not differ decidedly from standard notions of impartiality.[33] According to the standard notion of impartiality, for someone, A, to be impartial means that "*A* is impartial in respect *R* with regard to group *G* if and only if *A's* actions in respect *R* are not influenced at all by which member(s) of *G* benefit or are harmed by these actions."[34] It is a mistake to equate impartiality with justice or fairness.[35] Unjust and just laws can both be administered impartially, and action norms arrived at in impartial deliberations can be morally outrageous on all counts.

Does D_{FN} avoid the mistake of false equivalence between impartiality and justice? Yes. Or so it seems. In respect of properly participating in a rational discourse (of whatever particular type) and with regard to the entire group of participants, if D_{FN} holds then whatever A's reasons for A's communicative actions within the discursive space may be, they will not be reasons of benefiting certain group members while harming certain other group members. Reasoning as perceived by that group must appear impartial in regard to that group because otherwise some members can perceive it as posing a threat to them to which they have no reason to agree to.[36] This impartiality does not constrain the content of the action norm N whose validity (or invalidity) is to be determined by the discourse: N may be a way of acting which, judged by standards of justice or decency, would appear quite wrong (e.g., stealing food from the neighbor tribe whenever times are hard for us) yet if we are dealing with a pragmatic rather than a moral discourse (in which standards of justice and decency presumably would have to figure prominently) we might arrive at judging N valid (e.g., as the best means to secure our survival in hard times)—no matter how unjust N would appear from a moral point of view. N would be justified (by pragmatic standards) but unjust (by moral standards). Impartiality (in the standard sense that I have been considering) is only contingently related to justice and fairness. It is not essentially tied to either of these moral notions.

Impartiality, Morality, and the Practice of Evaluating Reasons

A further consideration may help to bring home the point made in the last section about the moral inertness of the impartiality inherent in whatever variety of argumentative discourse that is governed by D_{FN}. In discourse, participants' communicative actions will be of the reason-giving and reason-evaluating variety. Hence their communicative actions will be governed by the principles that rational persons let themselves be governed by when they invoke the concept of a reason. Here is one basic principle (R*) pertaining to the evaluation of reasons as good or bad reasons as we understand the concept of a reason: "(R*) If R is a good reason for agent S1 (in a certain respect, e.g. to adopt action norm N, or to believe *that p*) then there is some property F of S1 such that R is the same good reason (to adopt N) *for whomever is* F.[37]

I cannot *salva rationalitate* judge a reason to be a good reason (to do x) thinking that what makes it good for me would not make it good for anyone else in circumstances equal to mine. I maintain (but cannot prove here) that (R*) is the only *generic universalization principle*, that is, holding for argumentative discourse of whatever variety. Note that (R*) is a universalization principle: (R*) requires a good reason to be good from the point of view of *all* agents who are F. If this principle spells out the generic sense of impartiality that is part and parcel of argumentative discourse in virtue of the validity defining properties of argumentative discourse then such impartiality surely is "neutral" relative to differences between, and "more abstract" than, both law and morality. (R*) is a normative principle in that for anyone, S_i, to observe that S_j's claiming R1 to be a good reason (to do x) does not conform to (R*) gives S a prima facie good reason for disclaiming that R1 is a good reason (to do x). Thus (R*) itself serves as a reason in justificatory contexts where we judge claims concerning purportedly good (or bad) reasons. The trouble with (R*) is that it is anything but obvious how we can get from the unspecific normativity of (R*) to normative principles that are specifically relevant for evaluating reasons associated with moral and legal deontic judgments.

To say this is, of course, only to restate the problem Habermas lands himself in by defining D_{FN} so abstractly as to render D_{FN}—which I have interpreted by (R*)—a principle "still neutral" vis-à-vis the distinction between law and morality. Can that problem be solved at all? What kind of argument would do the trick? Roughly, the contention developed in the Apelian transcendental-pragmatic line of discourse ethics is the following: What is required is an argument in which someone, S, being involved in some justificatory context and actually judging claims concerning purportedly good (or bad) reasons reflectively identifies certain idealizing presuppositions without which it would be irrational for S (and indeed for anyone whom we recognize as a rational being like ourselves) to have confidence that S's own reason-evaluating acts conform to (R*). If a set of such presuppositions $P_1 \ldots P_N$ can be identified the next step of the argument consists in tracing out how this set or some of its elements constrain the practices of moral judgment of people who share an interest in avoiding irrational conduct in whatever dealings they consider morally significant. Differences in their initial conceptions of morality and rationality notwithstanding, it can reasonably be expected of people who share such an interest that whatever constrains their practices of moral *judgment* will also tend to constrain their ways of *acting* by providing them with universally prescriptive action-guiding reasons.[38] To develop this argument properly would take me too far away from the main objective in this chapter which is to diagnose difficulties in Habermas's exposition of D_{FN} rather than to provide a full-fledged alternative exposition.[39]

If D_{FN} Is Morally Inert, Whence Discourse Ethics?

In the sense just outlined, the impartiality of D_{FN} raises a number of questions. If the monistic principle D_{FN} as introduced in *BFN* represents Habermas's mature thoughts on his formal-pragmatic discourse-theoretical framework then either he has abandoned the original project of discourse ethics as *normative* moral theory—the disappearance of discourse ethics—or the former project has not been abandoned but the discourse-theoretical framework set out in *BFN* is seriously incomplete in that it is a normative dangler. I now state four questions that I think are crucial with regard to the status of discourse ethics after *BFN*.

1. *Whence the content of the moral point of view?* According to Habermas, the moral point of view has a certain (albeit formal) content in virtue of the premises (a) and (b). Habermas thus credits the moral point of view with content-giving premises (that persons must be respected and that their interests must matter)—premises that D_{FN} does not yet contain. Habermas does of course say that D_{FN} can be specified so as to yield the principle of morality.[40]

But where in *BFN* is this promissory note cashed in? Habermas mentions William Rehg's attempts to derive at least U, though not D, from presuppositions of argumentation but it is not clear to what extent Habermas endorses those attempts.[41]

2. *Whence the identity of the moral point of view?* If discourse ethics is a proceduralization of the moral point of view—(a) and (b)—then the original set of principles of discourse ethics—U and D—must be true to this view. The principle of dialogic universalizability (U) came close to capturing (b), equal consideration of the interests of all. And the distinctive principle of an ethics of discourse (D) came close to capturing (a), equal respect for everyone. But whereas the initial principle D was expressly meant to be a *moral* principle, D_{FN} now is not. Where Habermas in *BFN* now speaks of "the principle of morality" he is referring to U. So in *BFN* Habermas retains U— although its introduction remains gratuitous because nowhere in *BFN* (nor elsewhere) does Habermas provide U with a proper grounding. More disturbing though is another observation: U captures only part of the moral point of view. And D_{FN} cannot contribute what U fails to provide, namely (a), equal respect for everyone. So either the moral point of view Habermas describes in *BFN* is not the moral point of view he describes in previous writings. Or somewhere along the line in *BFN* there must be an argument furnishing D_{FN} with the moral surplus of the initial D. I can detect no such argument.

3. *Whence categoricity?* D_{FN} is a pragmatic definition of validity of action norms. Moreover, D_{FN} can be employed as a test for the validity of action norms. What D_{FN} cannot do, however, is command anything. D_{FN} does not oblige anybody to do anything. D_{FN} is not an imperative. Now if it were an adequacy condition for any normative moral theory to contain at least one imperative one might wonder as to the adequacy of discourse ethics. Yet what seemed clear to Immanuel Kant need not therefore be true. Maybe the idea of an unconditional moral ought or, for that matter, the idea of a categorical imperative cannot be redeemed so if we want to retain the idea of a rational morality at all we will have to do without. Given Habermas's frank inclusion of interests, and Kant's specification of "categorical" imperatives as those that obligate regardless of interests, it seems perhaps forced to strap Habermas with the attempt to generate categorical imperatives. However, Habermas has repeatedley and expressedly situated his version of discourse ethics as firmly within the deontological tradition of Kantian ethics. Should we conclude that this is, or has been, a self-misunderstanding on Habermas's part? These are deeply controversial issues. All the more so since Habermas seems to embrace a Kantian conception of the rational will and of practical reason as the source of imperatival obligation.[42]

4. *Cheapening morality?* I find Habermas's view unsatisfying and *ad hoc* where he contrasts postconventional morality[43] and law so that law comes out

as both a system of cultural knowledge and as an action system while morality comes out as merely cultural knowledge.[44] If morality were only a cognitive resource, as Habermas suggests, for correct judgment of the morally right and the morally wrong without substantive motivational links to rational conduct then why care about morality at all? *Pace* Habermas, it is not true psychologically that intellectually sublimated forms of morality must be "motivationally weak" owing to the cognitivism of such forms of morality.[45] Nor is it true sociologically that the practical reality such forms of morality gain is limited to their implementation in the personality system. Postconventional morality can be an indispensable part of powerful social movements.[46] And if the legitimacy of modern law rests "on a postconventional level" of justification in that its validity depends on arguments which, as Habermas maintains, appeal to an irreducible moral component alongside pragmatic and axiological components of legitimate law, then why not conceive of rational (i.e., "postconventional") morality as extending into, or loading into, modern (i.e., "postmetaphysical") law?

In order to think of postconventional morality as extending modern law in, for instance, the domain of human rights, it is not at all necessary to reduce law and juridical legitimacy to morality and moral rightness. Habermas is so anxious to avoid such reductionism that he juxtaposes morality and law as separate branchings in the sociocultural evolution of normative orders, that is, as coordinated yet essentially different normative orders.[47] Its functionalist sociological plausibility notwithstanding, Habermas's *bifurcation thesis* of law and morality is unsatisfactory as a thesis about the justificatory relations that link law and morality. Even if treating law and morality as parallel but unequal phenomena turned out to be the best approach for matters of empirical sociology it still would not follow that this approach served best concerning questions of normative justification. At various points in *BFN* it looks as if Habermas has simply substituted an explanatory-descriptive stance for a normative-justifactory stance because he thinks that modern law requires democratic procedures but not normative justification. The "form of law," Habermas says, is a historical *given* in modern societies.[48] However, accepting the form of law as a matter of historical fact cannot eschew the problem of the normative (as opposed to functionalist) rationale of that normative form. It can only kick the problem one step up the ladder. Historically one cannot help to notice that the form of modern law, after all, can exist in a wide range of societies with extremely different political configurations, for instance, in authoritarian states like Singapore. There does not seem to be any necessary (i.e., conceptual) link between the form of modern law and radical democracy. Or if there is, Habermas has failed to provide it. In any case, the specifically democratic configuration of the law-giving process cannot dispense with normative questions—now with regard to the normative rationale of democratic political arrangements themselves. A distinctively democratic configuration of the political process[49] is not self-justifying simply in virtue of its being distinctively democratic.

From a vantage point within discourse ethics, modern law has a moral dimension in that it is a way of coping with the very paradoxes of cooperation (free-rider problems and prisonerdilemma situations) that postconventional morality creates, as Karl-Otto Apel has shown.[50] This (normative) account is obviously different from Habermas's (functionalist) account of how law can compensate "cognitive" and "motivational uncertainty" of rational (postconventional) morality.[51] An in-depth exploration of the difference between Habermas's nonnormative account and Apel's normative account of the law-morality relation is an important task that I must leave for another occasion.

Notes

I thank Kenneth Westphal for linguistic help and for valuable comments.

1. "From the vantage point of discourse theory, the functions of the legislature, judiciary, and administration can be differentiated according to forms of communication and the corresponding patterns of argumentation" (*BFN*, 192).

2. "Like the postconventional level of justification itself—the level at which substantial ethical life dissolves into its elements—this principle certainly has a normative content inasmuch as it explicates the meaning of impartiality in practical judgments. However, despite its normative content, it lies at a level of abstraction that is still neutral with respect to morality and law, for it refers to action norms in general" (*BFN*, 107).

3. This principle is not stated very clearly anywhere in *BFN*; see *BFN*, 110. The gist of it is that the law must be such as to allow politically autonomous citizens to be authors of the laws they must obey as addressees.

4. For Jürgen Habermas's original dichotomy, see "Wahrheitstheorien," in *Vorstudien und Ergänzungen zur Theorie des kommunikativen Handelns* (Frankfurt, Germany: Suhrkamp, 1984), p. 176. For his revised, more complete typology, see *The Theory of Communicative Action*, vol. 1, p. 23. Habermas distinguishes five basic types of argumentation (theoretical, practical, aesthetic, therapeutic, and explicative).

5. See the diagnosis of "vestiges of subject-centered reason" in U in William Rehg, *Insight and Solidarity: The Discourse Ethics of Jürgen Habermas* (Berkeley: University of California Press, 1994), pp. 231–244.

6. Habermas, "Discourse Ethics: Notes on a Program of Justification," in *Moral Consciousness and Communicative Action* (Cambridge: Massachusetts Institute of Technology Press, 1990), p. 65.

7. Ibid., p. 66; a variant of D that has come to serve as the standard formulation of D can be found on p. 93: "Only those norms can claim to be valid that meet (or

could meet) with the approval of all affected in their capacity as participants in a practical discourse." Note that the conjunctive verb phrase "could meet" is ambiguous in that it could be taken to mean that for all affected people S1 . . . Sn, (a) if they are participants in a practical discourse about N, *then* they *will accept* N; *or* (b) *if* they are participants in a practical discourse about N, *then it is possible* for them to accept N.

8. "The aim of a practical discourse is to come to a rationally motivated agreement about the problematic rightness claims [for norms of action], an agreement that is not a product of external or internal constraints on discussion but solely of the weight of evidence and argument," Thomas McCarthy, *The Critical Theory of Jürgen Habermas* (Cambridge: Massachusetts Institute of Technology Press, 1978), p. 312.

9. "I have introduced U as a rule of argumentation that makes agreement in practical discourses possible whenever matters of concern to all are open to regulation in the equal interest of everyone," Habermas, "Discourse Ethics," p. 66.

10. 'U' and 'D' refer to principles introduced prior to *BFN*, and the subscript $_{FN}$ for the principles introduced in *BFN*.

11. Note that this validity formula clears up the ambiguity noted in D (see note 7) in favor of the second option (b).

12. "I understand 'action norms' as temporally, socially, and substantively generalized behavioral expectations" (*BFN*, 107).

13. D_{FN} supposedly "expresses the meaning of postconventional requirements of justification" (*BFN*, 107). Unfortunately, Habermas does not sufficiently explain his concept of a"postconventional level of justification" for action norms. Is a postconventional (as opposed to merely conventional) level of justification a level of justification where reasons that appeal to authoritative cultural traditions ones that are ruled out as justifying reasons for ought-claims? Does a postconventional level of justification imply a postconventional level of moral thinking? If a postconventional level of moral thinking, in Lawrence Kohlberg's sense of a prior-to-society perspective on moral obligation, were contained in Habermas's notion of a postconventional level of justification for action norms then Habermas could hardly claim D not to be a moral principle. These questions make it necessary to look more closely, in section 4.1, at Habermas's notion of a postconventional level of justification.

14. See *Justification and Application*, pp. 76ff. There Habermas maintains against Karl-Otto Apel that "an ultimate justification of ethics is neither possible nor necessary" (p. 84). See similar reservations already in "Discourse Ethics" where Habermas rejects the burdens of proof associated with "transcendental arguments," helps himself to what he considers to be lean "transcendental-pragmatic" arguments, and rejects Apel's theory of such arguments (namely, the theory of performative self-contradictions) without however providing any alternative theory of "transcendental-pragmatic arguments" (pp. 82ff.). See Apel, "The Problem of Philosophical Fundamental Grounding in Light of a Transcendental Pragmatic of Language," reprinted in *After Philosophy: End or Transformation?*, eds. K. Baynes, et. al, (Cambridge: Massachusetts Institute of Technology Press, 1987).

15. "This formulation [of D_{FN}] contains some basic terms that require elucidation" (*BFN*, 107).

16. See *BFN*, 23-25, 36f., 26, 60, and 95.

17. *BFN*, 96.

18. See *BFN*, 98, where Habermas confounds historical preponderance as a matter-of-fact with the superior rational status as a matter of justification: "It is here, at the level of personality and knowledge, that the logic of ethical and moral questions first asserted itself, such that alternatives to the normative ideas [of autonomy and self-realization] dominating modernity could no longer be justified in the long run." On Rawls, see *BFN*, 59.

19. "Like the postconventional level of justification itself—the level at which substantial ethical life dissolves into its elements—this principle [D_{FN}] certainly has a normative content inasmuch as it explicates the meaning of impartiality in practical judgments" (*BFN*, 107). D_{FN} "simply explicates 'the point of view from which action norms can be *impartially grounded*'" (Rehg, *Insight and Solidarity*, p. 30f.).

20. "Thou shalt not kill," for instance, is a general deontic judgment expressing that under any circumstance everybody is to refrain from killing anybody.

21. I say "intentional content" rather than "propositional content" because I am not convinced that the content of expressions used in order to express what someone is to do (e.g., "that passengers to Frankfurt buy tickets before they enter the trains") is best analyzed as a proposition.

22. See *BFN*, 107 and note 2.

23. I disregard for now the ambiguity pointed out in note 7.

24. See Habermas's paraphrase of the concept of rational discourse; *BFN*, 107f.

25. See *BFN*, 158-165. This part of *BFN* recapitulates sections of his article "On the Pragmatic, Ethical and Moral Employments of Practical Reason," in *Justification and Application*.

26. M. Kettner, "Habermas über die Einheit praktischer Vernunft. Eine Kritik," in *Pragmatischer Rationalität*, ed. Axel Wüstehube (Würzburg: Königshausen and Neumann, 1995).

27. *BFN*, 160f.

28. See A. MacIntyre, *Whose Justice? Which Rationality?* (Notre Dame: University of Notre Dame Press, 1989); and G. Skirrbekk, "Rationality and Contextuality," in *Rationality and Modernity: Essays in Philosophical Pragmatics* (Oslo: Scandinavian University Press, 1993), pp. 261-308.

29. See Charles Taylor, *Sources of the Self* (Cambridge: Harvard University Press, 1989), pp. 3–110 and 495–520.

30. A more recent example is provided by the battle of interpretations that surrounded the United Nations adoption of an action program addressing the problem of world population (overpopulation?) and development (underdevelopment?). Another example is the perennial "abortion debate." A third example the crisscrossing interpretations of the "nature of the problem" in debates about symptoms of Athe environmental crisis." I do not think that all rational persons with ecological and animal welfare concerns will have to agree to having their concerns categorized as "ethical" where this means (as in Habermas's categories it does) that what is at stake are particularistic values and not justice (see *BFN*, 165, where ecological problems are relegated to ethical discourse).

31. Susan Hurley, *Natural Reasons* (New York: Oxford University Press, 1989).

32. "equal respect for each person and equal consideration for the interests of all" (*BFN*, 97).

33. It should be noted, however, that Habermas sometimes couches the very idea of discourse ethics in terms of impartiality (see "Moral Consciousness and Communicative Action," in *Moral Consciousness and Communicative Action*, p. 122: "[Discourse ethics] establishes a *procedure* based on presuppositions [of] the impartiality of the process of judging."

34. Bernard Gert, *Morality* (New York: Oxford University Press, 1988), p. 80.

35. Ibid., p. 82.

36. Threatening someone beyond mutually conceded bounds disrupts the discursive space anyway. To develop this point would carry us too far afield here. See Apel, "Das Problem des offen strategischen Sprachgebrauchs" (manuscript, 1994).

37. For a discussion of some additional principles, see Kettner, "Kommunikative Vernunft, Gefühle, und Gründe," in *Auge und Affekt. Wahrnehmung und Interaktion* (Frankfurt, Germany: Fischer, 1995).

38. See Audun Ofsti, "Ist diskursive Vernunft nur eine Sonderpraxis?" in *Abwandlungen. Essays zur Sprachphilosophie und Wissenschaftstheorie* (Würzburg: Königshausen and Neumann, 1994), pp. 139–157.

39. For an attempt to flesh out this argument by drawing on Habermas's early views about "the ideal speech situation" as well as on Apel's transcendental-pragmatic approach, see Kettner, "Scientific Knowledge, Discourse Ethics, and Consensus Formation on Public Policy Issues," in *Science, Politics, and Morality*, ed. R. von Schomberg (Dordtrecht, Netherlands: Kluwer, 1992), pp. 161–180.

40. "The moral point of view first results when one specifies the general discourse principle for those norms that can be justified if and only if equal consideration is given to the interests of all those who are possibly involved" (*BFN*, 108).

41. *BFN*, 109.

42. See "Morality and Ethical Life," in *Moral Consciousness and Communicative Action*.

43. In the sense of the term made familiar by Kohlberg.

44. See *BFN*, 79, 107, and 113f.

45. "A principled morality thus depends on socialization processes that meet it halfway by engendering the corresponding agencies of conscience, namely, the correlative superego formations. Aside from the weak motivating force of good reasons, such a morality becomes effective for action only through the internalization of moral principles in the personality system" (*BFN*, 113-114); for a summary of empirical psychological findings on the relation of moral judgment and moral action, see Fritz Oser and Wolfgang Althof, *Moralische Selbstbestimmung* (Stuttgart, Germany: Klett-Cotta, 1992).

46. For an overview of the role of ethics in Latin-American liberation theology, see J. Brechtken, "Philosophische Ethik in der neueren Theologie," in *Die Vertkrise des Menschen*, ed. N. Huppertz (Meisenheim: Anton Hain, 1979); Enrique Dussel, "Auf dem Weg zu einem philosophischen Nord-Süd Dialog" in *Transzendentalpragmatik*, eds. A. Dorschel et al.; Apel, "Diskursethik als Verantwortungsethik," in *Ethik und Befreiung*, ed. P. Fornet-Betancourt (Aachen, Germany: Concordia, 1990); Cornell West, *The Ethical Dimension of Marxist Thought* (New York: Monthly Review Press, 1979); and Eduardo Mendieta, "Marxism in a Post-Communist and Post-Colonial World," *American Philosophical Association Newsletter* 93 (1994): 5–12.

47. In *BFN*, Habermas elaborates this point sociologically as the "co-originality" of law and morality; see *BFN*, 104f. The idea of branching or bifurcation of law and morality is a corollary of this co-originality thesis.

48. For Habermas's definition of modern law, see *BFN* 79, and 104. "The legal form is in no way a principle one could "justify," either epistemically or normatively" (*BFN* 112). On this premise Habermas proceeds to a functionalist sociological account of modern law (113f.). This account raises a conceptual difficulty that Habermas fails to notice: How is it possible for law and morality to stand as relata in a "complementary relation" with one relatum requiring normative justification and the other relatum not admitting of normative justification?

49. As outlined in *BFN*, chapter 7, "Deliberative Politics."

50. Apel, "Diskursethik vor der Problematik von Recht und Politik," in *Zur Anwendung der Diskursethik in Politik, Recht und Wissenschaft*, eds. Apel and Kettner (Frankfurt, Germany: Suhrkamp, 1992), pp. 29–60.

51. See *BFN*, 114f. At *BFN*, xl, Habermas dismisses Apel's approach as "normatively strained." By the same token, Habermas's approach could be chided for normative idleness.

10

The Erosion of Our Value Spheres: The Ways in which Society Copes with Scientific, Moral, and Ethical Uncertainty

René von Schomberg

Introduction

In this chapter, I will discuss the current social reaction to the ecological crisis and the ways in which society reacts to technological risks, which can be understood primarily as a reaction to scientific and moral or ethical uncertainty. I will first clarify what is meant by scientific and moral or ethical uncertainty. I will then contrast Max Weber's differentiation of science, law (*Recht*) and morality in the modern world with the process of dedifferentiation of these value spheres, a trend that can be observed in the present-day context of the ecological crisis and technological risks. We shall see that social contradictions emerge in the functional relationships between these value spheres, and that such contradictions go hand in hand with these value spheres or contexts of discourse either losing their original function or becoming transformed. Science forfeits its role as a functional authority and becomes a strategic resource for politics. Law becomes a basic constituent of an amoral form of negotiation, which can no longer be properly grasped in terms of legal categories. Morality is transformed into fear, and economics yields unprofitable practices. I will in conclusion attempt to open up the moral and ethical dimension of how to deal with uncertainty with the help of discourse theory (Apel, 1988; Habermas, 1996), as well as outline a possible solution.

Scientific and Moral Uncertainty

I will first discuss the ecological crisis and how society handles technological risks in the context of scientific uncertainty or scientific ignorance in

219

general. In 1976, the American climatologist Stephen Schneider published a best-seller about the threat of a new ice age, a hypothesis on which there was a consensus among certain sections of the scientific community. Less than a decade later, scientists agreed that another sort of climatic catastrophe was imminent: the greenhouse effect. Schneider's second best-seller, *Global Warming*, appeared in 1989. Once again, the author refers to a consensus among a section of the scientific community interested in publicity, but this time he is describing the well-known hypothesis that a greenhouse effect would ensue, something put forward as early as 1896 by Arrhenius, who cited the same reasons, but whose work fell on deaf ears. Such initial consensus is by no means cast in stone since one thing is clear: we will always have an incomplete knowledge of the crucial factors that would enable us to predict with certainty whether the greenhouse effect will or will not occur. We are then faced with the following dilemma: should we wait until a consensus has been reached among scientists, which will probably arise at too late a date, if it arises at all? Or must the public and those responsible for decision making rely on the one-sided hypothetical perspectives put forward by one individual scientific discipline—a commitment that appears more or less arbitrary, given the various scientific alternatives that can be found in political debate?

This kind of integrative perspective enables us to see that the individual disciplines, as they advance, are generating more and more knowledge on a small number of details, or microfields. However, they would appear to have to leave certain crucial questions unanswered since discussing ecological questions scientifically means attempting to understand open systems. As a result, certain epistemological viewpoints can be considered true only if we assume the existence of more or less plausible presuppositions, which we nevertheless cannot assume are exhaustive. Climatological and ecological theories cannot be applied as forecasts as if they were based on proven empirical, nomological statements. Rather, they are best put to use in explaining changes after the fact.

Taking the example of the discourses of science, the politics of science, and of politics itself on the ecological consequences of the deliberate release of genetically modified organisms into the environment, I have shown elsewhere that transferring issues that are epistemically conceivable in the context of politics to the level of science causes them to be inappropriately translated into a discourse on truth (see Schomberg 1993). This is expressed, for example, in the translation of prospective plausibility claims (that cannot be formalized) into predictions containing a probability value,[1] in the translation of illustrative data into proof,[2] and in the transformation of dangers into risks.[3] Through this process, technological risks receive a one-sided scientific definition, which becomes a resource utilized often by different interest groups in social debate. This kind of perspectivism robs science of its functional authority. It no longer serves to disencumber political discourse, but instead constitutes a strategic resource that one simply *has to* possess. The macabre discussion on the number of casualties resulting from the Chernobyl catastrophe (at the very beginning ranging from 35 (actual death toll at the site) to thousands; recent estimates put the figure at over 10,000) makes it clear just what such definitions are used to determine: they determine, among other things, the size of potential dangers, whether they can be localized, the social and biological characteristics of those affected as well as the cost and the likelihood that the risks will indeed become reality. These risks are new in character because they are collective and often irreversible, they are neither willingly nor intentionally taken, and cannot be limited either in time or in space, which ultimately makes identifying future victims an impossible task. This last feature corresponds to the principle that it is impossible to insure against such risks, and seems to be the greatest source of concern for the social actors involved (Beck, 1986). Thus, technological risks that are the products of society are given the same status as natural disasters.

Where technological risks are concerned, we are dealing not only with scientific uncertainty, but also with ethical and moral uncertainty. In this regard, technological development has opened up an ethical and moral dimension to discourse. The result is a form of uncertainty that is constituted by the undecided ethical status of animals, for example, or embryos, and/or through the wide gap or contradiction between the justifications of moral theory, on the one hand, and intuitions of ethics and morality, on the other. In other words, our ethical and moral knowledge does not suffice to solve the problems facing us in a manner that satisfies all those affected. Analogously to scientific uncertainty—for example, in the political discourse on the application of future medical technology—our existing (inadequate) ethical and moral knowledge is dominated by utilitarian concepts. The systematic point to be made here is that recognizable uncertainties are unilaterally and inappropriately transformed in political discourse into certainties.

The Diagnosis Proposed by Social Theory

According to Weber, modernity consists, on the one hand, of the differentiation of *value spheres*, which include science, law, and morality. These are the result of a cultural process of rationalization, and stand in contrast to the *systems* of "state" and "economy," which become differentiated as the result of a *societal* rationalization. Modern social theory has not managed to sidestep this differentiation, regardless of whether the spheres are understood as discourses (Jürgen Habermas), systems (Niklas Luhmann), or fields of argumentation (Stephen Toulmin). Traditional sociological theory assumes that value spheres and systems must be understood in terms of their autonomy and mutual independence. They are autonomous in the sense that what Habermas terms the specific validity claims—for example, claims to truth in science, or juridical claims rightness in law, or codes (see Luhmann: true/untrue, justice/injustice)—are generated, selected, and utilized in socially *authorized* discourses by a culture of experts. They are mutually independent in the sense that progress can be achieved within one sphere without this impacting on the results of the other discourses. Abstracting away from all other validity claims within a specific value sphere is necessary and essential for the successful development of that sphere.[4]

Seen from an empirical point of view, however, functional relationships arise between value spheres and systems. I wish to distinguish here between the *procurement function* and the *appellation function* of such relationships. Thus the procurement function of science for politics consists in science procuring authorized data for politics. This data then creates a consensual basis for further political discourses. As a result, science can perform the function of relieving political discourse of having to validate information. The appellation function of politics, for example, in relation to science, consists in the fact that politics calls upon science to tackle the various aspects of overly complex problems and to render them perceivable, or even controllable, in a form that has been reduced, simplified, and tailored to applications. The reaction on the part of society to overly complex problems and uncertainty requires that *all* value spheres of society appropriate the specific aspects of the problem. In this way, for example, *scientific, legal, and ethical* investigations all contribute to defining and classifying the concept of death or of the integrity of the human body. Here we are dealing with concepts that need to be redefined owing to developments in science and technology (i.e., in intensive care medicine).[5] Karl-Otto Apel (1988) has termed the fundamental validity claims of rationality, which can be explained through the presuppositions of the argumentation process, as *nichthintergehbar*, that is, we cannot go back behind them and thus avoid them. In modernity, there is a socially valid concomitant in the value spheres to these validity claims, namely, agencies for uncertain and complex problems that society *cannot sidestep*. Habermas (1996) has carefully tried to avoid thematizing the functional relations as they are actually present in modern societies. However, he has to assume normative premisses concerning the autonomy and independence of these value spheres.

In the following, I shall describe the functional interactions, that is, the existing procurement and appellation functions, of the value spheres and systems. Taking the specific empirical case of the social reaction to scientific and moral or ethical uncertainty in the context of the ecological crisis and the way in which the new technologies are being implemented, we can pinpoint specific contradictions by means of an analysis of such functional interactions.

As we shall see, the individual value spheres and systems, with their special codes or claims, are not capable of reacting adequately to new uncertainties. They display functional losses or appear to work against one another. The contradictions in the procurement and appellation functions can be summarized in the following formula: *the necessary is impossible (procurement function) and the impossible is necessary (appellation function).* This contradiction can be shown to exist in every functional relationship between the value spheres. The ineluctable coding systems of the value spheres "science" (true/false) and "law" (justice/injustice) can no longer, for example, be demonstrated in terms of a *desired output,* one that is moreover essential for society to be able to find an answer to uncertainty. I shall first devote my attention to the functional relationships between science—politics, law—politics, morality—law, the public sphere—politics, and, finally, law—economics as well as science—economics. The phenomena that are in need of description in this context are summarized according to the key words in the adjoining table.

The functional relationship between value spheres and their transformation

Relationship	Procurement Function	Appellation Function	Transformation	Tendency
Science-Politics	Consensus on outgoing data	Perception of phenomena	Science as strategic resource	Instrumentalization of science
Law-Politics	Scope for creating regulations	Potential for imposing sanctions	Law as practiced negotiation	Instrumental position of law
Morality-Law	Consensus on basic norms	Sensitiveness	Morality as fear	Defensive attitude
Public Sphere – Politics	Power	Integration	Desintegration of public decision-making process	Social conflict politics
Law- Economics	Property relations	Liability	Justice as injustice	Legal vacuum and loss of lawfulness
Science- Economics	Means of production	Technical foundation	Science as business undertaking	Economization of science

Science—Politics

The necessary is impossible (= *procurement function*): what needs to be done, namely, to translate scientific information into a basis for consensual political action, is impossible because authorized data cannot always be procured through science. The reason is that a certain degree of dissent cannot be completely eliminated within science itself, that is, it will always exist between the individual disciplines.[6] This gives rise to the structural problem that epistemic plausibilities are inappropriately redefined as probability or truth statements in the manner in which the value spheres normally do this. Politics is constantly anticipating new scientific consensuses that are obtained by assigning tasks to (interdisciplinary) research groups, which then produce data that constitute a fresh batch of explosive material to feed further discussion. Carrying out research on risk often serves, in this context, to provide a political alibi.[7]

The impossible is necessary (= *appellation function*): many of the questions posited by science and that arise within the scope of risk research cannot be answered by science, at least not in a realistically constrained time frame. So-called transscientific questions (Weinberg, 1972) should in particular be mentioned here. While such questions are of a factual nature, we cannot expect that they will be answered because they require experiments that are either ethically impossible to carry out (e.g., human testing) or empirically impractical (i.e., a large number of experiments to verify small probabilities), or because they demand a degree of overall knowledge of a field that can never be attained (i.e., a knowledge of all the factors relevant to the occurrence or nonoccurrence of the greenhouse effect). Such transscientific approaches are not normally included in the portrayals scientists give of the facts. Nonetheless, in situations where a political decision must be made, science may come under pressure from outside to produce "hard facts" in exactly those areas where it is not capable of doing so.[8] Although it is *impossible* to appeal to science directly, it is nonetheless *necessary* if we are dealing with problems that at least partially arise in fields that are the proper jurisdiction of science, and that are in addition so complicated that they cannot be perceived or made into an issue without the help of science. As a reaction to this uncertainty, science reacts to politics by dedifferentiation: it does not take on systematic problems as a challenge, but rather simply clings to the claimed truth of its statements. At this juncture, the function of science, namely, to reduce the complexity of things and to help lay the groundwork for political decisions, turns into its opposite: it becomes a strategic resource of political action. In such a situation, the interest groups participating in the discourse choose to cite those experts who subscribe to their political goals. Thus, in the political arena, scientific data is used as a weapon in the battle for access to information. Instead of serving to disencumber the political discourse, science contributes to burdening it down further by spreading dissent and sparking conflicts within the political arena.

Law-Politics

The necessary is impossible (= *procurement function*): the *necessity* of regulating technology systematically or of coming up with some kind of technology policy (by which I understand something more than indirect control via the market economy) can*not* be met on the basis of normative legal standards, because in the legal system, that which cannot be justified by science appears to be politics. In Germany, the controversy surrounding the fast breeder reactor in Kalkar has shown that the legislative is not duty bound to fulfill a normative function, and the decision regarding the safety of the reactor has been left to politics.[9] There is a strong trend in the field of environmental law to devise a legal form for all eventualities, although this does not guarantee that the desired goal will in fact be attained. Law is being instrumentalized by politics in order to achieve environmental objectives on the basis of norms and "scientific" standards that in practice cannot be controlled or adhered to. In the context of norms being set for dealing with new technologies and risks, the process of implementing the law is characterized by an informal practice of "bargaining." It is not possible for the public authorities to monitor the practices of those who operate all this technology, which means that opportunities to perpetrate environmental crime are inherent in the very structure of the system.

The impossible is necessary (= *appellation function*): citizens must be able to take legal action when their rights are infringed, and infringements of legal norms must be met with sanctions that are there for all to see. It is precisely these fundamental demands upon the legal system that can no longer be guaranteed in view of the problems arising from the uncertainty generated by science. To quote Rainer Wolf (1991): in this respect, law is shown to be antiquated. It is *impossible* to guarantee actionability, but at the same time this is a necessary element of a functioning legal system. The following four observations attest to the reality of this contradiction: (1) The principle that the person who has committed the offense is guilty, as well as the principle of causality, are inapplicable; neither perpetrator nor victim can be identified. For example, it is impossible for a "statistically possible victim" of the Chernobyl catastrophe to take the matter to a European court and provide sufficient evidence that the illness from which she is suffering was caused by the radioactivity released during the accident. When genetic engineering is used in agriculture, the following scenario is conceivable: possible negative results of such technology can no longer be distinguished from those that were caused by previously existing, or conceivably natural, factors.[10] (2) It is no longer possible to take legal action to serve rights because no one can explain their practical significance. As of 1983, the Dutch constitution has stipulated that a clean environment is a basic right. In an era when companies boast that their products sport the label for environmental responsibility (genetic engineering can also be defined as environmentally friendly technology) because the concept of "environmentally friendly" gives them sufficient leeway to do so, it seems that it is impossible in practice to file for fulfillment of such a basic right, even as environmental damage is increasing. (3) The permissible level of risk is correlated with the current level of technology, which means that the application of a precautionary principle is reduced to techno-logical progress. In many Western countries, nuclear law states that reactor safety shall be in accordance with the "state of affairs in science and technology." Thus, the acceptability of risks is equaled by taking the accepted current state of technology as the standard. (4) Social conflict between interest groups, each of which wants to get its *own* definition of risk politically accepted, cannot be overcome under the conditions of equality of power that form the basis for judicial decisions. Instead, these conflicts are handled via social unrest, where inequality of power is the prevailing condition. Moreover, degrees of risk depend on the awareness of individual citizens. However, individual citizens are no longer in a position to recognize the risks, or symptoms of being affected by risks, without having access to expert knowledge.

Morality–Law

The necessary is impossible (= *procurement function*): it is impossible to procure a consensual statutory basis within the context of ethical and moral uncertainty. However, this problem enters the awareness of the majority of the population only *after* technological innovations have already become established facts of society. Nevertheless, it is necessary to procure principles so that a consensus may be reached. Introducing an anticipatory precautionary principle would be a potential candidate. In the meantime, the scene is dominated by a typically knee-jerk, restrictive technological policy that is characterized by the selective and arbitrary perception of ethical and moral problems. The fears that are triggered within the population by the opaque and overwhelming development of technology are a crucial constituent element of this policy. Niklas Luhmann (1989) elucidates the situation as such: "he who has fear, is morally right." Fear is irrefutable, and reactions based on fear may very well be thoroughly understandable and even, for a certain period of time, legitimately fulfill a function. However, the result of allowing fear to transform the value sphere of "morality" is that the latitude for development within the legal system—which is *necessary* if technology is to develop in a constructive way—is replaced by a potential for fear, which functions restrictively at best.

The impossible is necessary (= *appellation function*): As concerns morally and ethically uncertain problems, it has been shown to be *impossible* to pinpoint principles of morality that can be generalized to the extent of creating a basis for legislation that would be compulsory for the general public. Moral dilemmas often arise when several incompatible ethical insights come into conflict with one another. Who could presume to have the last word, for example, in the debate on test-tube babies, or in the discussion on whether women over sixty years of age should also have access to in-vitro-fertilization technologies. The *necessary* development of law cannot appeal to a binding concept of morality, with the result that it simply follows in the footsteps of technological development, which in turn, uncontrollably, produces a fait accompli.

Public Sphere—Politics

The necessary is impossible (= *procurement function*): The contradiction between the public sphere and politics has, in my opinion, been in the public eye for quite some time as a result of the failures of environmental policy. It is *impossible* to procure the *necessary* power for those responsible for making decisions. On the one hand, politicians, who in any case are elected for relatively short terms of office, are unable or unwilling to pursue long-term environmental goals. On the other hand, the decision makers quarrel over how to define the problem and how to implement various measures outside of the domain of government, with science performing a mediating function. In a number of Western countries, the membership of environmental groups far exceeds the total membership in the major political parties. The fact that politics lacks legitimative powers has also extended to the apparatus of government. According to recent results, citizens trust information that has been provided by experts from environmental organizations more than the information they receive from the government.

The impossible is necessary (= *appellation function*): given this position, it is *impossible* for politics to take over the *necessary* task of coordinating the objectives of environmental policy, because the required trust on the part of the public is lacking. Any coordination tends to disintegrate as a result of the social confrontations between various interest groups. While some interest groups can promote the more or less popular environmental objectives, they do not need to concern themselves with transforming these objectives into policy so that they can ignore the problem of the politically and legally coordinative implementation of such objectives. In fact, at different points opposition to all available possibilities (e.g., the use of nuclear energy *and* coal *and* coal gasification *and* hydropower plants) can be mobilized. What is also problematic here is a governmental practice which, through appeals to the public, calls upon its citizens to behave ethically in their choice and use of consumer goods, but at the same time promotes the production of those same goods in a way that will benefit the economy regardless of ethical repercussions. This kind of interaction between state and the various interest groups contributes to an inappropriate moralizing of the problems involved.

Law—Economics

The necessary is impossible (= *procurement function*): the legal system has the task of clarifying the legal basis for property rights as a precondition of a functioning economic system. That such clarification is necessary hardly needed explaining in Germany, in face of the unclarity over ownership of property in former East Germany. However, this relationship between law and property cannot be smoothly transferred onto social discord over the possibility of patenting living organisms within the framework of potentially exploiting biotechnology in business terms in the fields of agriculture and medicine. It is also not applicable to patenting human genes within the scope of the "human genome project," which involves analyzing the total content of human genetic material. It appears impossible here to assert the degree of liability necessary for engaging in economic actions because, on the one hand, it is impossible to justify, scientifically and technically speaking, exactly what constitutes property, as is the case if an as yet unidentified human gene is to be patented. And, on the other, the consequences of using this property cannot as easily be thought through as if genes were real estate.[11]

The impossible is necessary (= *appellation function*): the impossibility of satisfactorily clarifying property rights, or in other words of a *necessary* precondition for economic action, renders the exploitation of genetic engineering for business ends a dubious undertaking. Most patents could be shown to be worthless because in practice they are presumably easy to circumvent. The peculiar compulsion (on the part of scientists) to establish a means of protecting their products with legal patents is also a result of the dedifferentiation of science and the economy. For scientists as well, the possibility of patenting their results and products (in addition to utilizing them for economic gain) functions as a motivation to carry out research. Science, and that which is sub-sidized by the state, is thus guided by economic motives without actually yielding economic practices that turn a profit. Industry need only wait until the results are published of the human genome project, which is receiving unparalleled financial support from the state as being culturally and scientifi-cally legitimate. Industry can then step in selectively and utilize only those patents that have proven to be lucrative. Any social or economic risks there-fore fall only upon the shoulders of the state, and must also be compensated by the state. So, as before, it is possible for human genome projects as a whole to prove economically unsound because none of the participating actors is truly compelled to carry out a cost (risk)- benefit analysis, and to use it to cre-ate a truly economic viable project.[12]

The possibility of establishing a patenting practice, and at the same time privatizing research, contradicts in principle the public availability of scien-tific knowledge within the context of science as a culturally differentiated value sphere. However, if one clings to the conception that genes should be merely mapped within the framework of the human genome project, in other words that they are simply waiting to be "discovered," then the project must be seen as a work of industrial production rather than a cultural undertaking. An interpretation of this nature comes much closer to the actual daily experi-ence of the scientists and subjects employed in the project. The demand that industry carry out and finance the entire undertaking (if it were still willing to do so under these circumstances) would then be logically consistent. This would have the additional advantage that the companies involved would also have to come up with risk calculations, while the scientists can once again devote their attention to deciding which basic questions still need to be clari-fied. The ideological demand by scientists that the human genome be researched "as fast as possible" would quickly disappear from public debate.

Discourse Theory's Evaluation of the Erosion of Value Spheres

The interaction between value spheres and systems that is triggered by the reaction to uncertainty seems to jeopardize the functions of the individual spheres and to call into question the differentiation between them. The inter-dependencies that were just elaborated upon show that value spheres and sys-tems are *eroding*, suffering functional losses and being transformed into their opposites. Reactions to uncertainty require an *unavoidable* coding system for value spheres and systems. This means that for society to cope with this prob-lem, detailed analyses must first be carried out within the value sphere affected solely with respect to truth (science), law, and morality. These codi-fications, for example, the true/false coding of science, cannot be established given the matter at hand; epistemic uncertainties cannot be understood in terms of truth, and moral and ethical uncertainties do not lead to universally applicable moral principles to which the legal system could appeal. However, codifications either ensue despite the uncertainties involved, or are left, undifferentiated, to some value sphere or other. In political discourse, the result is an inappropriate transformation of uncertainty into certainty and a legal vacuum arising with a concomitant lack of coding in the legal system. In this way, the current ecological crisis and new technological risks could trigger a social crisis also bringing the law into disrepute.

Discourse ethics is tailored to the problem of society's handling of uncertainty (Apel, 1988; Habermas, 1983). Discourses are sought where doubt and uncertainty prevail. The basis for the problem of uncertainty only becomes clearly recognizable by mediating all validity claims within a discourse. A discourse is called for precisely when we are confronted with the potential irreversibility of the consequences of proposed decisions. The circle of potential discourse participants, the need for available information, and the relevancy of the problem to the future are all factors here. Although discourse theory does not have any specific relevance to a particular field (see Apel and Kettner 1992, pp. 317–348), it is based on a specific starting point: the principle that conclusive arguments are simply not available. Discourse theory is ambivalent where the problem of uncertainty is concerned. It requires that all relevant validity claims be addressed and differentiated. At the same time, it demands that the various validity claims be integrated *after the fact*—in other words, after passing through the value spheres—and normatively opposes any universalization of one particular aspect of validity (e.g., it opposes utilitarianism, moralization, or aestheticization) as well as the use of one value sphere instrumentally or functionally to serve another. If discourse ethics is understood as the ethics of responsibility (in the sense of its so-called Part B justifications for the problems of application), then according to Apel neither law nor politics falls beyond its range of application (Apel and Kettner 1992, pp. 29–61). Law, says Apel, establishes itself between morality and politics as a responsible intermediary between the two. In contrast to legal positivism, stress is laid here upon the dependence of politics and law on morality, although there is of course no intention of moralizing politics or law (unlike the various versions of an environmental ethics, provided that this can be taken seriously as a philosophical ethics in the first place).[13]

Athough the reaction to uncertainty is well-suited to the point of departure taken by discourse ethics, the former yields no arguments for the application of latter. In my opinion, the question posed by moral theory as to the "best ethics" or the "best moral theory" cannot be answered by pointing to a practice in which the best ethics or theory *would* function. As a consequence, what is of prime importance is the morally justifiable demand that differentiated validity claims be mediated both procedurally and integratively. Against the backdrop of the contradictions discussed here, problems of legitimation arise, characterized by a state which, on the one hand, in its planning, cannot concur with opposing interest groups on how to interpret situations. On the other, it is confronted by citizens who are protesting against being overwhelmed by innovation processes that they are not allowed to decide upon.

The problem of legitimation and the phenomena just mentioned are only partially offset by the tendency of the administration to become increasingly involved in bargaining and negotiating processes with social groups. While a number of sociologists of science regard the extension of this kind of social consensus itself as a solution, in my opinion not much can be expected in terms of the quality of these consensuses, which, after all, arise in the context of strategic action and under conditions of unequal power. As I see it, what is far more important is whether there can be a *just procedural solution* to the historically novel problem of decision making under conditions of uncertainty. That we might need exactly this kind of procedural solution is, in my view, a consequence of the fact that in modern societies there are no pre-given notions that would clarify *which actors are to participate in which way* during decision-making processes in the context of such uncertainties. However, this question has not yet appeared on the political agenda.

The historically novel contradictions that exist between the value spheres cannot simply be eliminated through political decisions. The political system must react independently of the subjective will of political actors; for example, to the ongoing stream of information generated by science. In this way, a successful response to uncertainty is not a question of what the better political option might be, but rather a structural reaction to the growing problem of uncertainty, which could usher in a new evolutionary stage of social development. The essential hypothesis informing my analysis is that the need for differentiation of authorized discourses stands at odds with the impossibility of such differentiation on the level of the actual problems. There are two social responses to this: *dedifferentiation will ensue* within the value spheres and systems, or the various insights of the specialized discourses will be *subsequently integrated* via an intermediary. The first possibility (dedifferentiation within the value spheres and systems) leads, in my opinion, to regressive tendencies and to transformations of the value spheres: science surrenders its role as a functional authority and becomes a strategic resource for politics; law becomes a constituent element for an immoral negotiation practice that can no longer be correctly understood using categories of legality; morality is transformed into fear, and economics yields unprofitable practices. *The second possibility appears to be the progressive one, as I see it.* Here, the question arises whether democratic will formation can be extended to the problems of ecological crisis and technological risks. It is a matter of whether the social strife among interest groups can be settled through just, democratic decision-

making processes. This seems to bring with it the disadvantage of slow decision making. Often our attention is called to the supposed failure of Western
democracies; a plea is often sounded for the faster and politically more neutral decision-making capabilities of an elite group of specialized experts, for
example, in the second major report of the Club of Rome. However, this plea
fails to recognize that the problem is characterized by social argument. A democratic solution, if it were to be found, would also be more efficient. In other
words, from a social point of view the reaction to uncertainty oscillates
between progression and regression. Unlike systems theory and constructivist
approaches in sociology, discourse theory has the advantage of being able to
deliver normative justifications.

Seen from this angle, I tend to favor promoting the institutionalization of
discursive procedures, which must be organized for the specific case of uncertainty. They must also substitute for the functional relationship between the
value spheres and systems, as well as counter the contradictions and dedifferentiation of the latter. Within the scope of a *discursive procedure*, those interests that could hold universal appeal could be identified, thus preventing them
from falling victim to social conflict. In order to achieve this, a number of
general norms that can be justified by discourse theory would have to be given
the authority of administrative law:

- An information law entailing the right to obtain, and the obligation to
  provide, information
- A selective suspension of the majority principle, because this principle
  can no longer guarantee that political decisions remain open to revision; It might be possible to ensure the reversibility of decisions, for
  example, by approving only those epistemic risks that have a particular, limited time frame
- The elimination of unfavorable possibilities for action, which could
  give rise to irreversible damage or imply irreversible decisions

If a discursive procedure were integrated into the political planning
process and a procedural form of law, the following would become plausible:

1. A procedure for recognizing scientific dissent reduces scientific information being used as a strategic resource. This would also serve to contain the
tendency to politicize or instrumentalize science and law inappropriately.

2. Law can have a normative impact if discursive procedures can formally employ a recognized preventative principle as a means of fostering consensus. This would thus involve partially breaking away from a model of law
that is oriented toward conflict in favor of one that is oriented toward consensus. This would make it possible for significant decisions to be made based
on laws (as opposed to the current areas not subject to legal regulation and to
the loss of the meaningfulness of basic rights). Discursive procedures should

contribute to breaking up the usual sequence of actions—which involves first acquiring knowledge (in other words, the consensual use of science), and then making decisions—by applying anticipatory reason, which can create political regulations as a form of caution.

3. Pragmatic conditions, which constitute proof, are different in a scientific context than in the contexts of political planning. From a scientific point of view, the dangers of genetic engineering, for example, can*not* be refuted by pointing out that there have been no perceivable accidents for some years now. However, this is perfectly possible in the political arena, and even reasonable given certain conditions. However, in the case of social conflict concerning the consequences of officially controlled experiments in which genetically modified organisms are released into the environment, in view of epistemic uncertainty it can be questioned whether this pragmatic condition of the line of argumentation is indeed reasonable. Therefore, I suggest that we consider data that have arisen in this context not as normal scientific facts, but rather as a source of information for a mediating discourse in the framework of discursive procedures. Now, it would be possible to create a juridical basis for a pragmatic condition that has been altered in this way; it would have to replace the previous dictum according to which decisions regarding risks must correspond to the current level of science and technology. We can simply agree, pragmatically speaking, that *evidence* is not being established here, but rather that informed discourse is being enriched. Such a change in pragmatic conditions could preserve in fruitful discourses the rational core at the heart of contemporary activist protest (among others, destroying experiments involving genetically modified organisms).

4. The discursive procedure would have to be able, subsequently, to integrate the differentiated validity aspects of the various systems and value spheres. To this end, the state could create a legal framework for initiating talks among the typically antagonistic interest groups in a manner analogous to institutionalized collective bargaining between employees and employers. The state determines the rights and duties of the participants, that is, as concerns the procurement of information and scheduling. The talks could provide the scope for articulating common interests, which serves to keep the participants at the negotiating table. Simultaneously, the business world would get a glimpse of what might be desired and profitable from the point of view of society. Consumers and environmental organizations can draw ethical boundaries and help to determine in which direction technology will advance. The state would have to ensure that conditions exist for fair self-regulation, and in particular ensure that weaker parties would have access to adequate power. Perhaps an equivalent could be devised to the right to strike, an essential element of wage policy. Consumer boycotts have already gained importance as a means of pressure with respect to food products that have been genetically

modified. Clearly, such procedures can also clearly sow dissent. A minimum level of consensus among participants (e.g., on the willingness to compromise) is a precondition here—however, this is also true in the case of parliamentary will formation.

Luhmann (1991) has diagnosed a gap between those participating in decision making and those affected by possible damage. What I have been describing, however, is a more profound disintegration, because in my opinion it is not possible to distinguish between decision makers and those affected by technological development. They cannot even be identified as a group. We are faced with the impossible task of coordinating incompatible political, economic, and ethical objectives. At the same time, this very task appears to be necessary from the *abstract* perspective of making decisions that are valid within a prescribed period of time. The solution that I propose lays emphasis on expanding and reforming the scope of administrative law rather than on renewing constitutional rights (as Hans Jonas has suggested). Renewing constitutional rights would only further accentuate the diminished significance (and function) of law, and in any case are not necessary in the first place, because ecological objectives can already be considered as constitutional rights, in light of the fact that endangering the ecosystem also poses a threat to the survival of humanity.[14]

As I see it, in functionally differentiated societies, the only domain in which an ethics of responsibility can be applied is the sphere of a public that engages in critical thinking. The actors within this sphere must be truly free to act according to precepts of action that they have chosen themselves without having to limit themselves to some code or other belonging to only one value sphere and without having to concern themselves with whether their actions or the goals of their actions can be coordinated and achieved politically or legally. The possibility of making a normative appeal to the public is certainly of consequence for discourse theory. However, such an appeal does not clarify the problems of mediating between politics and the public, but instead allows them to be formulated in the first place. For example, the mere demand that the discourse be strategy-free would be highly quite problematic in terms of the ethics of responsibility: can one assume contrafactually that everyone would be able to accept the outcome of a given discourse? Many would dismiss delaying the decision-making process through discourse as unethical, or misunderstand it as being simply another dilatory strategy. The most important question is whether the process of reaching consensus *within* the scope of the rationality of political planning, driven forward with great effort over the years, can be partially replaced by a discourse involving the general public. Indeed, the political planning process would also have to be reconstructed as a discursive learning process, which the general public is hardly in a position to understand. At this point, the question arises as to what balance can justifiably be struck between the benefit of giving decisions more legitimacy by drawing social interest groups into the decision-making process and the risk of decreasing the substantive quality of the decisions. This question needs to be examined more closely in empirical terms.

Outlook

Expressed in terms of discourse theory, this loss of function seen among value spheres and system rationalities calls for new institutions. Assessment agencies and official inquiry commissions, can be seen as the (still) inchoate forms taken by discursive procedures, and also as the result of a social learning process. The new institutions would have to function as mediators between the value spheres and systems, acting as a discursive intermediary between differing validity claims. Although developed countries have begun to cultivate such intermediaries for the interface of science and politics, they are almost completely lacking in other areas. The problems discussed also urgently call for the conceptual reform of political planning and law. Discourse theory is continuing to tie its normative hopes to the quality of public opinion formation. Where the latter is concerned, the only thing that can be guaranteed is that truth prevails only to the same degree rational people prevail. However, any state that wished to guarantee more would be adopting a course leading away from democracy.

Notes

1. These probability values have to be constantly adjusted after new events or catastrophes have occurred. This insight has become common knowledge, at least since the Chernobyl disaster.

2. Thus, the results of ongoing experiments with releasing genetically manipulated organisms, should demonstrate the safety of gene technology as such.

3. For more information on how dangers are transformed into risks, see Evers and Nowotny (1987) and Bonss (1990).

4. This characteristic feature of Modernity leaves open the possibility for ambivalence that we may experience, for example, when we describe certain scientific or technical developments as progress, but at the same time perceive them as regressive in terms of ethics or morality. An example of such thought is given by Hannah Arendt in her impressive investigation of the question as to what extent conquering space will affect the status of humanity.

5. Experience has shown that scientists clearly exert more effort in defining these terms than legal scholars.

6. In this context see also the debate on releasing genetically modified organisms into the environment. Bonss, Hohlfeld, and Kollek (1992), Kollek (1993), and von Schomberg (1992).

7. In 1991, research on the dangers to the ecosystem that could arise from releasing genetically manipulated organisms was unable to provide quantitative data based on the then current standing of 284 research projects carried out around the world.

8. Ecologists, for example, must develop very thorough arguments with respect to the ecological consequences of releasing genetically manipulated organisms in order to get past the criticism that enormous expenses for testing would be necessary for a genuine prediction of those consequences. Some are less cautious, though, and demand that an isolated island be used for such tests (see Pimentel, 1987).

9. "The legislative is not obliged by the constitution to decide upon the possible kinds of risks, risk factors, the ways in which such risks shall be ascertained, or to determine fixed tolerance levels." German Constitutional Law 49, 131; quoted from Wolf 1993, p. 407.

10. For a comparison, see the court cases in among others, the Netherlandsand the U.S. Here, farmers claimed that their fields would be genetically contaminated through the use of genetically modified organisms (Dutch daily, N. R. C. Handelsblad, December 18, 1991). Also of interest in this context is a more recent judicial decision in the Netherlands in which compensation was awarded to the daughters of mothers who had been prescribed the hormone DES by their doctors during the fifties (without knowing that it could harm their daughters). This compensation must be financed by the entire pharmaceutical industry, as if it were a party, or collective perpetrator. It is no longer possible to prove the particulars of which manufacturer was responsible for which damages in which cases.

11. Where this in fact does occur, figures of speech result that are as interesting as they are characteristic. At the environmental conference in Rio de Janeiro, representatives from India complained that the Western countries are stealing the genes of the Third World—as if it were a fact that genes can also be property.

12. As for the rest, this kind of analysis could hardly be carried out because it would be difficult to weigh the hypothetical advantages (which, for ideological reasons, are often presented as concrete advantages) against the hypothetical disadvantages. However, in the current situation, if individual details of the hypothetical advantages become concrete, these could be used from the biased perspective of industry in order to promote genetic engineering.

13. Apel was right in warning us not to moralize law and politics directly as this could lead to a totalitarian politicization of society, the consequences of which are a lesson everyone should have learned from Stalinism. According to Apel, the impor-

tance of the differentiation of law, morality, and politics in the evolution of society is revealed through legal standards backed up by means of coercion. This is made possible by employing coercive force, limited and differentiated in the constitutional state, and thus relieving citizens of the burden of applying force that is morally justified. The individual citizen also no longer needs to be concerned with the political necessity of responsible mediation between moral, consensual behavior, and strategic behavior. Thus, modern citizens find themselves in the situation, on the one hand, of being able to act morally without taking risks; on the other hand, the state cannot require them to do so. It is part of the logic of Modernity that citizens can validly politically claim that they must be allowed to act morally without incurring punishment or other sanctions. This demand is on the political agenda, but has, of yet, in no way been fulfilled, the reason being that small steps taken by citizens toward acting in an environmentally friendly way still always prove to have economic disadvantages.

14. How much or how little Apel's ideal teleological supplementary principle of discourse ethics contributes to structuring a reasonable way of handling the uncertainty described here is a question I will have to take up elsewhere.

References

Apel, Karl-Otto and Matthias Kettner, eds., *Zur Anwendung der Diskursethik in Politik, Recht und Wissenschaft*. Frankfurt, Germany: Suhrkamp, 1992.

———. *Diskurs und Verantwortung*. Frankfurt, Germany: Suhrkamp, 1988.

Beck, Ulrich. *Die Risikogesellschaft*. Frankfurt, Germany: Suhrkamp, 1986.

Bonß, Wolfgang. "Zwischen Emanzipation und Entverantwortlichung—Zum Umgang mit den Risiken der Gentechnologi." In *Herstellung der Natur? Stellungnahmen zum Bericht der Enquete-Kommission "Chancen und Risiken der Gentechnologie*," edited by K. Grosch, P. Hampe, and J. Schmidt. Frankfurt, Germany: Campus, 1990. pp. 183–205.

Bonß, Wolfgang et al., eds. "Risiko und Kontext. Zur Unsicherheit in der Gentechnologie." In *Technik und Gesellschaft, Jahrbuch 6: Großtechnische Systeme und Risiko*, edited by G. Bechmann and W. Rammert. Frankfurt, Germany: Campus, 1992, pp. 141–174.

Evers, Adelbert and Helga Nowotny. *Über den Umgang mit Unsicherheit. Die Entdeckung der Gestaltbarkeit von Gesellschaft*. Frankfurt, Germany: Suhrkamp, 1987.

Habermas, Jürgen. *Between Facts and Norms*. Cambridge: Massachusetts Institute of Technology Press, 1996.

Kollek, Regine. "Controversies about Risks and their Relation to Different Paradigms in Biological Research." In *Science, Politics and Morality*, edited by R. v. Schomberg. Dordrecht, Netherlands: Kluwer, 1993, pp. 27–41.

Luhmann, Niklas. *Ecological Communication*. Chicago: University of Chicago Press, 1989.

———. *Soziologie des Risikos*. Berlin: De Gruyter, 1991.

Pimental, Donald. "Down on the Farm: Genetic Engineering Meets Ecology." *Technology Review* 1 (1987): 24–30.

Schomberg, René von. "Controversies and Political Decision Making." In *Science, Politics and Morality: Scientific Uncertainty and Decisionmaking*, edited by R. v. Schomberg. Dordrecht, Netherlands: Kluwer, 1993, 7–26.

Weinberg, Alvin. "Science and Trans-Science." *Minerva* 10 (1972): 209–222.

Wolf, Rainer., "Zur Antiquiertheits des Rechts in der Risikogesellschaft." In *Politik in der Risikogesellschaft*, edited by U. Beck. Frankfurt, Germany: Suhrkamp, 1991, pp. 378–424.

IV

Interview

11

A Conversation about Questions
of Political Theory

From Jürgen Habermas, *A Berlin Republic: Writings on Germany*
Trans: Steven Rendall (Lincoln: University of Nebraska Press, 1997)

WHEN YOU ADDRESSED *the Spanish parliament in 1984 you talked about the 'exhaustion of utopian energies.' We live in a time, you said, marked by a 'new impossibility of taking an overall view' and by a negatively invested future* (Die Neue Unübersichtlichkeit). *In our opinion this diagnosis has lost none of its relevance during the past ten years. The fall of so-called 'actually existing socialism' and the end of the Cold War have not led to a peaceful world. Instead we see ourselves confronted by civil wars, racism, new poverty, and almost completely unrestrained destruction of the environment. The hopes that the 'soft' revolution of 1989 instilled in quite a few people—Fukuyama even talked about 'the end of history'—were quickly revealed as delusions. With a view to these problems, in* Between Facts and Norms *you speak of a hope, born of despair, for the beginning of a universalist world order. Moreover, you hold fast to the socialist project. As the quintessential concept of the conditions necessary for an emancipated form of life—about which citizens must reach an understanding among themselves—socialism can be achieved only in the form of radical democracy. In saying this, you turn decisively against any form of utopia as the outline and goal of a fully spelled-out, ideal form of life. What matters in the procedural concept of democracy you have developed is the formal characterization of necessary conditions for the unpredictable forms of a successful life. In the preface to* Between Facts and Norms, *you write about the insight 'that under the sign of an entirely secu-*

'Ein Gespräch über Fragen der politischen Theorie.' *Res Publica* 3 (1994): 36–58 (in Swedish); *Krisis*, no. 57 (1994): 75–85 (in Dutch. The discussion took place in February 1993. The questions were asked by a Swedish colleague, Mikael Carleheden, and a Dutch colleague, René Gabriels.

larized politics a constitutional state is neither obtainable nor maintainable without radical democracy.' But is radical democracy even achievable? The question arises whether the realization of the necessary conditions of a democratic society—for example, equal opportunity for participation—is not too utopian in light of the previously mentioned problems and increasing social complexity. Would you agree with the thesis that the open-ended character of the 'modernist project' does in fact lack a utopian goal, yet cannot get along without utopian energies?

Of course, the thorn of skepticism must have penetrated deeply enough into the normative flesh for us not to end up once again merely arguing for the adoption of lofty democratic principles. As you say yourself: a skeptical evaluation of current world conditions is the background for my reflections. That is why my way can be distinguished from purely normative conceptions such as John Rawls's theory of justice, admirable as it is in itself.

First of all, I am seeking a *reconstructive* analysis, in order to prove what we always already tacitly assume, if we participate in the democratic and constitutional practices that have fortunately taken hold in our countries. A consciousness that has become completely cynical is incompatible with such practices—unless the practices were altered beyond recognition. As soon as the normative substance goes up in smoke—for instance, as soon as people feel they no longer have a chance of getting justice from the courts, as soon as voters no longer believe their voice can in any way influence government policy—law has to be transformed into an instrument of behavior control; and democratic majority decision turns into an inconsequential spectacle of deception and self-deception. A capitulation of constitutional principles in the face of overwhelming societal complexity cannot be ruled out. Should this occur, our concepts of justice and democracy will change, and citizens' normative self-understanding, which still exists in our latitudes today, will undergo a radical transformation. Because such conceptual interconnections explain social facts, it is worthwhile to undertake a reconstruction of the interrelated implications of a legal system that can draw its legitimacy only from the idea of self-legislation.

Secondly, I try to show that this normative self-understanding of our established practices is not from the start illusory. I see these democratic constitutions as so many projects on which legislators, along with the legal and administrative system, work each and every day—and whose continuation is constantly being implicitly fought for in the public political sphere. However, we have to let go of interpretations that have become dear to us, including the idea that radical democracy is a form of self-administering socialism. Only a democracy that is understood in terms of communications theory is feasible under the conditions of complex societies. In this instance, the relationship of center and periphery must be reversed: in my model the forms of communication in a civil society, which grow out of an intact private sphere, along with the communicative stream of a vital public sphere embedded in a liberal political culture, are what chiefly bear the burden of normative expectations. That is why you are right—nothing will change without the intervening, effective, innovative energy of social movements, and without the utopian images and energies that motivate such movements. But that does not mean that theory itself, as in Ernst Bloch's work, must take the place of utopias.

You criticized the republican idea of a radical democracy because, among other things, it cannot account for the inalienably systemic character and peculiar dynamics of politics. According to your view, politics should be analyzed not only in terms of a theory of action, but also in terms of a theory of systems. Popular sovereignty in the sense of self-determination programmed through laws rests on opinion- and will-formation involving communicative action, as well as on a political system directed via the medium of power. This raises the question as to how citizens can influence the political system through processes of opinion- and will-formation without simultaneously impairing the system's inherent dynamics. You developed two models for answering this question. The 'siege model' you proposed in 'Volkssouveränität als Verfahren' (1988), corresponded to the bi-level concept of society in Theory of Communicative Action. *This model implies that citizens besiege the 'political fortress' by means of political discourses that seek to influence processes of judgment and decision making without intending actually to take it over. In* Between Facts and Norms *your starting point is a 'sluice model,' in which the constituted political system consists of a center and a periphery. In order for citizens to influence the center, that is parliament, the courts, and the administration, the communication of influences has to pass from the periphery through the sluices of democratic and constitutional procedures. In the political circulatory system, law is the medium through which communicative power is transformed into administrative power. Now, in what respect does the precise status of this bi-level social model in* Between Facts and Norms *differ from that of the model proposed in* Theory of Communicative Action? *Don't your two metaphors—'siege' and 'sluice'—imply different connections between systems and life-world? According to the 'siege' model, democracy seems to be little more than a way of limiting the imperatives of a capitalist economy and of a paternalistic social state. . . . Doesn't the sluice model permit a much more far-reaching democratization of the economy and of political administration than does the siege model?*

At the time, my purpose in proposing the image of a 'siege' of the bureaucratic power of public administrations by citizens making use of communicative power was to oppose the classic idea of revolution—the conquest and destruction of state power. The unfettered communicative freedoms of citizens are supposed to become effective through—as Rawls says with Kant—the 'public use of reason.' But the 'influence' of the opinions that compete in the political sphere, and communicative power formed by means of democratic procedures on the horizon of the public sphere, can become effective only if they affect administrative power—so as to program and control it—without intending to take it over. On the other hand, the siege model is too defeatist, at least if you understand the division of powers in such a way that administrative and judicial authorities *employing* the law are to have limited access to the grounds mobilized in their full scope by legislative authorities in justifying their decisions. Today, the matters that need regulation are often such that the political legislator is in no position sufficiently to regulate them in advance. In such cases, it is up to administrative and judicial authorities to give them concrete form and to continue their legal development, and these require discourses that have to do with grounding rather than with application. However, to be legitimate, this implicit subsidiary legislation [*Nebengesetzgebung*] also requires different forms of participation—a part of the democratic will-formation must make its way into the administration itself, and the judiciary that creates subsidiary laws must justify itself in the wider forum of a critique of law. In this respect, the sluice model counts on a more far-reaching democratization than the siege model does.

You distinguish between politics as a form of will- and opinion formation, on one hand, and as administration on the other. These two forms of politics correspond to a conceptual division of political power into communicative and administrative power. One of the presuppositions of modern democracies seems to be that parliaments and the political parties are important institutions of will- and opinion-formation. But parliaments are now largely dominated by political parties that are primarily oriented toward the acquisition of power in order to govern. Various sociological studies have shown that the professionalization of politics, the growing gap between representatives and the represented—along with the commercialization of election campaigns— have led modern politicians to adopt a more strategic stance. For that reason, the room for deliberative politics keeps shrinking. To what extent can we still regard parliaments and political parties as institutions of opinion- and will-formation? And confronted by populism from 'above' and 'below'—to use Klaus von Beyme's language—how is it possible to control the political class in the party-state according to the principle of a radical democracy? Doesn't it seem necessary that the political system, precisely in order to maintain its inherent dynamics, be further democratized—that is, that more room for communicative power be created?

My analysis was intended suggest that conclusion. Insofar as political parties have been governmentalized [*verstaatlicht*] in the interim—insofar as their democratic substance has been internally exhausted—they are acting from the point of view of the administrative system within which they have established positions of power that they want to keep. The function they should primarily exercise—namely, the articulation and mediation of the process of shaping political opinion and will—they then fulfill only in the form of advertising campaigns. Thus they come into the public sphere as invaders from outside rather than operating from its center. The various functions the political parties fulfill must be more sharply differentiated. As Lefort rightfully says, in a democracy the symbolic place of politics should remain unoccupied: but it remains vacant only if democratic party leaders are regarded as people's representatives and not as officeholders or as potential administrative chiefs. This requires institutional imagination. The institutional measures that help increase the political parties' 'participation' in the formation of the political will, and could keep them from acting as organs of the state, would have to be in place at all levels—beginning with the organizational part of the constitution and going on to matters relating to plebiscites and even party bylaws.

In your essay 'Technologie und Wissenschaft als Ideologie' you write that since the end of the nineteenth century 'a growing interdependence of research and technology . . . has made science the primary productive power.' Nonetheless, scientific and technological developments are largely excluded from democratic codetermination and control. Decisions reached within the realm of science and technology, and whose transfer can have unforeseeable and sometimes unwanted consequences for all human beings (for example, decisions regarding nuclear power and genetic technology) are only rarely subjected to democratic principles. In view of the tendency for political decisions to become more scientific and the great interest taken by business in technological know-how, the shaping of many areas of society is largely in the hands of experts. We might ask how that definitional power could be democratically controlled and tamed, so as to exclude the threat of an 'expertocracy.' It is worth noting that your early work focused explicitly on topics such as 'the relationship between democracy and technology,' 'scientified political and public opinion,' and 'the danger of an expertocracy'—topics that have no systematic role in your most recently developed model of the political circulation of power. Is there a reason for that? Where would you situate the definitional power of science and technology within your model of the circulation of power? How could and must the danger of an 'expertocracy' be limited?

The differentiation among expert cultures that I described in *Theory of Communicative Action* is accompanied by risks running in the opposite direction—on one hand, the threat of an introverted encapsulation that hinders the spread of cultural knowledge and allows everyday communicative practice to dry up; and on the other, control over decisions that ought to be arrived at democratically exercised by those who understand the issues—that is, the danger of an expertocracy that concerns you. To be sure, the definitional power of science and technology is in this regard a relevant subject. I did not discuss it in my most recent book because today, in contrast to the situation in the 1960s, technocracy theories no longer play a role in the social sciences, and the planning craze and a naive belief in science have evaporated. In the broader public sphere, critical attitudes toward science have almost become the fashion. This shift in the climate of public opinion has had some positive consequences, as the growing awareness regarding the dangers of atomic and genetic technology shows. The evaluation of technological consequences has been effectively thematized in various arenas. In the process, a praxis of counterexpertise has become accepted, which recognizes that science is itself not a neutral authority and that the scientific enterprise is anything but monolithic—it splits into many competing conceptions that are also impregnated with values. These starting points for a politically related alternative science should be further developed and lent more weight in the public sphere and in parliamentary work. There are no questions so specialized that they cannot be translated when it is politically relevant to do so, and even adapted in such a way as to make it possible for the alternatives experts discuss to be rationally debated in a broader public forum as well. In a democracy, expertise can have no political privilege.

In your Theory of Communicative Action *you claim that unresolvable tensions separate capitalism and democracy. The self-understanding of modern societies expressed in democratic constitutional principles implies de jure the primacy of the lifeworld with regard to the subsystem represented by the economy and the state. This primacy, however, is undermined de facto by the neutralization of social inequalities, which are inscribed in capitalism in the form of paternalistic social services provided by the state. Citizens of the state frequently no longer see or rather perceive the possibilities of political participation inherent in citizenship. If we understand correctly, the emphasis in* Between Facts and Norms *is on the axis 'life-world state' rather than on the axis 'life-world/economy.' Compared with your earlier writings, in this book you devote little space to the problem of how the destructive forces of the capitalist economy can be democratically contained. Yet there are indications that the end of actually existing socialism is capable of lending the critique of capitalism a new impetus—as is shown, for instance, by the work of Friedrich Kambartel and Claus Offe on market socialism and a guaranteed basic income. Is your respect for the inherent systematic dynamics of a market-driven economy compatible with your conception of a deliberative politics and an ecological domestication of capitalism? In view of the tensions that exist between capitalism, ecology, and democracy, doesn't it become necessary to differentiate the concept of an inherent dynamics into a positive-exonerating one and a negative-destructive one? In what relationship do you think do capitalism, ecology, and democracy stand to each other? Confronted by a progressive destruction of the environment and a society in which the work to be distributed is becoming increasingly scarcer, wouldn't it be possible, on the basis of the system of basic rights you have developed, to justify a legally guaranteed basic income and to enlist a basic right to equal living conditions as a justification for a basic income? Faced with 'the end of the society of work' (André Gorz) isn't a basic income needed so as to provide the degree of self- respect and autonomy necessary for a properly functioning democracy?*

The point of the analysis of social modernization developed in *Theory of Communicative Action* was precisely to clarify the distinction you mention. We have to acknowledge the differentiation benefits of a capitalist economy, without concealing or accepting as a natural fate the social, cultural, and ecological costs that arise from a certain organization of economic production. I am interested in the processes of exchange that flow in both directions between life-world and system—as well as in the colonizing incursions of the money medium into communicatively structured realms of life, and the possibilities of damming up the inherently destructive dynamic of the economic system for the sake of environmental imperatives. From this theoretical perspective, the bankruptcy of state Socialism—that is, of the attempt to replace the directive function of money by extensive administration—cannot come as a surprise; but that is not to say that the historical events of 1989 did not surprise me.

On the other hand, the social theories developed in the Marxist tradition were too narrowly based on crisis analyses, so that constructive models are lacking today. All of us are rather at a loss as we confront the destructive consequences of a worldwide capitalism whose productivity we do not want to give up. That explains the renewed relevance of purely normatively based models for a 'market socialism.' These models pick up the correct idea of retaining a market economy's effective steering effects and impulses to innovation without at the same time accepting the negative consequences of a systematically reproduced unequal distribution of 'bads' and 'goods.' The crux of all these models is of course the vanishing possibilities for action. The old nation-state's political capacity for action (and also that of .the newer nation-combines, and of the permanently established international bodies) stands in no relationship to the self-steering mechanism of the global market network. The problems of a long overdue reorganization of world economic relationships therefore throw a new light on the desperate condition of international relations, and the role of the UN and other world organizations.

The idea of a guaranteed basic income discussed in the 1980s certainly has the interesting aspect that the material basis for citizens' self-respect and political autonomy would be made independent of the more or less contingent success of the private individual on the labor market. But these matters probably can be meaningfully judged only within the context of the complicated tasks of a reconstruction of the welfare state, which is in danger of being dismantled.

The critique made by dissidents and by the peacefully operating Citizens' Rights movement in eastern and central Europe lay at the foundation of the revolutionary events of 1989 and helped bring the concept of 'civil society' quickly into vogue among intellectuals in the West. This concept acquired a positive connotation because of its connection with the dissidents and the Citizens Rights movement. You understand civil society as 'the nonstate and noneconomic interconnections and voluntary associations that anchor the communication structures of the public sphere in social components of the life-world. Civil society is composed of these more or less spontaneously created associations, organizations, and movements, which locate, absorb, condense, amplify, and carry on into the political public sphere the response societal problems find in the realms of private life.' You claim that the political public sphere can find its sole support in a civil society 'that has moved beyond class demarcations and thrown off the millennia-old shackles of social stratifications and exploitations.' Doesn't this invite an empirical critique that would point out that the public sphere is not only dominated by media power but its civil-societal basis is still marked by inequalities of class and gender that the new poverty has increased rather than lessened? With your ideas about a democratic public sphere, aren't you attributing to citizens a post-conventional ego-identity that fails to correspond to the personality structure of most citizens? The response Shirinovshy finds in Russia, Le Pen in France, Schönhuber in Germany, and Allessandra Mussolini in Italy strengthens our impression that many citizens have a rather conventional ego-identity. The nationalistic regression shows that something other than democratic impulses also emanates from civil society. The concept of civil society has now also acquired a negative connotation because of right-wing pressure in the street. . . . How—on the basis of your discourse theory of justice and the democratic constitutional state—could one distinguish the undemocratic from the democratic impulses of civil society, and criticize them?

Well, if it is a matter of diagnosis, we can draw a sharp distinction, precisely from the point of view of a theory of communication, between populist mass mobilization in totalitarian states and democratic movements from the center of a civil society. Hannah Arendt already did so in her classic work *The Origins of Totalitarianism*, and she pointed to the important role played by the structures of the public sphere in this connection. Communicative power can be formed only in public spheres that produce intersubjective relationships on the basis of reciprocal recognition and make it possible to use communicative freedoms; that is, to take spontaneous positive or negative positions with regard to free-floating themes, grounds, and information. If these individualizing forms of an unimpaired intersubjectivity are destroyed, there arise masses of individuals who are isolated from each other' and who—once they are indoctrinated by leaders relying on plebiscites and set in motion—can then be provoked to participate in mass actions. Arendt's analysis was still designed for the forms of movement of collectives as we know them from the first half of our century—the classic mass demonstrations and mass strikes, the way the Nazi *Reichsparteitage* were conducted, military parades. In the posttotalitarian age of a Berlusconi, the image of the masses on the move has retreated behind the electronically interconnected network audience: even in 1989, the masses that revolted in front of party and government buildings acquired a different function when they were transformed into guests on live TV. So the images of the totalitarian state appear to have vanished, but the destructive potential of a new kind of massification has remained. In the public sphere of the media as well there are still structures that block a horizontal exchange of spontaneously taken positions—that is, the use of communicative freedoms—and simultaneously make the isolated and privatized viewers susceptible to an incapacitating collectivization of their conceptual worlds. Such *shaped* public spheres, which serve as forums for legitimation by plebiscite, differ from liberal public spheres in that the latter offer a vehicle for the authority of a *position-taking* public. Once a *public* starts moving, it does not march in unison, but rather offers the spectacle of anarchically unshackled communicative freedoms. In the simultaneously decentered and porous structures of the public sphere, the scattered critical potential is collected, activated, and bundled together. This certainly requires a civil social foundation. Social movements can then draw attention to certain subjects and dramatize certain contributions. In the process, the masses' dependency on populist leaders is turned around: the players in the arena are indebted for their influence to the approval they receive from a gallery that is trained in criticism.

Of course, a liberal public sphere requires a free form of association, domesticated media power, and the political culture of a population accustomed to freedom; it needs to be met halfway by a more or less rationalized life-world. To this correspond, on the side of personality structures, postconventional ego-identities. You will now object that even we in the Western democracies must reckon with an entirely different state of consciousness. Dispositions continue to exist that make a considerable portion of an over-stressed population susceptible to the Le Pens and Schönhubers, to national-ism and xenophobia. These facts are unchallengeable. But to what do they represent an objection? For it cannot be to the philosopher who—in the name of his normative theory and with the gesture of an impotent Ought—furthers a postconventional consciousness, thus sinning against a human nature that pessimistic anthropology has always led into battle against the intellectuals' dream dances. All we do is reconstruct the Ought that has immigrated into praxis itself, and we only need to observe that in positive law and the demo-cratic constitutional state—that is, in the existing practices themselves—prin-ciples are embodied that depend on a postconventional grounding, and to that extent are tailored to the public consciousness of a liberal political culture. This normative self-understanding introduces into our relationships, which are not what they ought to be, a certain dynamics: we see the constitution as a project we can continue working on—or abandon in discouragement.

In Between Facts and Norms *you regard the ideal communication community as a model of 'pure' communicative socialization. And in this connection you emphasize that one should not misunderstand the discursive character of the opinion- and will-formation essential for democracy by hypostatizising the ideal content of general argumentative presuppositions into a model of pure communicative socialization. However, the conception of an ideal communi-cation community rests on idealizations. In our opinion, the idealizations can be interpreted in (at least) two ways. Thus the assumptions humans always make when they raise validity claims—including the assumption that their arguments convince others and are not for the time being contradicted—can be interpreted as idealizations. These idealizations do not of course exclude the possibility that there might be arguments that could lead people to revise their validity claims. According to a second interpretation, idealizations can refer to a final consensus and to the assumptions regarding communication in an ideal communicative society human beings anticipate when they raise validity claims. Albrecht Wellmer has pointed out that this second interpreta-tion of idealizations does not make sense. If the ideal communication commu-nity were to be achieved at a future point in history it would mean the end of any form of human communication. In an ideal communication community, the conditions of the possibility of what is idealized are negated. In spite of this criticism, you have not given up the concept of the ideal communication community. The ideal communication community serves as a foil for detecting and articulating divergences from the model of pure communicative social-izations. It can be used to make it possible to perceive the unavoidable ele-ments of inertia that are inherent in the processes of opinion- and will-forma-*

*tion—for example, asymmetries in access to information as well as an
unequal distribution of competencies and knowledge. If our view is correct,
the model of pure communicative socialization is capable of two different
functions: first it can be of help if one wants to bring to light the unavoidable
elements of inertia; and, secondly, it can be used as a normative yardstick for
a critique of the existing power relationships in the political public sphere. Do
we even need the concept of an ideal communication community, as you
claim, in order to identify the unavoidable elements of inertia? Aren't the traditional sociological means sufficient for that? Or a philosophy like
Foucault's? And in any event don't the various globalization processes see to
it that the universal normative yardsticks crystallize out—yardsticks that are,
of course, indispensable for a critique of society? In other words, doesn't the
mounting cultural, ecological, and economic interdependence inevitably lead
to the development of a common language 'that is necessary for the perception and the articulation of global social relevancies and norms' (Between
Facts and Norms)? Couldn't we just as easily get along without the concept of
an ideal communication community and simply retain the previously mentioned first interpretation of idealization?*

If you introduce the life-world and communicative action as complementary
concepts and say that the life-world reproduces itself by means of communicative actions, then you lay values, norms, and especially the use of language oriented toward mutual understanding under a burden of integration
they could bear only in a society that met the demands of the intentionalist
mode of pure communicative socialization. I have already defended myself
against this hermeneutic idealism in *Theory of Communicative Action*. Along
with Bernhard Peters, I have now taken a different tack (in *Die Integration
moderner Gesellschaften*, Frankfurt am Main, 1993) to indicate my reservations regarding such an idealist misunderstanding of social integration, which
some people incorrectly ascribe to me. Such reservations could also be
expressed in terms of Luhmanrfs theory of systems or Foucault's theory of
power. Instead, I make a methodological use of the notion of an 'ideal communication community' to make visible the inescapable elements of societal
inertia. That cannot be the real point at issue.

Besides, like Wellmer, I criticize the conception of an ideal communication community as it was developed by Peirce and Apel, and even my own
discourse on the 'ideal speech situation,' as examples of the fallacy of mis-
placed concreteness.' These images are concretist, because they suggest a
final condition that might be achieved in time, which cannot be what they are
intended to suggest. But I continue to insist on the idealizing content of the
inescapable pragmatic presuppositions of a praxis from which only the better
argument is supposed to emerge. After we have abandoned the correspon-

dence concept of truth, the unconditional character of truth-claims can be explained only in relation to a 'justification under ideal conditions' (Putnam).

If we analyze the sense of 'truth' in terms of justification, we must avoid equating truth with rational acceptability; what was once accepted rationally as true can turn out to be false. We call an expression 'true' when we are convinced that it will withstand future objections—which does not exclude the possibility that we have made a mistake. But only if we consider propositions as *unconditionally* true, regardless of their fallibility, are we prepared to build bridges and board airplanes—that is, to assume the risks of acting on these propositions. However, this sense of unconditionality, which marks the difference between truth and rational acceptability, can be expressed in terms of justification only because we consider our justification praxis, that is, our argumentation, as in some respects a component of an ideal performance. Even today we must be able to form our convictions on the basis of the best available knowledge and arguments, without being coerced; that is, without being coerced except by the noncoercive coercion exercised by the better argument. In the section to which you allude in *Between Facts and Norms* I argue that 'the contra-factual presuppositions from which participants in an argument must set out open a perspective in which they can surmount the inescapable provinciality of their spatio-temporal context . . . and do justice to transcending validity claims. But with transcending validity claims they do not situate themselves in the transcendental Beyond of an ideal realm of intelligible beings.'

I also have to resort to such forms of argumentation in instances where validity claims can be resolved *discursively* if the legitimacy of law is to depend upon properties of the democratic process by which laws are made. Democratic procedure grounds a presumption of the reasonableness of results that have been achieved in conformity with procedures only when, if, and insofar as it guarantees—together with the legal institutionalization of corresponding forms of argumentation (and negotiations)—a discursive formation of opinion and will in the previously mentioned sense. Convincing normative yardsticks are formed only under such conditions. They are not simply produced naturally as a mere result of globalization processes.

The political public sphere is a place of equality only when it is formally considered; that is, the fact that every citizen has the same legal status in a particular state does not mean that there are also the same possibilities of influencing the formation of will and opinion. Political power is still unequally distributed according to class, gender, and ethnic membership. Examples include the emergence of an underclass in many democratic states, the underparticipation of women in politics, and the riots that occurred in Los Angeles after the acquittal of the policemen who mistreated Rodney King. To what extent is it possible, using your formal theory of political combat, to oppose not only a communitarian but also a Marxist critique of liberal formalism? What is your position on the question of quotas, for example for women or members of ethnic minorities, to increase their opportunities to participate in political power?

Struggles for recognition in the democratic constitutional state possess legitimate strength only to the extent that all groups find access to the political sphere, that they all speak up, that they are able to articulate their needs, and that no one is marginalized or excluded. From the viewpoint of representation and 'qualification for citizenship,' it is already important to secure the factual preconditions for equal opportunity to exercise formally equal rights. This is true not only for political participation, but also for social participation and for private rights to freedom, since no one can act in a politically autonomous fashion unless the conditions for private autonomy are guaranteed. In this connection I also support quotas: for example, I support a policy of 'preferred hiring' in all sectors of education and employment where that is the only way to secure the 'fair value' of equal rights for historically and structurally disadvantaged groups. These measures are intended to have 'a remedial effect' and are therefore only temporary in nature.

Considered from the point of view of the criteria for membership in modern democracies, people are members of a given society if they have citizens' rights. Consequently, the sovereignty of a people [Volkssouveränität] relates to all human beings who have Citizens Rights within a certain society. Citizens Rights are exclusive because they entail a differentiation between members and nonmembers, between citizens and foreigners. Since morally grounded human rights are not related to membership in a certain society, they are distinct from citizens' rights. Human rights are inclusive because—in contrast to citizens' rights, which, normally are bound to the territory of a nation state—human rights have a transnational, universal character. Political philosophy still continues to debate the question—as in the case of the debate between liberals and communitarians—whether human rights and citizens' rights are in competition or mutually ground each other. As becomes apparent in the system of basic rights you have grounded in a theory of discourse, in your view there is an internal relationship between human rights and citizens' rights. This connection 'lies in the normative content of a way of exercising political autonomy guaranteed, not so much by the form, of the general laws, as by the communicative form in which opinion and will are shaped discursively' (Between Facts and Norms). If we have understood you correctly, your derivation of the system of basic rights takes as its starting point the methodological fiction of a society without a state. Yet in harsh reality the positive legal status of human rights is precarious: many nation-states' positive legal systems are able to resist the moral pressure that emanates from these rights. So recourse to the sovereignty of a people legitimizes a situation that is unacceptable from the human rights perspective—the German 'asylum debate' being one example. Thus the question arises as to how one might be able to establish a bridge between the internal relationship between citizens' rights and human rights on the one hand, and, on the other hand, the area of conflict that actually exists between them. Do you see your system of rights as a critical foil used to denounce the precarious positive legal status of human rights? And can we establish, in the absence of a world society, a moral hierarchy of citizens' rights and human rights? Don't 'human dignity' and 'physical inviolability'—think of the example of the hot war that has succeeded the Cold War in the former Yugoslavia—have primacy in certain situations over a people's sovereignty? Isn't the status of human rights dependent on the realization Of world- citizens' rights and the monopolization of force worldwide?

You have asked several questions at once. First, I distinguish morally grounded human rights from legal human rights that have acquired positive validity through our constitutions; that is, they have been given a guarantee, within the pertinent legal order, that sanctions will be used to achieve them. It is because of their universal human rights content that these basic rights are pushing—as if on their own—toward the realization of a form of world citizenship in which human rights everywhere acquire the status and the validity of positive law. Such a situation cannot be achieved solely through international courts; for this we need a UN capable of reaching decisions and taking action, and that can, when it needs to intervene, employ military forces under its own command instead of delegating this function to the superpowers, which merely lend themselves UN legitimation for the conduct of their wars. The case is entirely different when valid basic rights are limited by parliamentary decision, and—as happened here in Germany in the case of the right to asylum—these rights are de facto hollowed out.

This is the case you mention in your second question as an example of an unfortunate competition between human and citizen rights—indeed, as a case in which the classic rights to freedom of life, liberty, and property are subordinated to the sovereignty of the legislative power. However, regarded normatively, the political legislative power is not permitted—in Germany or elsewhere—to limit or abolish absolute basic rights. The constitutional court can invalidate such decisions in the course of its review of norms. Whether the new asylum law is formulated so carefully as to withstand a constitutional court test is a question for experts, and I will not address it here.

Finally, you are interested in the relationship of a people's sovereignty to human rights in general. The example of the civil war in Bosnia, however, is not a very good choice if what you mean to stress is the importance of not deviating in any way from the liberal understanding of human rights. In my book I tried to show how it is possible to do justice to the intuition that human rights can neither be left to the sovereign legislative power nor simply converted into an instrument to be used for the latter's purposes. Private autonomy and citizens' autonomy mutually presuppose each other. And indeed the common origin of a people's sovereignty and human rights must be explained by the fact that citizens' practice of self-legislation in the form of institutionalized rights to political participation must be institutionalized; however, this presupposes the status of legal persons as bearers of subjective rights, and such a status-arrangement cannot exist without the classic rights to freedom. Without these rights, there is no positive law at all, and positive law happens to be the only language through which citizens can mutually assure each other of their participation in the practice of making their own laws.

The bilevel concept of society you presented in Theory of Communicative Action *afforded you an opportunity to diagnose and critique colonization of the life-world. Drawing on examples of the 'juridification' of communicatively structured realms of action, you show how, using monetary and bureaucratic means, the media-directed subsystems constituted by the economy and the state have made incursions into the symbolic reproduction of the life-world. The colonization thesis makes possible a critique of the medium of law. You seem to abandon this critique in* Between Facts and Norms. *What role if any do juridification tendencies continue to play in your critique of society? Have you given up the colonization thesis? What conceptual means does* Between Facts and Norms *make available to explain and criticize the negative effects of juridification in the realms of family, school, and social policy? And how, in this context, do you evaluate the shift of political decision making from parliament to the government and to the Federal Constitutional Court? For a democracy, doesn't this last development represent a threatening juridification of politics?*

I corrected myself on one point (cf. *Between Facts and Norms*). I no longer believe that juridification is an inevitable consequence of the welfare state. But juridification phenomena that I treat under the rubric 'welfare-state paternalism' continue to be relevant for me, because I want to show that today's return to the liberal model—praised as a 'society of private rights'—offers no way out of the dilemma constituted by the fact that when freedom is granted paternalistically, freedoms are simultaneously taken back. Starting from this way of framing the problems, I develop the proceduralist model of justice: in the complex relationships of the welfare state, private legal subjects cannot enjoy equal subjective freedoms if they fail, in their political role as co-legislators, to make use of their communicative freedoms by participating in public debates about how needs are to be interpreted, so that citizens themselves develop yardsticks and criteria according to which similar matters are treated similarly, and dissimilar matters dissimilarly.

So far as the juridification of politics itself is concerned, the constitutional court plays an unfortunate role to the extent that it exercises a subsidiary legislative function. The court ought not to confuse the constitution with a 'concrete order of values,' and in exercising its normative control it should essentially monitor the democratic character of the creation of laws; that is, it should ensure that the legislative process fulfills the exacting normative presuppositions of the democratic process. If our Federal Constitutional Court were to make such a proceduralist self-understanding the basis of its decisions, it could, for example, not simply send the abortion law back to the Bundestag, which had passed this law only after an exhaustive discursive preparation in the political public sphere and after repeated, conscientious consideration of all the arguments and counterarguments presented by all its members; moreover, it passed by a decisive, thoroughly bipartisan majority vote. At least the court ought not to have sent the law back unless it could produce other grounds for its decision.

The Federal Republic of Germany established a halfway reasonable democracy after 1945. In our opinion, basic rights and democratic institutions do not guarantee a properly functioning democracy. If citizens no longer perceive the possibility of participation, and have lost faith in politics—'protest voters' and 'disgust with politics' are symptomatic of this—democracy is endangered. That is why in our view democratic learning processes—which are determined by historical experiences and education, among other things—are very important for a well functioning democracy. In your essay 'The Second Lie of the Federal Republic: We're becoming Normal Again,' you speak of two 'life-lies' or collective self-deceptions that haunted the Federal Republic after 1945. The first originated during the Adenauer period: 'We are all democrats.' You claim that since 1989 a second life-lie has emerged: 'We have become normal again.' Could you explain to us what you mean by the 'second life-lie?' This is not immediately apparent to Scandinavians, who are not very well versed in German history. To what extent have these two lies diminished the democratic learning processes in the Federal Republic? Don't the years 1989–1990 mark a decisive break in this respect, because during the unification process the opportunity for a republican refounding of Germany was neglected?

I presume that the disgust with politics, which of course is not found solely in the Federal Republic, has different, contrary, and mutually reinforcing causes. On one hand, citizens are unhappy because they see too few opportunities to be meaningfully engaged politically along the well-trodden paths of a nationalized party landscape; the nonactivities of the local chapters of our political parties show how much unused energy is administered and laid to rest there. On the other hand, this wish for more democracy is intersected by the authoritarian wish to simplify an overly complex world by means of a simple recipe and strong men. The old stereotype of apolitically turning one's back on 'mere talk' [Gerede] and 'party squabbles' is receiving new impetus from fears about losses in income and status attributed to a politically out-of-control economic development that follows the pattern of 'jobless growth.' Clearly, politics has become overburdened by problems that are worldwide, and now also internally proliferating. It was not capitalism that won in the system competition with state Socialism but a capitalism that had been tamed by the welfare state during the favorable conjunctures of the postwar period, and which currently finds itself in a state of disintegration. This objectively difficult situation demands new solutions, but so far the imagination necessary to find them has been lacking.

It is against this general background that the Federal Republic has to digest the consequences of a precipitous annexation of the former GDR—a process conducted administratively and pushed through with confusing slogans. How far social disintegration will go, and how great the dangers it poses to internal stability will grow, no one can now say. In the general population, nationalist tendencies with regard to the internal German problems of distribution are not very marked. What we observe is an elite nationalism, cosponsored by intellectuals, which seeks to fill with backward-looking constructions the moral gap left by the anxiously avoided 1990 republican refounding. What worries me is that those who have always refused to acknowledge the political-cultural break of 1945 are the very ones who are now most loudly crying 'new normality' and 'goodbye to the old Federal Republic.' The political civilization of the Federal Republic made headway until 1989; the question is whether we will be able to continue this process in the enlarged Federal Republic—or whether the past will catch up with us again. One fortunate thing is that so far Kohl is stubbornly continuing to insist on a speedy unification to Europe.

In your article 'Citizenship and National Identity you criticize the European Union's lack of democracy, but express 'cautiously optimistic expectations' (Between Facts and Norms) regarding European development. However, it seems much easier to internationalize democracy than to internationalize the economy and administration. The reason for your cautious optimism is not entirely clear to us. Doesn't the transnational character of an organization like the European Union make new demands on democracy? How extended and differentiated can a political public sphere be without completely exceeding the capacities Of individual citizens faced with a highly complex society

and the impossibility of gaining a comprehensive view of it? Can a radical
democracy be realized within the framework of the EU at all?

We Germans need the political union if only to protect ourselves against the
fantasies of 'a great eastward-looking power in the heart of Europe' that are
beginning to be revived. For the same reason our neighbors should be interested in bringing Germany into mutual foreign and security policies. But that
can be effectively done only within the framework of a common European
constitution. So far, in Scandinavia and elsewhere opposition is directed only
against a Brussels bureaucracy; that is, against a systematically created unity
that still lacks a corresponding mutual political life-world, but such impulses
might yet be able to translate themselves into a longing for a democratic
Europe. The only genuine obstacle is the lack of a common political public
sphere, the lack of an arena where subjects that have a common relevance can
be negotiated. Ironically, whether such a communication context will develop
depends on the intellectuals more than on another group, yet they go on end-
lessly arguing without doing anything to help.

Contributors

KENNETH BAYNES is Professor of Philosophy at the State University of New York at Stony Brook. He is the author of *The Normative Grounds of Social Criticism: Kant, Rawls and Habermas* (SUNY, 1992) as well as numerous articles in social and political philosophy. He is the editor of the SUNY Series in Social and Political Thought.

JAMES BOHMAN is Danforth Professor of Philosophy at Saint Louis University. He is the author of *Public Deliberation* (MIT, 1996) and *New Philosophy of Social Science* (MIT 1991) and the editor of several volumes including, most recently, *Pluralism and the Pragmatic Turn: The Transformation of Critical Theory* (MIT, 2001).

HAUKE BRUNKHORST is Professor of Sociology at the Faculty of Social Sciences at the University of Flensburg, Germany. He is the author of several books, including *Adorno and Critical Theory* (Wales, 1999) and *Hannah Arendt* (Beck, 1999).

ANDREW BUCHWALTER chairs the Department of Philosophy at the University of North Florida. He is the author of *Culture and Democracy: Social and Ethical Issues in Support of the Arts and Humanities* (Westview, 1992) and is currently completing a book on the contemporary significance of Hegel's political thought.

PETER DEWS is Chair of the Department of Philosophy at the University of Essex. He is the author of *Logics of Disintegration* (Verso, 1987) and *The Limits of Disenchantment* (Verso, 1995) as well as many articles on contemporary European philosophy.

JÜRGEN HABERMAS is Professor of Philosophy and Sociology, Emeritus, at the Goethe University in Frankfurt, Germany. He is author of more than twenty books, including *The Transformation of the Public Sphere* (MIT, 1989) *The Theory of Communicative Action* (Beacon, 1984), *The*

259

Philosophical Discourse of Modernity (MIT, 1987) and *Between Facts and Norms* (MIT, 1996).

MATTHIAS KETTNER is Lecturer in Philosophy at the Goethe University in Frankfurt and he is in charge of a bioethical research project at the *Kulturwissenschaftliches Institut* in Essen, Germany. He is the author of *Angewandte Ethik als Politikum* (Suhrkamp, 2000) and numerous articles in moral and political philosophy.

INGEBORG MAUS is Professor of Political Science at the Faculty of Social Sciences at the Goethe University, Frankfurt am Main, Germany. She is the author of *Zur Aufklärung der Demokratietheorie* (Suhrkamp, 1992) and other books.

GEERT MUNNICHS is a Research Collaborator in the Department of Applied Philosophy of the Agricultural University in Wageningen. He is author of a book on Habermas in Dutch, *Publiek ongenoegen enpolitieke geloofwaardigheid. Democratische legitimiteit in een ontzuilde samenleving* (Holland, 2000).

WILLIAM REHG is Associate Professor of Philosophy at Saint Louis University. He is the author of *Insight and Solidarity: The Discourse Ethics of Jüergen Habermas* (California, 1994), co-editor, with James Bohman of *Deliberative Democracy* (MIT, 1997) and *Pluralism and the Pragmatic Turn* (MIT, 2001), and the translator of Habermas's *Between Facts and Norms*.

WILLIAM SCHEUERMAN is Associate Professor of Political Science at the University of Minnesota. He is the author of *Carl Schmitt: The End of Law* (Califonia, 1999) and *Between the Norm and the Exception: The Frankfurt School and the Rule of Law* (MIT, 1994).

RENÉ VON SCHOMBERG has held positions at Dutch universities and recently works as a scientific officer at the European Commission in Brussels on socio-economic issues of Science and Technology. He is the author of numerous articles and monographs. Recent edited books in English include: *Science, Politics and Morality: Scientific Uncertainty and Decision Making* (1993), *Contested Technology* (1995), *The Social Management of Genetic Engineering* (co-edited with Peter Wheale) (1998), and *Democratizing Technology. Theory and Practice of Deliberative Technology Assessment* (1999).

Index